Sidel
LIVES

CW00550118

KIRSTEN IRVING has edited more than a dozen poetry anthologies, covering everything from monsters to magpies. She is the author of the collections *Never Never Never Come Back* (Salt, 2012) and *What To Do* (Happenstance, 2011). Her poetry has been translated into Russian and Spanish, widely anthologised and thrown out of a helicopter. Not in that order. @KoftheTriffids

SEBASTIAN MANLEY received his PhD in Film Studies from the University of East Anglia in 2011. His first book, *The Cinema of Hal Hartley* (Bloomsbury), was published in 2013. He lives with some humans and a cat in London.

lives beyond us

lives beyond us

POEMS AND ESSAYS ON THE
FILM REALITY OF ANIMALS

edited by sebastian manley and kirsten irving

sidekickBOOKS
www.sidekickbooks.com

First published in 2015 by

SIDEKICK BOOKS

www.sidekickbooks.com

Printed by
ImprintDigital

Typeset in Vollkorn with Helvetica World and BPreplay for title page
Sidekick Books logo font: Roman Antique

Typesetting and cover design by Jon Stone.

Image sources: DoverPictura (licensed); Wikimedia Commons;
Pixabay (User: Nemo) under the Creative Commons
CC0 1.0 Universal Public Domain Dedication
(http://creativecommons.org/publicdomain/zero/1.0/deed.en)

'The Wolf Man' by Abigail Parry was first published in *Poetry London*.

~

ISBN: 978-1-909560-20-8

Supported using public funding by
ARTS COUNCIL
ENGLAND
LOTTERY FUNDED

for Mitchell

Contents

15

Introduction by SEBASTIAN MANLEY

19

'I quite deliberately dressed wild animals in tame costumes of my imagination': Animals as Special Effects
PAUL WELLS

39

Post-production
JOHN CLEGG

41

Representations of Animal Advocacy in Film
LOREDANA LOY

63

The Human–Animal Dialectic in Animated Movies
TÂNIA REGINA VIZACHRI

73

Extras / Commentaries / Owls
MIKE WEST

75

Significant Others: Of Horses and Men
in The Wild Horse Redemption
AMANDA GILROY

99
Gender Trouble and The Horse Whisperer
ANGELA HOFSTETTER

121
Blurring the Boundaries: Big Cat Diary
CAROL FREEMAN

145
Bear #141
SAMUEL PRINCE

147
BEAR INTERVENTION!
JON STONE

159
The Avant-Garde among the Animals
WALTER C. METZ

185
grrrrrrrrrrrrrr
SOPHIE MAYER

187
Asta: The Screwball Dog and the Hollywood Crime Film
NICOLAS PILLAI

197
Ambrosius
CHRISSY WILLIAMS

198

A Pirates of the Caribbean *Bestiary*
ANTHONY ADLER

201

Les Chiens de Mon Oncle
SIMON BARRACLOUGH

221

Alien vs Jonesy
ANGELA CLELAND

223

The lion handler's advice to a young Melanie Griffith
REBECCA WIGMORE

225

*Analytic Animals: Agency at Some Interfaces
within Chronophotography*
CLIFF HAMMETT

249

A cat called Orangey was in a number of movies,
MARK WALDRON

251

Machine-Age Comedy Gone Rural: Hustlin' Hank *(1923)
and the Problem of Animals on Film*
KEVIN M. FLANAGAN

265
The Wolf Man
ABIGAIL PARRY

269
*'Does zoology include people?' Human and Animal Identity
in Hitchcock's* Marnie *(1964) and* The Birds *(1963)*
SEBASTIAN MANLEY

281
Empire of the Ants
JUDE C. MONTAGUE

284
Tallow
JAMES COGHILL

287
*Death of a White-Tailed Deer
in David Lynch's* The Straight Story *(1999)*
JULIE ANN SMITH

307
A Very Special Case
NICK MURRAY

310
The Pitch
RICHARD EVANS

313
*Easy Rovers, Raging Fur Balls: How Animals Did a Wee-Wee on
Hollywood and Humped Louis Mayer's Favourite Armchair*
OLLY GRUNER

333
Writers' Biographies

Introduction

OFTEN it takes only a slight shift in perspective to see a whole new world: this was the familiar truth brought home by my first explorations into the subject of animals in film, sometime around the start of this decade. I had a background in film and something of a background in animal ethics, but it wasn't until I happened across some pieces with a specific focus on animals in cinema that I began to hold in my mind the possibility of writing on a subject that combined two of my most enduring interests. This book is an attempt to add something to what is now a burgeoning body of writing on animals and their significance in and for film. It is almost certainly the first book of both criticism and poetry on animals in film, and it is my and Kirsten Irving's hope, as co-editors, that the mix will be enlivening, and perhaps point readers beyond the familiar horizons of the film world, as it has done for us.

The contributors to this volume – writers, academics and poets, mostly – each offer a distinct way in to thinking about the relation between animals and films, film genres or film history. We are living through an upheaval in the position of animals in film and in culture generally, and it's hardly surprising that many of the contributions express feelings of unease or sometimes horror at the way animals have been represented in films, or how little some films seem to register concern for the lives of real animals. An edge of criticism or protest in particular distinguishes several of the essays, including Walter C. Metz's 'The Avant-Garde among the Animals', a critique of the terminally anthropomorphic natural history filmmaking tradition and a call for a new, avant-garde tradition to take its place, and Loredana Loy's 'Representations of Animal Advocacy in Film', which explores a range of ostensibly 'pro-animal' films, finding in them both resistance and surrender to the mainstream human ideologies that relegate animals to the realms of the trivial and the abject. Olly Gruner, in his essay, adopts the tone of a Peter Biskind Hollywood exposé to deliver an imaginative retelling of the history of 1960s and 1970s Hollywood from the perspective of animal actors – with poignant and sometimes lurid contributions from 'Pickles Gabor' (the Dostoevsky-channelling spaniel who played Rocky in *The Panic in Needle Park*), 'Bruce Fairfax' (the nice-guy shark who starred in *Jaws*) and other representatives of what Gruner calls 'the animals that saved Hollywood'. Something of Gruner's piece finds a reflection in Nick Murray's *Free Willy*-inspired poem 'A Very Special Case', another account of an animal actor's day in the sun and the shadows of exploitation and patronisation that cannot ever be fully put out of mind. 'Life is all slow circles / in between films. / Cheap tricks and / trying to remember / you're at the apex of your career': as much as humans, animals are the victims of a film industry hungry for bodies to turn into profits, whatever the cost for the individuals involved.

Critique and disquiet are mixed throughout the collection,

and within many pieces, with a different kind of response to films featuring animals (or ideas of animals), one that speaks of the multiplying imaginative possibilities that come with looking at something familiar in a new way. In the poem 'ALIEN VS JONESY' by Angela Cleland, we are given a chance to re-experience *Alien* as a sort of mythopoetic clash of wills between two lifeforms: the cat Jonesy and the alien. Here, human characters are pushed to the margins, Brett (played by Harry Dean Stanton in the film) intruding into the narrative as an almost comic distraction, his understanding of the full reality of the situation hopelessly limited. Abigail Parry's poem 'The Wolf Man' is a vivid testament to the enduring importance of the figure of the animal to our self-conception as human beings – that idea, often crystallised in fairy tales and horror stories, that there is something primal and animal vibrating in the heart of the modern human. This is a theme that also surfaces in my essay on Hitchcock's *Marnie* and *The Birds*, which reads Hitchcock's great late films as darkly imaginative tales about the animal nature of human identity.

Other pieces take a variety of critical and creative positions to probe the possibilities of subjects as diverse as the animated animal (John Clegg, Paul Wells, Tânia Regina Vizachri), animals in chronophotography (Cliff Hammett) and the assorted fauna of *The Night of the Hunter* (Mike West). I hope readers will find opportunities to make connections between the pieces and come away with some fresh understanding of the compelling, enigmatic and often disturbing nature of cinema's engagement with the world of non-human animals.

Sebastian Manley

P<small>AUL</small> W<small>ELLS</small>

ೀ

'I quite deliberately dressed wild animals in tame costumes of my imagination': Animals as Special Effects

A <small>SMALL</small> Jack Russell dog stands on its hind legs staring at the camera. It holds a placard that says 'I'm Dead'. When I first saw David Shrigley's playful artwork, I was reminded of Tex Avery's direct-to-camera gags and the way they sought immediate communication with the audience: a mode of shared recognition that transcended the form – in Avery's case, the Hollywood cartoon – and represented the artist speaking specifically to the viewer, insistent that the spectator get the joke. Shrigley's dog also insists we get the point. This dog is indeed dead, but it has been manipulated, suggesting perhaps the perverseness of taxidermy, the seductiveness of anthropomorphism, the surreal finality of death, and, certainly, the ease with which the animal could be made to become something it wasn't, and could not be, in life. This kind of animal image-making, though, is nevertheless custom and practice in the cartoon. I have written elsewhere about this relationship between animation and the representation of animals (Wells 2009a; 2009b: 96–110; forthcoming), offering an analysis of the status of the animal within the freedoms of the animated langue, exploring the contradictions and complexities of coming to terms with the use of animals as representative cinematic forms. The following discussion will draw from those analyses, but in this case look more specifically at both the status of the animal and the animated form when it is used in the guise of a visual effect.

I am careful to immediately employ the term 'visual effect' here, since effects are no longer really 'special' but the fundamental condition of cinema itself in the digital era. It is crucial that there is no longer an obvious disjuncture between the grounded literalness of live action performance and acts of spectacle and fantasy but that they are now the seamless whole of the contemporary moving image. As McClean has noted, though:

> *On the one hand, the effects are designed to meet the highest standards of photorealism so that they can maintain the diegetic world without drawing attention to themselves, yet on the other hand even the desire to examine the images to determine whether they have attained a sufficient degree of convincingness serves to distract from the narrative engagement.* (McClean 2007: 36)

This stringent hyper-realism also seems at odds with the plastic freedoms of the animated cartoon, but nevertheless it is the very versatility and malleability of the animated form that actually allows for the extremes and exaggerations of action-led visual storytelling to take on compelling plausibility and conviction. It is important to remember, though, that in the case of the representation of animals there has always been a tension in how such naturalistic persuasiveness might be achieved, whether through the use of trained animals, the deployment of a 'man in an animal suit', the use of animatronics or the flexibility of animation. The measure of 'the animal', then, has often been commensurate with registers of 'the real', or at the very least, what I am terming the *point of relatability*, when the animal is understood and accepted *as an animal*, and not merely as a vehicle to accommodate human characteristics, design idioms, brand values or the sheer arbitrariness and exigencies of animation itself. It should be said that this does not discount the 'talking animal' of much animation, but positions the animal as a phenomenon measured through degrees of verisimilitude in relation to its behaviour, habitat, natural inclinations, and so on.

It was this ontological question that preoccupied the film critic André Bazin. Seung-hoon Jeong (2011) has traced Bazin's film reviews, noting the way in which Bazin aligned his theorisation of film with the representation of animals. Bazin initially held the view, for example, that anthropomorphism is achieved in traditional fiction, or indeed non-fiction, cinema through the use of montage (most obviously perhaps in the stirring lion in Sergei Eisenstein's 1925 film *Battleship Potemkin*), but in essence, he concluded that the use of such montage effects denied the *real* animal in a way that the single, extended shot did not. Jeong notes, though, that 'this aesthetic credo does not rule out all types of cutting. If montage "tricks the film" by deceiving the spectator, *decoupage* – the script or planning for spatiotemporal unity – "films the trick" by allowing the spectator to invest belief over knowledge' (Jeong 2011: 179). This is the essential illusionism of most cinematic practice, of course, but the assumption here is that animals are not, and should not be, manipulated by film form, but in some way be *apprehended* by it: not controlled or directed, but made familiar within the shot or the sequence.

Even though many documentaries prioritise this model of apprehended actuality, Bazin noted difficulties, however, in relation to Disney's 'True Life Adventures', natural history films employing narrative voiceovers telling the story of a variety of animals in their own habitats. Disney himself, though, was quite clear about their outlook and purpose:

> *Our aim in these pictures is to present animal nature honestly, in all of its phases of comedy, and sometimes tragedy, its family life, training of the young, heroic defense of the helpless and the elemental emotions which govern their existence as our fellow creatures on this earth. So presented, they tug at our sympathies and understanding and therefore more humane regard. I am sure that children all over the world – and their parents as well – have a kindlier attitude toward wild creatures after having seen them in our True-Life Adventures.* (Jackson 2006: 69)

Such an approach, however, has been strongly criticised for its over-determined anthropomorphic stance, directly allying animals with humans in ways that arguably misrepresent the animal (see Bouse 1995). Disney's view, though, is clear: his method is concerned with encouraging sensitivity towards the animal by insisting that humans are more like animals than might be freely acknowledged. Disney notes: 'purists in the world of nature criticize me. They say "Disney personalizes these little animals". That's the way I see little animals. I can't help it [...] I personalize them. It's an intuitive thing with me' (Jackson 2006: 110). Disney inherently finds associations with the animal that helps him to understand their very difference and to narrativise them. Bouse argues, though, that 'the True Life Adventures were not concerned with exploring real places or documenting real events, but with creating mythic places that conformed to the Disney style' (Bouse 1995: 31). While this may have the inevitable consequence of placing animals within inappropriate social and moral infrastructures, and moreover misrepresenting them, it is indeed the bigger mythic and archetypal narrative that was important to Disney. Disney is concerned not with apprehending the animal, but with *assimilating* it in an assumed schemata in which humans and animals share a symbiotic relationship and continuum. Disney's approach is intentionally inclusive, resisting 'difference' to suggest 'relatedness'. Brode has persuasively argued, too, that though Disney personifies animals, he is careful to balance nature's 'dark (Darwinistic) side' with 'its positive (Wordsworthian) counterpart' (Brode 2004: 135) and does not descend into simplistic notions of archetypal struggle. Rather, as the narrator of *The Living Desert* (James Algar, USA, 1953) insists, 'nature knows neither hero nor villain, she's impartial to all'.

Though these nature documentaries often manipulate live-action footage and stage events – the scorpion square dance in *The Living Desert*, for example – this is not new in documentary construction, and is clearly in a spirit of dramatising habitat and ritual in an accessible way. Importantly, these films do not at any time seek to disguise such dramatisation and storytelling, trusting the viewer to be intelligent enough to be entertained and informed, to believe and to know. This becomes a heightened 'realism' of using the actual footage but

23

playing with the projected frame rates to 're-animate' it. This strategy is problematised yet further by sometimes integrating live-action footage with animation itself, for example in films like *Perri* (N. Paul Kenworthy Jr and Ralph Wright, USA, 1957), featuring a young female squirrel. Brode argues that this 'blending' is fundamentally what 'the Disney sensibility is *about*' (Brode 2004: 140), going so far as to suggest that this kind of work represents the view that fantasy and reality *as lived experience* are indistinguishable, and that Perri's dream sequence in the film is essentially Buñuelesque in the way it naturalises the apparently surreal as a condition of the real (Brode 2004: 160). Such assumptions significantly disregard certain kinds of anxiety about the misrepresentation of animals, and the imposition of human agendas. Further, and crucially, they amount to an embrace of philosophical principles and aesthetic interventions to accommodate them, which repositions the whole engagement with these issues. Though Disney was criticised for these strategies, they fundamentally anticipate the idea of animals as visual effects in the contemporary era, certainly in films like Jean-Jacques Annaud's *The Bear* (France, 1988), which deploys animated dream sequences, as well as animatronics. Further, they anticipate models of narrative predicated on a mode of 'magic realism' that situates everyday experience in more surreal, supernatural and spiritual environments. This wider picture has almost intrinsically accommodated animals as part of a more natural or cosmic schemata partially beyond human comprehension. This will be further addressed later in my discussion, in relation to Ang Lee's film *Life of Pi* (USA, 2013).

Related to this 'magic realist' principle, *Perri*, like *The Bear*, insists upon a specific relationship between live action and animation as a continuity achieved by turning one into the other, and vice versa. For Bazin, such an approach inevitably dramatises situations on terms and conditions which sit outside the material reality of animals, domesticating and sanitising them, on the one hand making them seemingly more familiar and allied to humanity, while on the other misrepresenting, or simply not representing at all, their fundamental difference. As Jeong again notes, 'Now the animal appears like an amalgam of the real and the imaginary, documentary and fiction, but also of actual and animated documentaries, which is the same as actual and animated fictions' (Jeong 2011: 180). Interestingly, for all of Bazin's insights about the construction of realism thereafter, it is this permeability between representational verisimilitude and animated interventions that remains the actual condition of animal-related narratives more than fifty years later. While Bazin guards against anything that might be viewed as visual exploitation, embraces the self-reflexive presence of the camera within the context of the recording, and points to the ways in which the appropriation of the real is often suggestive of the proximity of death, for him, it remains the case that the animal appears 'on the threshold between the seen and the unseen, between positive and negative imprints, between subjectivity and nothingness' (Jeong 2011: 181). In the contemporary era, it is important to rewrite Bazin, though, since this apparent invisibility of the animal is fundamentally changed in the visual-effects-laden digital era. While arguably the contemporary effect may be viewed as something that evacuates the animal altogether, perhaps endorsing Bazin's perspective, the very presence of the animal *as sometimes indistinguishable from a real animal* calls into question the very premises of its existence. As McClean notes:

The basic quality of the invisible effect is that it should be completely

undetectable. There should be no reason for the audience to suspect
that effects have been used at all. Everything about the shot must
be physically possible. For example, digitally added rain must
conform to the principles of real rain, and, from a narrative point
of view, rain must be possible and plausible within the world of the
story in the context that it is used. (McClean 2007: 78)

In directly engaging with the presence of the animal, then, whether in its disputed status as an unsatisfactory amalgam of representational forms or in its apparently plausible literal and material form as a reconcilable visual idiom, a specific method of analysis is required to evaluate it. This prompts a discourse that reflects these tensions and that I have termed elsewhere *bestial ambivalence*, in which the 'pure animal', the 'critical human', the 'aspirational human' and the hybrid 'humanimal' mix and oscillate in any one model of animal representation. The 'pure animal' is when the animal most approximates real animal behaviour; the 'critical human' is when the animal is used to critique humanity; the 'aspirational human' is when the animal is used to advance or endorse human endeavour; and the hybrid 'humanimal' is when already embedded codes, conventions and mythic and social meanings of the animal are deliberately referenced and employed. So, for example, in *Rise of the Planet of the Apes* (Rupert Wyatt, USA, 2011), the story of Caesar, a baby chimp saved from a research laboratory and brought up as a human child, the 'pure animal' is concerned with primate hierarchies and physical/violent mobilities. This is set against the classic tension, particularly in science fiction, between the 'aspirational human' agenda to understand nature better and cure human medical failing, and the 'critical human' perspective that objects to animal testing and the *Project Nim*-style mis-endeavour of attempting to bring up an ape as if it were human.[1] The hybrid 'humanimal' aspect of the film is directly engaged with animal sentience, so often embedded in most animal narratives as an anthropomorphic device, but on some occasions, like *King Kong*, implicitly suggested in the assumed affection a gorilla has for the young woman sacrificed to him. Another important element of this, of course, is the notion of the 'circle of life' or the 'great chain of being', or ideas associated with the work of Charles Darwin related to determining how close humans and apes actually are biologically, physiologically and, ultimately, psychologically and emotionally. On top of that is a broader theme in the film of the presence and effect of a 'virus'. The bestial ambivalence paradigm, thus, engenders the animal as 'live' and the catalyst for the simultaneous achievement of both 'belief' and 'knowledge', one supporting the other, without undermining the premises of narrative or representation. Arguably, as has already been implicitly suggested, this collapses only when either the effect is unpersuasive or the knowledge is implausible, a premise tested by the film version of Yann Martel's 2001 novel *Life of Pi*.

The omniscient narrator of the novel, Piscine Molitor 'Pi' Patel, muses, 'I quite deliberately dressed wild animals in tame costumes of my imagination' (Martel 2001: 47). He fully recognises the dangers and difference embodied in animals but, like many of us, deliberately finds ways in which the animal can be made safe and conducive to human control, if only in the imagination. It is this, though, that enables all

---

[1]   Project Nim *(James Marsh, UK/USA, 2011) is a documentary about a research project in which a young chimp is brought up in close proximity to humans in order to advance methods by which they can communicate through sign language and domesticate the bond. Perhaps unsurprisingly, things don't work out well.*

creative artists to find connection and empathy with animals. Those who work directly with animals, or feel particularly close to domestic animals, may claim clear bonds and relationships, but in my view, the relationship with animals is ultimately best mediated by creative discourses, since these suggest other means of understanding animals beyond those inevitably embedded in anthropomorphism. This is normally related to the recognition of the physical and behavioural (in)difference of the animal, and the specific use of habitats. When not operating as 'pure animals', then, animal characters are essentially 'bi-creatures', who operate with degrees of *continuity*, *communion* and *complementariness* – the first, demonstrating a deep primal relationship between animals and humankind; the second, when humanity and animality become allied and indistinguishable (often in 'imaginary' creatures); and the third, where humans and animals operate in dialectical tension and have parallel existence. Ang Lee's film adaptation of *Life of Pi* is especially interesting because it places the 'pure animal' at the centre of its story while addressing all three aspects suggested in 'bi-creatures'. This is only achieved, however, by using the 'tame costume' of animation, which I wish to argue succeeds in foregrounding 'the animal' through possessing inherently animistic traits in its execution and vocabulary. This in turn creates deep empathy in the animators creating and interpreting the animal, and in the spectator, prompted by the authenticity of its depiction. In creating the computer-generated tiger 'Richard Parker', a representation with no distinguishable difference from a real Bengal tiger, the creators of the film ensure there is no suspension of disbelief – crucial in a film whose subject matter is entirely concerned with systems of belief.

'Pi' Patel is a Tamil boy brought up in Pondicherry, a

former French colony in India, where his father runs a zoo in a botanical garden. Tired of being teased by other boys, who call him 'Pissing' Patel, the boy insists on being called 'Pi', and this is the first key metaphorical clue to the heart of the story, since Pi's status as an irrational and transcendental number signals the idea of abstraction, irresolution and the infinite – the condition of the universe that the narrative deals with. Pi's childhood is characterised by his spiritual curiosity, and his mutual engagement with Christianity, Islam and Hinduism, a pluralist eclecticism that sits uneasily with his father's rationalist Enlightenment sensibility. This becomes directly symbolised in a dramatic confrontation in which Pi's father seeks to demonstrate that 'the tiger is not your friend' by making him watch a tiger consume a goat. He seeks to show Pi that the tiger is essentially 'unknowable' as a spiritual creature, and 'knowable' only as an efficient carnivorous predator, implicitly insisting that the tiger has no continuity or communion with Pi, but only a necessarily distant complementariness; the tiger is pure animal, and beyond Pi's spiritual schemata. Pi is then pitched into existential chaos when he is the only survivor when the freighter carrying him, his family and a menagerie of animals to a new life in Canada is sunk during an extraordinary storm. He is then left in a lifeboat in the company of 'Richard Parker', the Bengal Tiger, an injured zebra, an orang-utang and a hyena. It is this microcosm of animal life that becomes the focus of the story, and Pi's 227-day ordeal, in which the complexities, instabilities and awesome conditions of the natural world – rendered real and imaginary, material and mythic – becomes a complex analogy for spiritual enlightenment. The use of hyper-realist animation in this case is even more compelling, since it revels in its own illusionism, here bound up with issues of memory, hallucination and belief. The very 'animism' of the story and the techniques by which it is told suggests the idea of powerful primal forces beyond our contemporary recognition or comprehension.

It is important to remember that for the film to work at all the central premise of the story – a young man co-existing with a tiger on a lifeboat in the middle of the ocean – had to be resolved as a visual system. The visual effects supervisor on the film, David Conley, notes:

We had to convince the audience that Richard Parker was a real tiger on the boat with Pi and that Pi was in real danger. Ang [Lee] was adamant about that. I don't think he would have done this movie if the tiger would wind up looking CG. (Duncan 2013: 2)

This remark is telling in the sense that already, after what is a comparatively short time, there is a sense that 'CG' can often seem a *transparent* visual idiom: a noticeable and intrusive aesthetic, sometimes obvious when something seems too weightless, or impossibly shiny, or too elastic. McClean notes, too, that

Animated characters have a tradition of acceptance. Mickey Mouse, Bugs Bunny, and Lara Croft have legions of fans who are little influenced by the fact that the characters are not 'real'. Although a great deal more could be said about why and how animated characters have obtained this acceptance, the pertinent issue to address is that CG characters have been subjected to considerably different kind [sic] of analysis rather than those created with traditional animation. (McClean 2007: 60)

This issue is closely related to context and intention. If a character operates in a quasi-cartoonal world, it is permitted more cartoonal freedoms. If, however, a character functions as part of a nominally real world, even in a fantasy story, it must obey the laws of that reality. Failure to do so, for whatever reason – whether at the level of 'perceptual verisimilitude' (McClean 2007: 142), where the image is unpersuasive, or at the cognitive level, where, simply, whatever the quality of the effect, its use cannot overcome common knowledge and plausibility – results in the collapse of the suspension of disbelief. Though all audiences will accept comic book exaggeration, there are certain times when narrative and conceptual premises fail. For example, anyone who has seen the relentless power and destructive force of the arachnids in *Starship Troopers* (Paul Verhoeven, USA, 1997), who simply overrun humankind, might ask why at the beginning of the sequel the arachnids now have sufficient respect for their adversaries to have to secretly infiltrate their base, when surely they could just destroy it! This is nothing to do with the excellence of the animated visual effects, and everything to do with not properly adhering to the already established logic of the story world.

Under these conditions, the 'CG' of films like *Starship Troopers* and *Hulk* (Ang Lee, USA, 2003), for example, might be understood as having more of the characteristics of the traditional cartoon, but within the context of a narrative like *Life of Pi*, the CG animation produced *must* attain an unobservable verisimilitude. Bill Westenhofer, who actually animated Richard Parker in *Life of Pi*, suggests that

> *A CGI tiger was really the only way you make* [sic] *this movie. You couldn't do an animatronic tiger, and you couldn't use a real tiger throughout. Even if you had a perfectly trained tiger and you*

could get the studio legal department and the insurance company to allow that tiger to interact with a kid, they were going to be trapped together on a small boat. There was no way that could happen. (Duncan 2013: 2)

These issues are echoed in the narrative itself in that Pi has to come to terms with what it means to co-habit with a tiger, and to train it accordingly, knowing all the while that its behaviour is still not predictable or guaranteed. Ironically, here, then, Westenhofer and his team had to create an animated character – Richard Parker – and achieve a level of acceptance normally accorded to animated characters, but only on terms and conditions that would mean the viewer would never question that the tiger was indeed animated. This is made all the more problematic, though, by the fact that the novel, like the film, deliberately engages with notions of 'magic realism', consciously using different registers of the real to address issues of faith, belief and the human capacity to tell stories in the service of making sense of experience.

Three sequences in the film are instructive in understanding how the use of animation must be persuasive in relation to both its context and its implicit meaning. I wish to return to my three conditions of the bi-creature – *continuity*, *communion* and *complementariness* – in order to illustrate this. Richard Parker is at once a literal animal – a Bengal tiger – and also a conduit for, and point of access to, the physical and psychological worlds Pi becomes party to. He is a constant reminder of the dialectic tension and exchange between humankind and animal, and serves to embody a natural ecosystem, which once more is 'impartial to all'. When Pi and the tiger finally reach an island after their troubled travail, both rediscover their own *continuity* with forces and imperatives that underpin the natural order. The island, rich in vegetation and fresh water pools, and populated by thousands of meerkats, initially seems a welcome idyll for Pi, who eats and refreshes himself. Richard Parker, too, indulges in a diet of meerkats, and the sense of animal hierarchy and predatory instinct reasserts itself. Earlier sequences on the boat had seen a hyena devour a zebra, and ultimately kill an orang-utang, before itself being overcome by Richard Parker. At night, though, the meerkats retreat to the trees and the tiger to the boat, and it becomes clear that the island itself is carnivorous, poisoning the water and eating living creatures. This is Darwinian adaptation at its clearest: nature at once providing and recalling, recycling and renewing, Pi and Richard Parker necessarily adjusting to survive, and to recognise their place in a wider primal order. Pi discovers a plant with a human tooth hidden in its bud, and knows that other Crusoes who have preceded him have been unwittingly eaten. Though the island's activity is correspondent to the known cycles of the natural world, it is nevertheless clear that the story remains ambivalent about the existence of such an island, and the veracity of Pi's account. The idea is made plausible, of course, by the animation of the island, and the visual effects that ensure that the events are entirely believable. Once again, in the tradition of the more progressive interpretation of Disney's 'True Life Adventures', the surreal apparently becomes a condition of the real; fantasy and reality a matter of perception; animation the very animus of the island.

In another sequence, Richard Parker stares out into the night sky, and Pi requests of him, 'Tell me what you see'. The tiger turns his head and stares into the water, followed by Pi. The camera zooms in towards the tiger, implying that the imagery that follows is in some way a visualisation of consciousness. Marine life forms encounter each other; never-before-seen creatures swim uninhibitedly; stars and cosmic clouds appear; the shipwreck and the menagerie of animals released into the ocean also appear, as do the image of Pi's mother and suggestions of religious icons. The camera zooms out from these images, though, to the face of Pi, the sequence implying that there has been *communion* between Richard Parker and Pi, where each is temporarily effaced once more by forces beyond them, but which inherently connect them. Pi is essentially revealed to himself through his animality or, more precisely, through a heightened awareness of his animality as it experiences its deepest connection with the universe. Crucially, here, it is the capacity for animation to visualise this state of being that ensures that the viewer embraces the abstraction of the moment but invests it with symbolic validity. This is not a memory or a hallucination but a communion that accepts that the unknowable, the unfathomable and the unspeakable are the common bond shared by human and animal.

On the island, Richard Parker followed his instincts and appetites; on the boat in the midnight hour, he embodied stillness. When a storm raged he swam, flailing against the powerful flow of the water. When fed, his own power was undiminished, but without food, and subject to sickness, he becomes emaciated and weak. Such is the verisimilitude of the animation that none of this is questionable, nor the moments when Pi can actually comfort the stricken tiger as he lies dying. Both the novel and the film are careful, though, that the viewer is not seduced into the belief that there is any shared reconciliation in the bond. Pi has partly trained Richard Parker, and partly seen the tiger rendered less strong and more relative in his status by the elemental circumstances surrounding him. At a metaphoric level, his struggle in the storm, for example, conveys the sense that physical materiality – for both animals and humans – denies them access to God. Richard Parker has not become 'a pet' or cultivated the anthropomorphic awareness to accept his relationship with Pi as if it were conscious. Rather, when the boat reaches the shore, the tiger simply leaves 'unceremoniously', not looking back, staring only intently into the jungle, and then onward into its lush vegetation. Despite all that they had apparently shared, Pi is left to accept the *complementariness* of their relationship – their inherent and intrinsic separateness. Pi is heartbroken, and as a mature adult recollecting his experience, he insists, 'I have to believe that there was more in his eyes than my own reflections staring back at me, I know it, I felt it, even if I can't prove it'. Importantly, then, Pi is looking to assert his relationship with Richard Parker, a relationship the viewer has witnessed, and a relationship that the animation both has facilitated and, at another level, is instrumental is denying. As Westenhofer points out,

> *it's very easy to anthropomorphise animated characters. You can go in with every intention to make it a real animal; but you know what each scene is trying to accomplish, and so there's a tendency to say, 'Maybe we should make it more clear that Richard Parker is holding Pi's gaze here', and then you've blown the 'animalism' of it. To work against that, we found a reference clip for every shot, and we stayed true to that.* (Duncan 2013: 22–23)

Conventional animated characters in drawn, clay, paper or puppet form, even more than characters in any other kind of fiction, first and foremost foreground their constructedness and illusionism, so arguably they call upon the investment and belief of the viewer to a greater degree. They are literal and iconic at the same time, and most animated films must sustain both aspects simultaneously to succeed. Motion in animation is a deliberate choreographic choice, so it must carry with it narrative and purpose. In the case of the animated animal, this usually involves taking into account the way that the animal actually moves and the way in which its anatomy and habitat affect its behaviour. In the case of the animal as a hyper-realist visual effect – Richard Parker – this representation of motion is heightened in such a way that the 'pure animal' is privileged, and the orthodox, some might say dominant, characteristics of anthropomorphised animated characters are reduced or denied. The interesting aspect here becomes the way in which Westenhofer uses reference material; this is the apparent guarantor in sustaining realism over personalisation, animalism over the self-reflexive presence of animation. Crucially, though, animation has been used to access more complex continuities between human and animal kind – primal encounters, higher natural cycles, fundamental and irreconcilable difference. The discourse that sustains the hyper-realist animated animal, then, is a combination of Disney's assimilative model and Bazin's mode of apprehension. Richard Parker is in effect the logical consequence of Disney's ambition to blend live action and animation, and to use what McClean has called 'transubstantiation' (McClean 2007: 47) – the capacity to transcend and transform characters and context using digital animation – to create (magic) realist conditions. In essence, then, Richard Parker, for all his artifice and illusionism, is a *re-substantiation* of the animal: a character and a living being testing the limits of belief, but ultimately insisting upon the discourse of the pure animal in the face of narratives, technologies or social conditions that might deny it. In believing in Richard Parker, we believe in the 'tame costume' of animation, we believe in the animal, and we believe that stories can make sense of, and shape, existence in ways that at least temporarily make our often chaotic, complex and contradictory experience conscious and comprehensible.

References

Bouse, D. (1995) 'True Life Fantasies: Storytelling Traditions in Animated Features and Wildlife Films', *Animation Journal*, 3(2), pp. 19–39.

Brode, D. (2004) *From Walt to Woodstock: How Disney Created the Counterculture*, Austin: University of Texas Press.

Duncan, J. (2013) 'The Calculus of Pi', *Cinefex*, 132 (January), iPad edition, pp. 1–32.

Jackson, K. M. (ed.) (2006) *Walt Disney: Conversations*, Jackson: University Press of Mississippi.

Jeong, S-H. (2011) 'Animals: An Adventure in Bazin's Ontology', in D. Andrew (ed.) *Opening Bazin: Post-War Film Theory and Its Afterlife*, Oxford; New York: Oxford University Press, pp. 177–186.

Martel, Y. (2001) *Life of Pi*, Edinburgh; New York; Melbourne: Canongate.

McClean, S. (2007) *Digital Storytelling: The Narrative Power of Visual Effects in Film*, Cambridge, MA; London: MIT Press.

Wells, P. (2009a) *The Animated Bestiary*, New Brunswick, NJ; London: Rutgers University Press.

— (2009b) '"Stop writing or write like a rat": Becoming Animal in Animated Literary Adaptations', in R. Carroll (ed.) *Adaptation in Contemporary Culture: Textual Infidelities*, London: Continuum, pp. 96–110.

— (forthcoming) '"You can see what species I belong to, but don't treat me lightly": Rhetorics of Representation in Animated Animal Narratives', in M. Lawrence and L. McMahon (eds) *Animal Life and the Moving Image*, New York: Columbia University Press.

JOHN CLEGG

Post-production

A CGI orang-utang
falls from his perch to knucklewalk
along the jungle track, a forward
roll which never quite completes
the way the bracken rendering
swims up toward a focus which
it never reaches – drag and drop
another file in the script
to break his gait and make him stop
and howl and howl and howl and howl
to breaking point, to make him turn –
another file in the script
will never finish – hold the mouse
and spin around a focal wedge
of broken rendering, the way
his pixels never quite cohere
along the jungle track, a backward
fall from knucklewalk to perch
to skin to frame to loading screen

LOREDANA LOY

ಹ

Representations of Animal Advocacy in Film

Iɴ ᴍᴏᴅᴇʀɴ times[1], animals have been marginalised both physically and culturally (Berger 2009). Physically, urbanisation removed animals from sight and obscured their exploitation, while industrialisation reduced them to mere raw materials, commodities and property. Culturally, animals were rendered invisible because they were defined solely through anthropocentric lenses and denied a meaningful presence in culture.[2] Anthropocentrism is the cultural ideology that assigns

---

1   *That is, the periods of industrialisation and post-industrialisation, beginning with the nineteenth century.*

2   *Berger points out that in pre-industrial times, animals were an important part of human culture, not as objects and products of exploitation, but as symbolic participants: 'to suppose that animals first entered human imagination as meat and leather or horn is to project a 19th-century attitude backwards across millennia. Animals first entered the imagination as messengers and promises' (Berger 2009: 12).*

humans the utmost importance in society. This ideology is fundamental to the process of concealing and making animal exploitation acceptable by casting it as natural and necessary.

Because animals' marginalisation and removal from sight has contributed to their invisibility and hence to their unchallenged exploitation, cinema might be a particularly powerful way to challenge anthropocentrism by reinstating the visibility of animals within the cultural context. Movies as a form of culture represent a site for the production and perpetuation of meaning (Burt 2002). The pedagogical strength of Hollywood is well documented, with Giroux (2002) even claiming that cinema influences its audiences to the extent of consciousness building.

With some exceptions, representations of animals in cinema usually follow the hegemony of anthropocentrism. In this view, films tell anthropomorphic stories that teach erroneous lessons about animals and our relationships with them. However, a dominant way of representing certain types of animals, such as the animals used in the industrial complex, is not representing them at all. Nibert points out that 'the virtual invisibility of other animals – similar to that of devalued groups of humans – teaches that their lives and experiences are irrelevant and insignificant' (2002: 208). Furthermore, Nibert argues, due to the power of the media conglomerates and their continuous efforts to manipulate consumers and influence cultural ideas, everything we know about animals we see in corporate terms.

The majority of mainstream films in which animals or animal-related themes do get represented are thoroughly speciesist, naturalising animal exploitation and its culturally accepted behaviours, such as meat eating, fur wearing, treating animals as 'cute' objects and depicting the killing or harming of animals as comedic. Baker claims that animals in popular culture have been belittled such that they exist as mere objects of entertainment and that they have come to represent 'all that is taken not-very-seriously in contemporary culture; the sign of that which doesn't really matter' (2001: 174). Porter (2006) explains that most humans experience animals as commodities. However, Porter claims, this is one reason why representations of animals in cinema matter, because these representations are a way to experience animals as 'embodied wholes' rather than dismembered products. On that note, Molloy (2011) observes that animal imagery is ubiquitous and that in the mainstream cinema box office of the last decade (2001 to 2009), at least one animal featured in the ten most financially successful movies each year, which points to the immense popularity of certain types of animal narratives, but most importantly to their profitability. Molloy also argues that these media representations are key in the formation of attitudes towards animals.

While cinematic representations routinely reinforce anthropocentrism, Burt (2002) gives an account of the power of movies to challenge traditional anthropocentric beliefs. In 1949 the filmmakers of *Gone to Earth* were prevented from shooting the final scene of their movie by an association of foxhunters. The scene depicted the heroine and her 'pet' fox running from a pack of foxhounds. The association claimed that the film would encourage anti-foxhunting sentiment: 'it is surely absurd to create propaganda out of a work of art and to create the most undesirable publicity', said the letter from the association (Burt 2002: 7). Even though the movie did not involve any graphic scenes, the symbolic messages behind this image were enough to create a stir. This means that there are films that are significant in terms of articulating a pro-animal stance. These films can create an opening for the introduction of a less anthropocentric view of the world.

The purpose of this essay is to discuss representations of such pro-animal stances by looking at movies that include messages that, though not perfect, might inspire audiences to consider animals in non-anthropocentric ways. What follows is a survey of such movies and a discussion of their narratives from an animal-centric perspective.

It must be noted that the list below is not intended to be, or presented as, exhaustive; it is a work-in-progress list of movies and genres. The reader will probably be reminded of many other movies that should be included on this list.[3]

THE 'ECO-FILM'

These films aim at delivering an environmental message to audiences. There are many types of eco-films and a few of these can be discussed in terms of the animal-related messages included in them. Alas, the connection between protecting the environment, animal exploitation and liberation is missed by most movies in this genre. This analysis operates on the assumption that animal liberation and environmental protection go hand in hand and that there is an intrinsic connection between the two movements and philosophies, exemplified by the links between factory farming, pollution and climate change, species extinction and environmental destruction (Jamieson 2002).

In *Avatar* (2009), after exhausting Earth's resources, humanity has moved on to exploit those of Pandora, a planet

3   *To suggest other movies and to contribute to this evolving survey, please write to the author, Loredana Loy, at loredana.loy@nyu.edu.*

populated by a humanoid species that has a special connection with their natural environment. The movie decries the loss of wilderness and promotes the myth of primal purity. This type of narrative reflects cultural trends often labelled as returns to 'traditional' ways of living that existed prior to industrialisation, and seems to express disenchantment with our modern society. Nonetheless, it also romanticises native people and their ways of living (see Ingram 2000: 45). Most importantly, the manner in which the natives' connection with nature is portrayed perpetuates the model of human domination over nature. The natives hunt some species of animals and use others for transportation. Ironically, individuals belonging to species that are killed for food join the natives in the fight against humans to save the planet. As much as this seems to promote the animals' sentience, the spectator is left to wonder if these animals will be returned to their utilitarian roles once humanity has been driven out and the original order has been restored. Thus, although *Avatar* has an overt ecological agenda, it paradoxically ends up delivering a conflicted message about protecting the environment while continuing to exploit some species of animals.

Also in the eco-film category are films that advocate for the protection of the natural environment and of certain species of animals. *Star Trek IV: The Voyage Home* (1986) furthers the idea that our species' survival is dependent on other species' survival. The movie's narrative implies that if humanity does not save the whales in the twentieth century, aliens who are only able to communicate with whales might destroy the planet in the twenty-third century, since the species that they are looking for no longer exists. Thus, the film plays on the philosophical idea that humanity is hindered in imagining types of intelligence other than our own. As Wittgenstein said:

'If a lion could talk, we could not understand him' (2010: 223). The film also includes some poignant scenes depicting whale extermination presented as historical material in the museums of the twenty-third century.

CHANGING PERSPECTIVES

These movies invite audiences to evaluate *otherness*. They promote a change of perspective by prompting audiences to consider some of the 'non-human others' as being similar to us. Some of these films end up delivering a speciesist message as well, but there are also exceptions that include a well-rounded animal liberation message.

In *How to Train Your Dragon* (2010), the inhabitants of an idyllic island are in a perpetual war with flying dragons. The main protagonist is a young boy who himself is an other within his group because he doesn't display warrior traits. He befriends an injured dragon and unravels the true nature of the 'beasts', who themselves are enslaved by a much more powerful dragon. After the protagonist manages to convince everyone of the dragons' true nature with the aid of his now 'pet' dragon, the humans join the fight against the tyrant dragon and defeat him. As a 'reward' the colony of dragons become 'pets' for humans and serve as means of transportation, roles that they seem happy to embrace, thus exchanging one type of enslavement for another. Thus, the dominant role of humans is replicated even in this fantasy world. Furthermore, the 'be kind to others because they are ultimately very much like us' message does not extend to the creatures who continue to be feasted upon, such as the sheep and chickens, whose carcasses adorn the festive tables. Such images of dead animals might appear to be common tropes employed to represent celebration. Nevertheless, the message about embracing non-human others is diluted this way.

In *Powder* (1995), the main character Powder (Sean Patrick Flannery) is a young albino boy who is shunned by society because of his striking appearance and who also has supernatural powers. His state as an outcast and his emotional intelligence allow him to be in tune with the suffering of others on a level that is not experienced by the average human being. In one scene Powder telepathically 'connects' a hunter with his dying deer victim and makes the hunter live the fear and agony of the animal. After the traumatising experience of seeing the world through the eyes of the dying deer, the hunter swears never to hunt again.

A similar scenario is found in *Starman* (1984), in which an extra-terrestrial from a more advanced planet ends up on Earth and takes human form. Starman (Jeff Bridges) witnesses a scene with a group of hunters and their dead deer victim, who is tied to the trunk of the hunters' car. In an effort to understand what happened to the deer he asks his companion, 'Do deer hunt men?' He brings the deer back to life and releases her. Later on when describing his own world he says that on his planet 'the strong do not victimise the helpless'.

CHARISMATIC SPECIES

This category includes movies that contain a deliberate animal advocacy message focused on an animal species generally regarded as more deserving of being protected, either for cultural reasons or because of the 'cute' or intelligence factors.

In *The Misfits* (1961), Gay (Clark Gable) is a cynical hero who

47

doesn't think twice about an opportunity to make money. When he takes his lover Roslyn (Marilyn Monroe) along to catch mustangs for the pet food industry, she laments and decries the cruelty of the act. When Guido (Eli Wallach), Gay's partner, offers to stop the carnage if Roslyn can provide 'a reason to stop it', she replies, 'Do you need a reason to be human?' This is an incredible statement in support of animals. This movie presumably caused the collapse of the horsemeat pet food industry.[4] On the down side, though, even though our heroine shows compassion towards horses, in an earlier scene she wears a fox fur. The fox's fate remains obscure because the fox is not included in the circle of beings that deserve moral consideration.

Another example is *The Day of the Dolphin* (1973), in which dolphins are taught human language, in a story that presents them as a superior species, morally pure and incapable of grasping human deception.[5] Even though this movie's message and portrayal of dolphins is emotionally touching, there are issues involved with the film's production as well as with parts of its narrative. Besides using captive dolphins, some of the experiments portrayed are incredibly cruel, such as one in which the protagonist dolphin is separated from his companion in order to force him to speak to his captors. The movie's redemption lies with the heart-breaking representation of the loving and pure nature of dolphins and the acknowledgement of their sentience.

---

4   *The popular series* Mad Men *centered an episode on this story –*
'The Gypsy and the Hobo', 25 October 2009.

5   *The film is based on the book* A Sentient Animal *by Robert Merle.*

There is a whole genre of movies that take a stand against human activities that exploit animals or affect their lives, particularly hunting, entertainment, the fashion industry, human urban expansion and travel.

In *Bambi* (1942), the forest is destroyed by hunters who leave a fire unsupervised.[6] Yet, the strongest anti-hunting message is delivered when Bambi's mother is killed by a hunter. *Bambi* was labelled by the American hunting lobby as 'the worst insult ever offered in any form to American sportsmen' (Burt 2002: 9). Movies such as *Bambi* have often been criticised for anthropomorphising animals. Invoking the use of anthropomorphism to deconstruct the validity of pro-animal arguments delivered through animal representations in films is common. Talking and feeling animals draw the wrath of pundits even today. However, from an animal advocacy perspective, Taylor (2011) points out that by imbuing an animal with the characteristics of a human, the superiority of the latter is challenged. This, she argues, has practical consequences, because if animals are like us, it is more difficult to find justifications for their exploitation. Two other Disney movies, *One Hundred and One Dalmatians* (1961) and *Finding Nemo* (2004), condemn animal exploitation industries, the fur and the aquarium industries respectively, while *Lady and the Tramp* (1955) brings attention to the plight of unwanted dogs.

All the Little Animals (1998) addresses another issue – the killing of animals by drivers on public roads as well as the connection between animal cruelty and human violence.

---

6   *The film is based on the book* Bambi: A Life in the Woods *by Felix Salten. The book was banned in Nazi Germany because it was considered that the story of the animals was an allegory for the country's treatment of the Jews.*

Mr Summers (John Hurt) travels around looking for animals who have been killed on roads and buries them. A particularly poignant scene shows a driver attempting to hit a fox intentionally. The immense number of animals killed on roads is rarely discussed, and this movie provides a rare opportunity to consider this pervasive issue.

TAKING ACTION FOR ANIMALS

These are movies that focus on delivering a well-thought-out animal advocacy or liberation message.

In *Year of the Dog*, Peggy (Molly Shannon) quits her job and becomes an animal rights activist after being exposed to the realities of animal exploitation. The movie tries to advance an animal liberation agenda by hiding behind a plot that revolves around our generally accepted love for dogs. Hence, the narrative of the movie unfolds on two scenes. On the front scene we have the story that is palatable to the general public, the one about our love for dogs. Behind this scene we have the 'hidden transcript', the more serious message about speciesism and animal rights. The movie ultimately fails in its attempt to deliver a serious message because of its apologetic tone, Peggy's activism being justified as just another personal choice that people *should* accept. In addition, Peggy is portrayed as socially inept, a misfit who blurs the lines between acceptable and unacceptable social interactions. In one instance, Peggy hides in her neighbour's closet to scare him as she jumps out with a knife and simulates an attack. She wants to give her neighbour, who is a hunter, a taste of what it is like to be hunted. However noble this idea might seem, this type of portrayal certainly hurts the audience's chance of identifying with Peggy's character and with her struggles and transformation. The question is, why would the writers make this character act in such an unlikely manner if they wanted to send out such an important message? Animal advocates already have to bear the brunt of activism stigma. Ultimately this movie self-sabotaged its message because it caricatured its characters.

Bold Native (2010) follows Charlie (Joaquin Pastor), an animal liberationist who spends two years travelling around the country recruiting other activists to stage a series of animal liberation projects. His recruits come from all walks of life and include his university professor. Charlie's father (Randolph Mantooth), a corporate paeon of the fast food industry, receives a visit from the FBI to inform him that Charlie is considered a domestic terrorist under the Animal Enterprise Terrorism Act. *Malcolm X* (1992) features scenes from the Rodney King police brutality video to remind audiences that the struggles of African Americans are not history (Guerrero 1993). In the same manner, *Bold Native* intertwines reality with fictional narrative. The movie intercuts footage from factory farming operations in order to create a feeling of urgency and give the viewer a sense that these things are real and happening now. At the end of the movie the audience is informed that 'Animals were harmed during the making of this movie. But not by us.' The screen goes on to list the staggering numbers of animals killed in the US alone in the animal industrial complex.

ADVOCACY THROUGH ALLEGORY

These films contain symbolic narratives that have to be deciphered by audiences. The interpretation of their messages

51

depends largely on the views that the audiences already hold. In a society in which the consumption and exploitation of animals is sanctioned and is the social norm, the animal industrial complex will fear and fight the infiltration of messages which threaten to usurp its hegemony. Under such constrictions, how can animal liberation messages be promoted? One possibility: in an allegorical manner.

A human-created virus has wiped out almost the entire human population in *Twelve Monkeys* (1995). The survivors live in a totalitarian regime in complete darkness under the surface of the planet. A group of scientists are in control while the rest of the population lives in cages. When Cole (Bruce Willis) is sent back in time to gather information about the origin of the epidemic and the Army of the Twelve Monkeys that apparently is responsible for spreading the virus, he meets Jeffrey (Brad Pitt), the son of a virology expert who owns an animal testing facility. The virus that caused the pandemic was stolen and released by a misanthropic scientist who worked in the facility. The film overtly condemns vivisection. In one scene, Cole and Jeffrey have a dialogue about animal testing while images of animal testing are played on the TV screen behind them, with the voiceover announcing that 'animal activists have obtained footage which has outraged the public'. Jeffrey, looking at the screen, says, 'Testing, torture, we're all monkeys!' Cole asks, 'Did they hurt you?' Jeffrey responds: 'Not as bad as what they're doing to the Easter bunny.' As the camera closes in on a rabbit who is being administered the Draize Test,[7] Cole looks up at the screen and says: 'Look at them, they're just asking for it. Perhaps the human race deserves to be wiped out.'

7   *The Draize Test is a toxicity test devised in 1944 by the Food and Drug Administration. The procedure involves testing substances dripped in the eye or on the skin of restrained, conscious animals.*

The triumph of nature over humanity is also extolled by this film. The opening scene tells us that 'Once again the animals will rule the world.' When Cole comes up to the surface of the post-apocalyptic planet to collect samples of living organisms, he is greeted by the roar of a lion resting on top of a building and by a brown bear roaming the streets. When Cole is sent back to 1990, he stops in front of a window that displays a stuffed brown bear. In the end, the Army of the Twelve Monkeys reveals itself to be just a group of kids who want to free the zoo animals. As they succeed and the zoo animals walk free through the city in the last scenes, the film shifts its visual tones to an exuberance of colour, contrasting the earlier dark tones. Humanity's demise is greeted with joy.

INVERSION AND INFERENCE

Some movies invite a look at the injustice of animal exploitation by portraying humans being treated the way animals are treated in the animal industrial complex and in our society in general.

In *Fantastic Planet* (1973) an alien race is exploiting humans, using them as pets and managing their population in much the same manner in which wild animal populations are 'managed' today. A few aliens become aware of the humans' sentience and attempt to advocate an end to their exploitation. Other movies such as *War of the Worlds* (1953, 2005) and *Soylent Green* (1973) also explore the idea of humanity being exploited and used for food; however, these movies do so in an anthropocentric fashion and not from a perspective that leaves room for interpreting the injustices as a parallel to the injustices inflicted on animals. Another film, *Never Let Me Go* (2010), explores the idea of exploiting human clones for the health industry, and the disregard and contempt for cloned human life invites the parallel to the case of animals.[8]

A rather unusual example is *The Texas Chainsaw Massacre* (1974), in which the industrial slaughter process is replicated and inflicted upon a group of human victims. The movie clearly intends to make audiences connect to what happens to animals. For example, in the slaughter scenes cries of animals can be heard, although the victims are human and no animals are present. There are many other references to animals and the meat industry, including one character describing slaughterhouse work and another one commenting that people should not kill animals for food.

ANIMAL AGENCY

These movies showcase animal agency in a unique fashion by following an animal's interaction with humans throughout the course of the animal's life and within the very limiting context of the animal's existence in a world dominated by humans.

In *The Turin Horse* (2011) the audience is presented with the destiny shared by many 'beasts of burden'. The female horse, whose name we never learn, is worked to exhaustion, carrying her 'master' to town and back in freezing cold and scathing winds. The opening scene of the movie is a glimpse of her life as an enslaved being, her torment and her inescapable doom. But she decides that there is an escape, one that most humans would not even consider accessible to her kind – she stops eating because she does not want to live like this. This is the only action available to her. The man who owns her tries to

8   *The film is based on the book with the same title by Kazuo Ishiguro.*

force her to work, pushes and whips her. Perhaps some might say that the horse has sensed the impending doom that is the destiny of this family, but regardless of how audiences decide to interpret the plot, this is one magnificent way of giving animals a real voice.

In the same way, *Au Hasard Balthazar* (1966) follows the life of Balthazar, an adorable donkey, from the moment that kids snatch him from his mother's teat to make him their pet. He spends a few years of happiness with Marie, who loves him dearly. Later on, her family gives him away to replace him with a tractor. Balthazar is passed from owner to owner, their cruelty only matched by Balthazar's increasing misery. Just like the Turin horse, Balthazar attempts to resist his fate through the limited means that are available to him. He tries to run away a few times, and even manages to get back to Marie for a short period of time. However, every time his inescapable destiny claims his freedom again and he is put back to work. He is beaten, starved, left to freeze in cold rain and snow, and even has his tail set on fire by Marie's sadistic boyfriend. A surreal moment ensues when Balthazar is forced to become part of a travelling circus, as he comes face to face with the caged animals for the first time. A tacit conversation takes place between him and a tiger, an elephant, a chimp and a polar bear, as they glance at each other, and Balthazar realises that their lives are even more wretched than his. In the end, he is abandoned on the top of a mountain with a cargo of smuggled goods on his back, while his tormentors run away from the border patrols. Balthazar is shot, but looks around and understands that he is finally free. The bleak but realistic message conveyed is that for the majority of animals exploited by humans, freedom can only mean death.

These are the films that tell the story of animals after they have escaped exploitation, and are some of the most powerful yet rare stories to be found in cinema.

In *The Plague Dogs* (1982), Snitter and Rowf are two dogs who escape from an animal experimentation facility only to find that the outside world is just as cruel.[9] They try to survive in the wild with the help of a fox. After the facility spreads a rumour that the dogs are carrying the plague in order to hasten their capture, the media generate a commotion around their escape. Hunted by the military and the farmers, upon whose sheep the dogs feed in order to survive, chased and feared by people due to the potential infection anxiety, the dogs' journey is a harrowing one. The film is told from the perspective of the animals. There is very little human presence. In fact the only contacts between the animals and the humans on screen always end in disaster. The film also touches on the so-called 'dirty trade' of selling animals from shelters and pounds to biomedical research.[10] Snitter is born in the facility, but Rowf ends up as an experimentation subject after his guardian passes away. The experiments portrayed in the movie are inspired by real experiments. The opening scene shows Snitter drowning in an endurance experiment which he is put through over and over, being revived once he drowns.

These types of films are imbued with misanthropic tones. They reflect humanity through the eyes of animals. For example, because his view of the world is determined by his sole life experience, that of being tortured by humans, when he

---

9   *The film is based on the book with the same title by Richard Adams.*

10   *The sale of unwanted companion animals to biomedical research labs is well documented (see Vetri 1987).*

sees snow for the first time, Rowf says: 'Ooohhh they're clever, they really made it too cold for us to live.' Most importantly, these films do not stand in for some metaphorical human story – these stories could not be the stories of humans.

ANIMALS AS SYMBOLS FOR HUMAN MYTHS

These movies cannot be considered to be advocating directly for animals because of their anthropocentric focus. They connect femininity with innocence and purity, as portrayed by the special relationship between women and animals. Their message is that protecting animals and being loved back by them makes one pure and even magical. However, these movies also promote the idea that this type of purity and innocence is in essence feminine – most importantly, *childlike*, which is problematic for reasons that are beyond the scope of this essay.

In *The Sorceress* (1956), Ina (Marina Vlady) is a young Swedish girl who lives in the forest with her grandmother away from civilisation. The two of them are regarded by villagers as witches. Ina rescues and releases animals from hunter traps during her peregrinations through the forest. She is hated by the villagers and in the end is killed by them. The last scene of the movie shows her lying on the forest floor, comforted by the baby deer that she had saved.

And finally, *Green Mansions* (1959) is a similar story set in the Amazonian rainforest. Rima (Audrey Hepburn) lives with her grandfather, also away from civilisation, and has a special connection with the animals who live in the forest. The grandfather hides his meat-eating ways from his vegetarian granddaughter. Most importantly, Rima's vegetarianism is justified through her love for animals. Paralleling the tropes of *The Sorceress*, Rima is killed by the natives because she is considered a witch.

These are just some examples of movies and genres that can be discussed from a pro-animal perspective. As mentioned in the opening of this essay, this list is open-ended and is not presented as complete. It is certainly missing important genres which could not be included due to space limitations, such as the 'Animal Revolution' genre, in which *The Birds* (1963) and *Rise of the Planet of the Apes* (2011) would be the guests of honour. This essay endeavours to start a conversation about ways of seeing animal representations in movies and invites readers to pay attention to the manner in which some stories can be interpreted as advocacy for animals.

As argued in the opening, visual animal representations are essential determinants of attitudes and behaviours towards animals. These representations can prompt audiences to question animals' actual circumstances in real life and provoke ethical and moral considerations. As Burt (2002) points out regarding *Gone to Earth*, the association of foxhunters wanted to prevent a movie from offering audiences a glimpse of the reality of foxhunting. Similarly, we have seen how some of the movies discussed in this survey might have the potential to provoke audiences to think critically about the subject of animal exploitation.

Duncombe says that in our spectacle-dominated time, 'truth and power belong to those who tell the better story', and that by imagining tales of resistance we can 'manufacture dissent' (2007: 8–9). Duncombe argues that entertainment can be used to make people dream about a better world and that activists need to harness fantasy in order to make people aspire to these dreams and create the world that they are seeking. Therefore, for the vision of animal liberation, cinema represents one of the few settings in which a better world can be not only imagined, but also visually and symbolically constructed and promoted to millions of people.

References

Baker, S. (2001) *Picturing the Beast: Animals, Identity, and Representation*, Chicago: University of Illinois Press.

Berger, J. (2009) *Ways of Seeing*, New York: Viking Press.

Burt, J. (2002) *Animals in Film: Locations*, London: Reaktion.

Duncombe, S. (2007) *Dream: Re-imagining Progressive Politics in an Age of Fantasy*, New York: The New Press.

Giroux, H. A. (2002) *Breaking in to the Movies: Film and the Culture of Politics*, Massachusetts: Blackwell Publishers Malden.

Guerrero, E. (1993) *Framing Blackness: The African American Image in Film*, Philadelphia: Temple University Press.

Ingram, D. (2000) 'Ecological Indians and the Myth of Primal Purity', in *Green Screen: Environmentalism and Hollywood Cinema*, Exeter: University of Exeter Press.

Jamieson, D. (2002) *Morality's Progress: Essays on Humans, Other Animals, and the Rest of Nature*, New York: Oxford University Press.

Kashani, T. (2010) 'Hollywood and Nonhuman Animals: Problematic Ethics of Corporate Cinema', in B. Frymer, T. Kashani, A. Nocella and R. Van Heertum (eds) *Hollywood's Exploited: Public Pedagogy, Corporate Movies, and Cultural Crisis*, New York: Palgrave Macmillan, pp. 219–234.

Molloy, C. (2011) *Popular Media and Animals*, New York: Palgrave Macmillan.

Nibert, D. (2002) *Animal Rights/Human Rights: Entanglements of Oppression and Liberation*, Lanham, MD: Rowman Littlefield.

Taylor, N. (2011) 'Anthropomorphism and the Animal Subject', in R. Boddice (ed.) *Anthropocentrism: Humans, Animals, Environments*, Leiden: Brill Academic Publishers.

Vetri, K. (1987) 'Animal Research and Shelter Animals: An Historical Analysis of the Pound Animal Controversy', *St Louis University Law Journal*, 31, pp. 551–575.

Wittgenstein, L. (2010) *Philosophical Investigations*, New York: Wiley-Blackwell.

TÂNIA REGINA VIZACHRI

ॐ

The Human–Animal Dialectic in Animated Movies

ANIMATED features have a high appeal due to their technological craft, creativity and moral message. They have a significant influence on people's imaginations. It is interesting to note that the protagonists of these movies are usually anthropomorphised animals. Adults usually understand these animal representations as metaphors for our society or humanity. So, we can ask ourselves: Is anthropomorphising ethically valid? What does it show about our culture? What about our relationship with other animals?

The anthropomorphisation of animals is the attribution of human characteristics to non-human animals. There are suggestions that the onset of anthropomorphic thought dates back at least 40,000 years, to 'Paleolithic art representing a conversion from totemic representation – of humans in animal form – to the inverse' (Mithen quoted in Horowitz and Bekoff 2007: 31). 'Anthropomorphism might be considered a product of natural selection, a "tentative adaptation" to our environment' (Horowitz and Bekoff 2007: 31). Evolutionary psychology suggests that anthropomorphisation of the animal is natural among humans. This mechanism is necessary to protect the species, as well as to anticipate potential hazards or necessary aid. In their book *When Elephants Weep*, Jeffrey Masson and Susan McCarthy quote the British philosopher Mary Midgley, who, discussing elephants and their trainers in India, argues that although the trainers may misinterpret some aspects of elephants' behaviour because they rely on anthropomorphism, if they were misinterpreting the basic feelings of elephants day to day – when they are angry or suspicious, for example – they would have problems beyond the professional; they would also be risking their lives (Masson and McCarthy 1995: 21).

If we turn to a consideration of Native Americans, what can say?

Lévi-Strauss (2009) said that Native Americans and the majority of primitive people believed there was a natural harmony between humans and animals and that they could communicate with each other. He shows that even now we are nostalgic for that primitive harmony, exemplified by our plastic and plush animals, as well as – I would add – our liking for looking after animals and pets, and admiring them in children's animation.

The Brazilian anthropologist Viveiros de Castro (2002) adds to this example of nostalgic anthropomorphism when he discusses Native American perspectivism. While anthropologists believe in multi-naturalism, where the assumption is that there is only one nature and several indigenous cultures, Native American perspectivism assumes that there is one spirit and a variety of bodies. So animals perceive themselves as persons and other species as prey. Perspectivism, then, can also be thought of as a form of anthropomorphism.

We can say that cartoons adopt a perspectivist view. They imply that animals have intentions and views like our own. This viewpoint allows us to understand animated films as having a social function. Such animation serves as an imaginary solution to tensions, conflicts and contradictions that cannot be solved within reality. Therefore, we can say there is a mythical function in animated movies (Hirschman and Sanders 1997). This means it is important that these narratives are decoded.

As cartoons have a cultural meaning, it is important to understand this meaning. Many people see them as simply metaphors for society. But animals cannot be reduced to a metaphor; this would be to treat them as a smaller area of interest, less worthy of academic study (Baker 2001). And it is not true! Animals have a representative history that has specific connotations linked to ethics and welfare (Burt 2002). So animals are more than a simple metaphor. We should see representations of animals as an expression of our relationship with them.

There is an unsolved dialectic between non-human and human animals in our society that is reflected by these kinds of movies. Cartoons can reinforce the dominant ideology, reproducing the need for animal exploitation, but they can also show us other possibilities, representing our relationship with animals in more ethical and respectful terms.

After all, the media doesn't just transmit stories that reinforce the ideology. Stories can also question the ideology (Kellner 2001). These messages need to make sense and they need to be in accordance with cultural receptors. The cultural industry's main characteristic is the standardised production and reproduction of goods, the function of which is to satisfy consumers' needs (Adorno and Horkheimer 1972). If the products weren't aimed at satisfying consumers' needs, they would not be accepted without resistance.

Therefore, we can understand animated movies as dialectic movies in which relations of exploitation and subversion are intertwined. *Bee Movie* is a good example of this dialectic relation: until the middle of the film, the human–animal relationship represented appears to be something deep and liberating. There is a friendly relationship between a human and a bee – due to the insect's modest ability to induce empathy in humans. The bee gets to the point of having its rights recognised by human society. But in the end a great inversion occurs that restores order: the bee works for the human again, and a bee lawyer persuades other bees that it is necessary to work for humans, because it is part of the natural cycle. If animals did not work for humans, nature would be unbalanced and this would be the end of life.

The representation of animals in animated film has changed: they are now presented in quite a sophisticated and credible way (Malamud 2007). These animations engage in moral or environmental discourses about our relationship with animals which reflect a cultural change in our relationship with them. However, although these films offer truer, more naturalistic representations and moral discourses about animal rights, we know that the animal voices in animated movies are the creation of a cultural industry and that they represent the interests of the society in which they were created. Therefore, they show us how our society views animals and our relationship with them. This goes some way to explaining why the end of *Bee Movie* is so cathartic.

Bee Movie pleases those who defend animal rights because it raises real questions about the possibilities of human–animal relationships. But it also pleases the beekeepers and animal exploitation industries because it creates a fake necessity for the consumption of honey, deeming it normal, natural and necessary (see Joy 2010).

Although we see messages at the end of some movies which suggest that animal abuse is not acceptable (along the lines of 'No animals were harmed in the making of this picture'), such messages do not cover rhetorical violence. Even though we may pay lip service to animal rights and independence, our actions are connected to our own desires and emotions (Malamud 2010). When we watch animals in movies, we see ourselves, our culture. These movies impose a human narrative, a human cultural aesthetic, on animals. Randy Malamud asks us a question:

Millions of people have seen these films, crossover blockbuster hits. Does this testify to our increasing interest and concern for other animals, or does it mean that we've dragged these creatures down to the level of mass entertainment, which is inherently anti-ecological and anti-animal because of the hegemonies of consumption culture in Western industrial society? (Malamud 2010)

However, is it entirely true that animated films exist solely to reproduce and legitimise the capitalist order? Do these cartoons show us any other vision of nature? After all, these

67

animation movies also give the animals a chance to defend themselves and sometimes do justice to the wronged ones, as in *Chicken Run*.

Animations like *Madagascar*, *Ratatouille*, *Chicken Run* and *Bee Movie* show changes in our view of nature and animals. They portray a greater concern for their animal protagonists and their feelings (Malamud 2007). They suggest the possibilities of human–animal relationships and also alternatives – though inexplicit – to animal consumption.

Fewer and fewer people live in the countryside, and the majority cannot experience animals in their natural habitat. The world is becoming increasingly urbanised and prevents children from becoming acquainted with animals. Nowadays, few children live close to animals, except dogs, cats, fish and birds. So, animal representations in different media are responsible for filling a gap in children's imagination. In the absence of contact and coexistence with animals, children receive these images and process them. Therefore, the way these animals are represented is very important for children's mental formations of who the animal is, particularly when these films are shown at the cinema and released on DVD to reach the widest possible audience.

Increasingly, children spend their time in front of visual media rather than out in the streets. Such media play an important role in children's identity formation. Studies of reception have shown that these messages are not simply accepted by passive receptors; rather we should consider these receptors as subjects who draw up and re-frame media messages (White 1998). The subject receptors re-frame the messages which they have access to. Therefore, the process of giving a new meaning to movies is dialectic, and the receptor has limited liberty in this process. For example, *Chicken Run* and

Bee Movie offer an important reflection on animal consumption. Children reflect spontaneously on this issue when they question the origin of meat, and they are very often horrified when they make the connection to the reality of their food's origin. However, children's reflections on this discovery are often repressed by their parents. In this context cartoons can often, in an engaging manner, stimulate children's reflection.

Like adults, children are not passive receptors, and they give a new meaning to messages according to their environment. Animation does not wield isolated power for change, transformation or alienation. Its interpretation depends on its social use and the contexts in which it is watched. The message presented in animated movies will inform children's construction of signification and comprehension of the world. These movies have become an important part of our narrative production and cultural consumption because they tell us something about who we are, who we want to be and who we should be. As many adults do not allow or stimulate children's reflection on the consumption of animals, children frequently do their own reflection and elaborate their thoughts according to what they watch. They can also reflect when talking to other children, or they may simply forget the message, because the context in which we live invites us to embrace obliviousness, particularly where the origin of food is concerned.

Animated film can bring discourses of either reproduction or subversion of animal exploitation to viewers' attention. This contradiction constitutes a Marxist dialectic because the films show us the different interests surrounding the human–animal relationship and seek a way to overcome this contradiction. But just like myths, such films seek to overcome the problem using the imaginary. Unfortunately, this is far from a full solution in a real or even symbolic sense.

We should not expect ethical messages from the cultural industry. This is an industry that aims to achieve the highest profit possible and to bring pleasure to the greatest possible audience. It is crucial that, in our roles as parents and teachers, we instigate reflection and elucidate the problems and contradictions of this type of animated film, contradictions which pass unnoticed when we merely enjoy the movie.

References

Adorno, Theodor and Max Horkheimer (1972) 'The Culture Industry: Enlightenment as Mass Deception', in *The Dialectic of Enlightenment*, New York: Herder and Herder.

Baker, Steve (2001) *Picturing the Beast: Animals, Identity, and Representation*, University of Illinois Press.

Burt, Jonathan (2002) *Animals in Film*, London: Reaktion Books.

Chauí, Marilena (2007) 'Desafios e obstáculos para o educador democrático', conference paper, E. E. Rui Bloem, São Paulo, 5 August.

De Castro, Viveiros (2002) 'Perspectivismo e Multinaturalismo na América indígena', in *A inconstância da alma selvagem e outros ensaios de antropologia*, São Paulo: Cosac and Naify.

Hirschman, Elizabeth C. and Clinton R. Sanders (1997) 'Motion Pictures as Metaphoric Consumption: How Animal Narratives Teach Us to Be Human', *Semiotica*, 115(1/2), pp. 53–79.

Horowitz, Alexandra C. and Marc Bekoff (2007) 'Naturalizing Anthropomorphism: Behavioral Prompts to Our Humanizing of Animals', *Anthrozoös*, 20(1), pp. 23–35.

Joy, Melanie (2010) *Why We Love Dogs, Eat Pigs and Wear Cows: An Introduction to Carnism*, San Francisco: Conari Press.

Kellner, Douglas (2001) *Culturas da mídia*, Bauru, São Paulo: Edusc.

Lévi-Strauss, Claude (2009) 'A lição de sabedoria das vacas loucas', *Estududos Avançados* (São Paulo), 23(67).

Malamud, Randy (2007) 'Animal Animated Discourse', *Chronicle of Higher Education*, 19 October.

— (2010) 'Animals on Film: The Ethics of the Human Gaze', *Spring*, 83, www.english.gsu.edu/pdf/Spring.pdf.

Masson, Jeffrey and Susan McCarthy (1995) *When Elephants Weep: The Emotional Lives of Animals*, New York: Dell Publishing.

White, Robert A. (1998) 'Recepção: a abordagem dos estudos culturais', *Comunicação e educação*, 12, pp. 57–76.

MIKE WEST

ॐ

Extras | Commentaries | Owls

Rabbits?
Tortoise?
Spider's web?
I flew into Miss Gish's trailer,
but see the clock?
bam! four udders.
Oh, Charles wanted to –

but Mitch
because this
Finally, cast all the cows you want
twisting your head

Puppets.
Clockwork.
Mitch drew that:
got an eye pencil,
One hour, on the beak,
Didn't fake the udders.
"A fellow in Dryden Street
made Beerbohm Tree the
most exquisite
imitation udders,"
he says don't schvitz:
this was fifty-five.
without

over your shoulder.
That milk drip?

like manna.

Up there
we watched
on a horse
on a pony
without giving
I kiboshed the tattoo;
so Mitch
but Charles said "Dear boy,"

that branch
the preacher
that was the midget
red scare, black list
a left hand HOOT.
I don't eat rabbits
Mitch was kvetching
he said "if she kills it
that's one thing and if she
doesn't that's another
thing but really
who's to say?"
I flew off that branch.
was fifty-five:

so she flies
I tell you, this
perspective
without bobbing your head

like they're fixing a rope.

AMANDA GILROY

❧

*Significant Others: Of Horses and Men
in* The Wild Horse Redemption

IN THE opening shots of Canadian director John Zaritsky's 2007 documentary *The Wild Horse Redemption*, wild mustangs gallop through rugged foothills in Northern Wyoming pursued by a helicopter.[1] As they speed through the snow and across the screen accompanied by stirring music, their hoofbeats conjure up images of the frontier wilderness, evoke the aura of cowboy culture, and recall those quintessential American values of endurance and independence that are celebrated in so many classic Westerns. Subtitles in the long expository prelude

---

1   *Subsequent citations of* The Wild Horse Redemption *(Point Grey Pictures, 2007) will abbreviate the title to* WHR. *In-text references are to the film's chapters; screenshots are identified by chapter and time.*

inform us that these horses are the legacy of the European conquest of the Americas, give details about the Bureau of Land Management's protection of the breed since 1971 and note its decree that public lands in ten western states can support 27,500 mustangs. Thousands of horses are taken annually from the herds to maintain both population and habitat stability. Following some of the mustangs put into training for sale or adoption, the documentary focuses on the horses that end up at East Canon Correctional Complex in Colorado.[2] If the big skies of southern Colorado remind us throughout of the horses' loss of freedom, the film is interested in what is gained as well as what is lost. What modes of equine agency are visible within the clearly demarcated limits of their new social sphere? How do the captive horses and imprisoned men connect and communicate with each other? The intertwined narratives of horses and inmates are played out principally in the theatrical space of the training ring, where the techniques of 'natural horsemanship' transform both participants.[3]

In this essay, I will argue that the documentary has two dominant narrative and visual/technological registers.

2   *The 1971 Wild Free Roaming Horses and Burros Act designated mustangs as 'living symbols of the historic and pioneer spirit of the West' (quoted in Behar 2010). See Dalke (2010), Behar (2010) and Walker (2010) for a discussion of the controversies around the political ideologies that fuel the management of mustangs. To the best of my knowledge, the present essay is the first on the documentary.*

3   *'Natural horsemanship' is a training system that is perceived by its practitioners to be kinder than traditional methods. It has gained global popularity through famous 'horse whisperers' such as Pat Parelli and Monty Roberts (the inspiration for Robert Redford's film, discussed in this volume). See Lynda Birke for an excellent overview of the cults and cultures of natural horsemanship.*

The first I call an *aesthetic of alignment*, whereby the horses and men are understood in terms of parallel stories and plot trajectories. Of course, the setting itself establishes the linkage of horses and men: both are disenfranchised and disempowered, if unequally so, and both are guests of the federal government, dependent on its schedules and policies. As Carol Walker (2010) observes, 'These horses are in jail, separated from their families, their homes, and yet they are innocent of any wrongdoing. They are simply guilty of living on our public lands.' The film gives substance to this simple structural analogy, recording and reinforcing interspecies symmetry through cross-cutting, visual links and spoken commentary. In the process, species boundaries start to become blurred. The second register is an *aesthetic of attunement*, whereby new identities are produced by the intimacies of interaction.[4] The training ring is a type of 'contact zone', to use Mary Louise Pratt's term: a 'social space ... where disparate cultures meet, clash, and grapple with each other' (Pratt 1992: 4). In tracing these aesthetics through the film's four primary horse/human partnerships, I will show how it is both the document and the agent of a '"contact" perspective [that] emphasizes how subjects are constituted in and by their relations to each other' (Pratt 1992: 6). The encounters between humans and horses can be understood as forms of what Donna Haraway calls 'becoming with' animals, that is, as material, semiotic and affective practices of interaction and transformation.

---

4   *I borrow the term 'aesthetic[s] of attunement' from Kari Weil (2012: xx, passim).*

'I'm like you.' ('Fragile World', written and performed by Mack Starks in *WHR*)

From the outset, the operational logic of the film establishes parallels between the captive horses and the imprisoned men. The opening sequence cuts between scenes of the horses being herded by helicopter into a chute and then onto trucks and scenes of the men being offloaded from a bus in handcuffs. Jump-cuts shift between the legs of the horse and the legs of the inmates, and later between a group of men and a group of horses. A horse is branded with its identifying number while an inmate (Jon Peterson) talks about his DOC number (chapter 2). Images of fences and chains of various sorts (the tangled wire of the prison security fence; the fences of the pens within which the horses jostle; chains hanging from the guards' uniforms; the sides of the horse trucks) form a visual rhetoric that links the two imprisoned species. In the first of many

Mustangs in transportation, chapter I: 2.49.

such scenes, we look through the apparatus of containment at the horses, and sometimes they look back from the frame (chapter 1).

Similarly, the inmates look out at the landscape and horse pens through the windows of the bus. These shots figure an emotional framework of constraint and longing, of what one might call a shared structure of feeling. The aural soundtrack reinforces the structural parallels, especially in the recurring sounds of gates and doors slamming. At the end of chapter 6, the image of inmate Brandon in a snow storm fades out to a scene of a mustang herd in the snow; the species are correlated not only by the camera technique and shared weather, but also by the song that accompanies the second scene, with its pointed lyrics, notably 'I'm like you / Haunted by whatever I can't do / Like you' (the whole scene has focused on horse/human anxieties).

This aesthetic of alignment subtends the written and spoken commentary as well. An early subtitle claims that the inmates' new job 'will pit them against a creature wilder, stronger, and more dangerous than they are'. The senior staff trainer, Guy McNulty, constantly compares humans and horses. Thus, if they 'get excited, [they] don't think good' (chapter 3); Samson (one of the documentary's equine protagonists) is 'hard to change, and Jon Peterson [the trainer with whom the horse is paired] is the same way'. Anthony Edwards, the senior inmate trainer who is released during the course of the documentary, says, 'I see a lot of me in the horses'. Brian Hardin, the director of the Wild Horse Inmate Program, jokes to camera that with the new gentler training methods, 'the recidivism of the horses is way down'. Discussion of anger issues among inmates is followed immediately by a scene of horses fighting and biting each other (chapter 3). There is much comment on the 'moods' of the horses, and inmates identify 'their' horse as being 'like me'. Peterson comments that 'When Sam kicked me ... I didn't hold it against him. I knew he was just scared. ... I was a fighting fool' (chapter 7). Thus he understands Sam's behaviour by analogy with his own past.

The film asks us then to consider the similarities between men and mustangs. This strategy has a number of effects. On the one hand, the men's (and the movie's) compulsion to identify with another's experience is anthropomorphic: they project human qualities onto horses in a potentially narcissistic erasure of the boundaries of difference. On the other hand, as critics have noted recently, this type of identification is precisely what moves people to care for and about other animals. Most importantly, the structural parallelism of their twinned imprisonment focuses our attention on the shared response of men and horses to captivity and training. The loss of freedom provides the framework for an exploration of equine agency, with agency defined less as something innate than as something produced and performed in a particular context (see Burt 2002: 31).

Both participants are disempowered when they make contact in the training ring. While the contact zone typically involves colonial relations of domination and subordination, here both inmates and horses are subject to a disciplinary technology. The training methods of natural horsemanship might be gentler than the older, more brutal ways of horse 'breaking', but nevertheless it is worth noting that the programme's acronym is WHIP. As Anthony Edwards observes, the training programme rescues horses and men from 'chaos' and gets them to 'conform' to social norms. We witness the process by which docile bodies, and minds, are produced. The horses who kick against the metal sides of the round pen behave like horses and function as well as metaphoric substitutes for the human subjects, whose participation in the programme is contingent on their continuing good behaviour. The men must 'abide by the rules', as Guy puts it, and the horses have to learn that there is 'another way to conduct themselves'. As becomes clear through the film, the inmates internalise the disciplinary regime; the documentary posits that the horses do the same, in a gesture that defines them as thinking creatures. As reviewers are fond of noting, both horses and men are 'gentled'.

Critical writing about 'animal-assisted' programs like WHIP tends to focus on the dual benefits to the incarcerated men of the acquisition of vocational skills and life lessons.[5] The horses (or dogs, as used in some prisons) are the means to transform and rehabilitate the prisoners. Learning patience, empathy and self-discipline, the men learn 'to feel human again' (Deaton 2005: 49). Thus, the horses have instrumental and exchange value (they generate profit for the prison and the Bureau of Land Management through their sale), but little attention is paid to their subjectivity. In *WHR*, however, the horses are what Jonathan Burt calls 'participant observers in visual culture' (2002: 37). Observation is one of the primary motifs in the film, from the surveillance tower and cameras that preside over the complex to the involved observers at each training session and the horses that look at the camera. Significantly, there are close-ups of horses' eyes in almost every chapter of the documentary. Vision is the dominant human sense

---

5   *The documentary colludes with the idea that the programme prepares inmates for the labour market, not least in its attention to Anthony Edwards, who gets a job training thoroughbreds, though his exceptional status is encoded in both his equestrian talent and his romantic-lead good looks. In practice, most inmates would find it hard to enter the equine industry, which is full of people willing to work for a pittance because they love horses.*

(though not the dominant equine sense) and historically has been privileged over the other ways of experiencing the world. To focus on the animal's eye is to suggest again its link to the human and to posit its interiority and potential for thinking and understanding. The film is careful in its articulation of the limits of the visual. It annotates differences as well as similarities between the look of the human and the look of the horse. As I noted already, both horses and men look out of windows, from the bus or from their prison cells, or through fences and trucks. However, the camera rests *inside* with the human protagonists looking out, while it is *outside* looking in at the horses, who look back at it and us. In this sense the film resists imputing meaning to the equine gaze and suggests that we may never fully understand what we see.

That said, in the documentary's most significant scenes in the training ring, the shared look between men and horses is a key site of mutual comprehension. In the next section, I want to explore Jonathan Burt's notion that the cross-species exchange of looks is the foundation of 'a social contract':

> *The very fact of screening the mutual gaze between human and animal to an audience means that film is always going to play on a number of different registers that relate to both psychological and social aspects of visual culture. This effectively means that this exchange of looks is not just a form of psychic connection but also determines the practical interaction taking place. In that sense the exchange of the look is, in the absence of the possibility of language, the basis of a social contract.* (Burt 2002: 38–39)

In outlining the 'aesthetics of attunement' that structure the stories of the equine/human partnerships, I want to attend also to the ways in which the documentary moves *beyond* the hegemony of the visual to engage with other modes of shared understanding.

'Queer messmates in mortal play' (Haraway 2008: 19)

The cover image of the 2008 DVD depicts a cowboy with his arm round a horse, and the line 'Can two creatures help each other to a better life?' The film's title plays with the notion of redemption for both parties, and many online reviews talk about the 'transformation' that takes place in the men and the mustangs. What are the constituents of this transformation, and how is it enacted? What does 'attunement' signify? What new identities are produced by the interaction of men and mustangs? As we have seen, critics claim that prisoners are 'humanised' by their relationships with the horses: they are no longer the violent and anti-social figures of popular media representations – more human, less animal, in other words. While the film annotates this acquisition of humanity, the interspecies symmetry that it works so hard to enforce means that the mustangs are humanised, too; not only are they tamed, but human qualities and characteristics are attributed to them. And, perhaps more radically, the men undergo a process of what I would term 'horsification'.

The documentary tells the intertwined stories of four human/horse combinations, as well as the post-prison narrative of one former inmate. Though I will discuss each partnership separately, in the film itself the stories are not self-contained but loop through the narrative, so that activities recur in a rhythmic, repetitive pattern that gives the plot a type of organic authenticity. The most dramatic transformative activities take place in the 'contact zone' of the training ring; this is the space in which transculturation –

the upending and translating of conventions and merging of cultures – takes place. Transculturation is not an easy process: it includes the aspect of struggle, the sense of 'grappling' to which Pratt (1992) refers, as represented in the comical scene when the camera cross-cuts between inmates, who recount their litany of injuries. Thus, to a banjo backtrack, we hear how they have been kicked, bitten, stomped and bucked off (chapter 7). Recently, Donna Haraway has picked up and started to run with the notion of the contact zone as the space where species are constituted by a 'dance of encounters'; as she puts it, 'the partners do not precede the meeting' (2008: 4). Haraway writes about dog agility training and the ways in which training establishes relations between creatures with different corporeal and linguistic vocabularies, who get attuned to each other's languages and share conversations. This is the process we see in *WHR*, whereby emotional (and physical) conflict is transformed into 'hearing and mutual recognition' and the contact zone becomes a space 'in which to construct shared understandings, knowledges, claims on the world' (Pratt 1992: 587).

There are two younger inmates, both of whom are paired with horses who mirror their temperaments and personalities, or vice versa. It is worth observing that the equine protagonists are all individualised: like their human counterparts, they are named and brief details are given about their origins (just as we learn how the inmates ended up in prison), and, significantly, they are all male. Brandon Clay is a young black inmate with a track history of truancy, drug use and petty theft. He is paired with a fearful three-year-old Pinto gelding called Apache, from the Lost Creek, Wyoming Range. Scared of horses, initially Brandon works as the book clerk. It is only after *playing* at being a cowboy by roping a dummy steer that Brandon decides to become a trainer. Subsequent scenes continue the emphasis on performance but destabilise the species roles. In a wonderful role-play scene, Guy helps newbie Brandon deal with some training issues: Guy takes over the role of trainer and Brandon performs as the horse, moving around in response to his trainer's actions.

Guy and Brandon, chapter 4: 25.20.

Horse and human seem to be mobile subject positions that can be occupied by either species. Thus, the film encodes a parallel rhetoric of zoomorphism, whereby humans are imagined as animals, to match its discourse of anthropomorphism. In a key scene, Peterson first lassos Brandon before roping Apache, linking them together through his act (chapter 8). He instructs Brandon to 'see his eye', and the camera offers a close-up of Apache's eye. Here Brandon's own fear sensitises him to Apache's fear. While he professes to understand the horse through this visual engagement, their most significant interaction is when Clay takes off his gloves and touches the horse. When he rides Apache for the first time, he nervously rubs the horse all over following Guy's advice to 'let him know you're partners, just be part of him'. Brandon is not a natural rider, and bounces around the ring, but horse and rider are bonded. A long camera shot shows them walking back to the pen together, an image of intimacy that will be repeated with other partnerships.

Barad replaces the notion of 'inter-action' with 'intra-action' to emphasise that the actors in a performative relationship are less distinct entities, acting upon each other from 'outside', than intertwined agencies that mutually construct each other (2003: 815). Haraway writes that 'touch ramifies and shapes accountability. Accountability, caring for, being affected, and entering into responsibility are not ethical abstractions; these mundane, prosaic things are the result of having truck with each other' (2008: 36). Their comments speak to the intra-action that Zaritsky observes here. Brandon is very emotional to find that the horse trusts him, and movingly says he wants to adopt him. But both actors remain constrained by the scripts they inhabit: Brandon is released two months later, and an ironic subtitle, positioned immediately after Brandon's wish, tells us that Apache was adopted by a woman in Texas. We hear no more about the horse, but Brandon has been changed by his affective encounter. He tells us he's learned 'patience', but perhaps more importantly, though the documentary does not overtly engage with the issue of racial disprivilege, the meeting of species propels Brandon into the inheritance of alternative histories and identities. Thus, he acknowledges the legacy of black cowboy Bill Pickett, whose iconic status highlights the classically white discourse of cowboy culture, and embraces his performative identity as 'Cowboy Troy' (the name of a black country rapper).

Articulate but inscrutable behind his round glasses, former drug addict Matt Peeples connects with Chad, a similarly enigmatic dark horse from the Crook Mountain, Wyoming Range. Plump, quietly spoken and thoughtful, Matt is teased by the other inmates. As part of the desensitising process for his gelding Chad, Matt has to move round the horse jumping up and down, while his trainer Tim calls Matt 'cute', comments on the horse's moustache and claims they are 'look[ing] at Peeples' big boobs bouncing up and down'. Held within that spectatorial gaze, Matt is positioned by others as the feminine part of this equation, and, in the context of an all-male prison, subjected to the discourses of homosociality and homosexuality. In an important later scene, Matt and Chad 'join up' as horse follows rider round the ring after their first ride, a tribute to Matt's ability to move harmoniously with his partner. Both subjects display their openness to being transformed by difference in the training process. Chad's new docility facilitates his adoption by a home for at-risk youth, where he will help to transform others. He steps confidently onto the horse trailer that will take him away. Matt undergoes an extreme makeover. Physically, he loses forty pounds in three months, and we see him reading books on horse training and planning a career as a vet. Most significantly, *enacting* the relationship with Chad validates Matt's self-worth outside the boundaries of the prison house of gender. It is not that he moves from femininity to the security of masculinity, but that he can talk confidently about 'feeling love from animals' without fear of sexist commentary. A discourse of domestication supplants the focus on gender discrimination. Horses become part of Matt's family unit, as the camera observes in its movement from family photos on the notice board by his bed to the horse books above the bed and in his hand (chapter 5).

Both of the older inmates are released near the end of the film. Tim Schoenleber's horse Nash has already been adopted by the US Border Patrol, and we see him only a few months later behaving perfectly at a town parade. Though Tim says he will be 'walking on eggshells' after his release, Nash's easy transition into *his* new life augurs well for his partner. The final relationship that I'll discuss is that between Jon Peterson and Samson. It forms the emotional core of the film. Their stories frame the narrative: they are the first pair we meet and the documentary concludes with their fates. At the age of forty-four, Jon has spent twenty-seven years in prison. Jon 'loved the adrenalin rush of running the streets', and old photos show a young man at home in the urban wilderness. Samson, or Sam, is a four-year-old sorrel stallion. If the two alpha males have 'got an understanding', theirs is nevertheless the most conflicted of the relationships we witness, and Samson's training the most problematic.

Straight after Guy confirms that 'Peterson is in the top end of the tough ones out here', Samson runs from his pen to the training ring, charges out again when the gate is not closed quickly enough, and then barrels around the ring when he is back inside (chapter 3). Talking quietly to him all the time, Jon approaches Samson to make their first tactile contact. The camera frames both participants in a moment of visual equality as they stand looking at each other.[6] The reframing of community in terms of mixed species continues as Jon touches Sam's face, with the camera switching sides to give us the alternating perspectives of horse and human. This mutual gaze allows us to speak about the ways in which the animal 'regulate[s] its symbolic effects' (Burt 2002: 37), and thus to

6   See also the later scene in chapter 4 when Sam and Jon look at each other and the subsequent close-ups of Sam's head.

think about equine agency. But *WHR* does not fetishise the gaze. Jon's words are matched by Sam's snorting, which dominates the soundtrack. Towards the end of the scene, Jon's hand and Sam's nostrils and eye fill the screen like a kinaesthetic collage. Instead of elevating language as the sign of human superiority, Zaritsky foregrounds the reciprocal semiotics of species.

Jon and Samson, chapter 3: 19.55.

The embodied communication between Jon and Sam continues in a paradigmatic scene in chapter 6, when Jon puts his weight on Sam's back and eventually lies stretched out along his length with his arms around the horse's neck and his face buried in Sam's tangled mane. Again, the camera asserts their visual connection, but more importantly we hear Jon's breathing and panting as he labours to get on the horse; Sam's nostrils and ears move in constant response, and he too snorts. Ann Game's notion of 'entrainment' speaks to the experience we witness here:

The therapist R.D. Laing notes that 'Once open to the presence of someone else … you start breathing together, like a mother and baby breathing together. There is a rhythm of breathing which is a duet of breath … you entrain your rhythm' [...] In this vein, [...] training can be thought of as entrainment: learning to be carried along in the flow, learning to become in tune with or in the train of. For this to happen, one needs [...] to be receptive, letting go of will and self-consciousness. (Game 2001: 3)

In Sam and Jon's rhythmic duet it is hard to tell where one species ends and the other begins. Other men watch or help at various points, and other horses participate in the process of co-creation. Thus, Dexter, another horse with whom Jon has trained, helps to teach Sam how to run clockwise around the ring.

Samson, Jon and Dexter, chapter 9: 1.08.48.

How might we categorise the relationship between horse and human? Jon simply calls it 'love'. He is remarkably unselfconscious about annotating his feelings for 'his' horses. In a voiceover at the end of the chapter 6 training scene, Jon comments on the bonding process: 'It's like falling in love. You know, you bond with a woman. I bond with my horse … Every horse that I've trained, I've loved. I love my horses'. At the end of chapter 10, Jacob Golden's haunting ballad 'Zero Integrity' accompanies Jon and Samson as they walk between the stalls and then as Jon lunges the horse in the ring, fading out on the repeated line 'No one's ever loved you like I do'. 'I' and 'you' are interchangeable positions in the grammar of their love affair. On Jon's last day in the programme, he finally rides Sam for the first and only time; like the previous pairs, they join up after the ride as the horse follows Jon round the ring, and Jon showers him with kisses. Jon reflects that it's 'been a learning experience for both of us'. With segues from Jon's declaration of love into a sunset scene (chapter 6) and romantic backing tracks, along with Jon's own allusion to bonding with a woman, the documentary flirts with the notion of the horse as a stand-in for an absent woman and the whole scenario as a displacement of heterosexual romance.

However, conventional romance itself seems a pallid substitute for horse love. This is oddly confirmed by the single figure who *does* have a relationship with a woman: in the scene preceding Sam and Jon's joined-up breathing, we've watched Anthony Edwards riding through golden fields in his new job training thoroughbreds at a private ranch; in a voice charged with emotion, he says: 'The horses have changed my life … horses are my life'. In a later scene, we meet his new wife Melonie. Though they hold hands while Melonie does most of the talking about their dating and their wedding, this seems a less intense relationship than Anthony's equine ones. It is fortunate, perhaps, as the subtitle informs us, that Melonie now has a job working with Anthony at the ranch. The human couple does not quite live up to Jon's avowal of 'equal partnership' with Sam (chapter 11). As Jon and Sam walk back between the pens after their ride, they are absorbed in each other. We are excluded from the conversation (there is no sound for this segment), but the camera quietly observes their intimacy and the equality of synchronised movement.

Samson and Jon, chapter 11: 1.21.52.

Their synchronicity recalls earlier images of horses moving in sync with each other (such as the horses' legs at the opening of chapter 7).[7]

Some days before Jon's release, Sam has a sore foot, and two weeks later the vet is called out to look at it in the scene immediately following Jon's leave-taking. He recommends

---

7   *On corporeal synchrony and communication, see Gala Argent (2012).*

some treatment, and Samson is led limping back to his stall. We follow Jon to his new job at a landscaping company, and learn that a month later he broke his foot at work. Even apart, the human and non-human pair are so closely associated that they might share molecular codes or psycho-somatic connections. They have matching wounds (Jon's left foot and Sam's left foreleg hoof). Thus, the film encodes Haraway's provocative speculation about 'potent transfections' (2008: 15), that is, the literal transfer of DNA between two creatures intimately enmeshed in a complex social and technological network. Sam gets turned out to long-term holding facilities, neither back in the wild nor adopted, the horse equivalent of the half-way house where Jon must live. Despite Guy's sense that Jon's attitude hasn't changed, Jon himself says he has 'learned to relax' and control his emotions. The final shots of the film switch between Sam among a group of horses and Jon limping away down a corridor. Sam faces the camera and looks back at the spectator (or for Jon) while Jon is seen in a reverse shot, as though they are two sides of a coin. Guy's voiceover comment, 'He's not wild, just a little hard-headed', comprehends both species.[8]

8   John Zaritsky updated me on their fates: 'Sadly, I have to report that Jon Peterson committed another felony shortly after being released from the program and was sent back to prison until next year when he will be eligible again for parole. Even more sadly, Samson, shortly after Jon's current incarceration, broke a leg trying to jump a fence and had to be put down. Two incorrigible characters' (personal email, 16 September 2013).

Though *WHR* is primarily a film about humans and horses, I want to conclude with a black and white cat. Fat Petey, as the human inmates call him, is featured four times as he roams around the complex. With the camera at cat level, we see him in the tack room and being picked up by Jon; a horse looks up at Petey as he stalks along straw bales outside the horse pens; a close-up of his eyes follows a close-up of horses' nostrils; and in our final encounter, the camera gazes again at Petey's eyes, which look back at us.

Fat Petey, chapter 9: 1.09.39.

As the spectator makes eye contact with Petey, we might think about what he is thinking and feeling. However, apart from a detail about how he likes to be picked up, we know far less about him than the film's equine protagonists. He reminds us how much we do *not* know about animals and their lives. Indeed, recurring shots throughout *WHR* show horses interacting with other horses in their own ongoing plots of befriending and defriending. Connecting with both the men and the horses, the cat gestures as well towards other off-screen stories about cross-species encounters. I like to think of him as a signifier of the cat's cradle by which Haraway figures the enmeshed networks of interdependent species. The film invites us to witness

> *situated histories [...] in which all the actors become who they are* in the dance of relating, *not from scratch, but full of the patterns of their sometimes-joined, sometimes-separate heritages both before and lateral to* this *encounter. All the dancers are redone through the patterns they enact. The temporalities of companion species comprehend [...] the [...] rhythms of conjoined process.* (Haraway 2008: 25)

As witnesses, we join the community of feeling articulated by viewers who register their 'compassion and hope' for the men and the mustangs in online reviews (Marchetti 2013), and potentially get involved in the adoption programme, to which the end credits direct us. Above all, the film asks us to think about and embrace our responsibility towards animals as active participants in the cat's cradle of entangled lives.

References

Argent, Gala (2012) 'Toward a Privileging of the Nonverbal: Communication, Corporeal Synchrony, and Transcendence in Humans and Horses', in Julie A. Smith and Robert W. Mitchell (eds) *Experiencing Animal Minds: An Anthology of Animal-Human Encounters*, New York: Columbia University Press, pp. III–128.

Barad, Karen (2003) 'Posthumanist Performativity: Toward an Understanding of How Matter Comes to Matter', *Signs: Journal of Women in Culture and Society*, 28(3), pp. 801–831.

Behar, Michael (2010) 'The Mustang Redemption', *Mother Jones*, 35(I).

Birke, Lynda (2007) '"Learning to Speak Horse": The Culture of Natural Horsemanship', *Society and Animals*, 15, pp. 217–239.

Burt, Jonathan (2002) *Animals in Film*, London: Reaktion Books.

Dalke, Karen (2010) 'Mustang: The Paradox of Imagery', *Humanimalia*, I(2).

Deaton, Christine (2005) 'Humanizing Prisons with Animals: A Closer Look at "Cell Dogs" and Horse Programs', *Journal of Correctional Education*, 56(I), pp. 46–62.

Game, Ann (2001), 'Riding: Embodying the Centaur', *Body & Society*, 7(4), pp. I–12.

Haraway, Donna J. (2008) *When Species Meet*, Minneapolis and London: University of Minnesota Press.

Marchetti, Cindy Q. (2009) 'Mustangs Offer a New Life for Men Behind Bars', customer review of *The Wild Horse Redemption*, Amazon. com, 8 March 2009 (accessed 8 August 2013).

Pratt, Mary Louise (1992) *Imperial Eyes: Travel Writing and Transculturation*, New York: Routledge.

Walker, Carol (2010) 'Wild Horses: The Adobe Town Wild Horses in Prison', *Wild Hoofbeats: Saving America's Vanishing Wild Horses*, http:// www.wildhoofbeats.com/blog/wild-horses-the-adobe-town-wild-horses-in-prison, 6 December 2010 (accessed 6 August 2013).

Weil, Kari (2012) *Thinking Animals: Why Animal Studies Now?*, New York: Columbia University Press.

ANGELA HOFSTETTER

Gender Trouble and The Horse Whisperer

Rᴇᴀᴅᴇʀs of the interdisciplinary publication *Equus* believe that natural horsemanship is the single most important phenomenon of the last twenty-five years (Kilby 2001: 67). Noted for its inherent respect for the horse, natural horsemanship's emphasis on partnership rather than domination has changed the lives of animals – equine and other – lucky enough to meet the clinicians dressed in faded Wranglers and Stetsons who travel the countryside in their old pick-ups. The underground movement found a global audience after Robert Redford not only adapted Nicholas Evans's international bestseller but brought on Buck Brannaman, the inspiration for *The Horse Whisperer*'s Tom Booker, as technical adviser to rewrite the training scenes to convey the authenticity associated with this auteur. Adaptations of successful novels are always plagued by questions of fidelity, but for many equestrians it was natural horsemanship, rather than Evans's novel, that excited viewers, and they saw it as a medium to share important truths about interspecies communication. Indeed, Brannaman saw the film as an opportunity to honour a way of life, dutifully following in the steps of Ray Hunt and the Dorrance brothers (Brannaman 2001: 234).

Reception of *The Horse Whisperer* challenges the boundaries between fact, fiction and fantasy. By opening up the production to the Horse Industry Alliance and other equine groups, Redford created a direct line to the horse world that arguably had a significant impact in disseminating the philosophy of natural horsemanship even to the unreceptive audiences, from bronc riders to dressage queens. Equestrian journalist Diana Deterding insists it isn't just another horse story. It is 'a slice of life':

> *Tom Booker may only be a fictional character, but his methods, his spirit and his philosophy are very real. Through* The Horse Whisperer *Redford has a chance to expose millions of people to a training philosophy that replaces the bronco-busting approach that has been a part of our culture for over two hundred years with a kinder, gentler way to work with horses.* (Deterding n.d.)

Deterding claims the film has done 'more for the treatment of horses in 2 1/2 hours than all the gentle training advocates have been able to do in the past twenty years' (n.d.). Redford and Brannaman's collaboration increased the already sizable number of enthusiasts following other clinicians like Pat Parelli, John Lyons, Monty Roberts and Clinton Anderson, who fill international stadiums rather than the small, dusty arenas of yesteryear. Similarly, the *Equisearch* exclusive 'Horse Whispering: Method or Myth? Montana Native Tom Booker Carries on Ancient Tradition' (Anon. 2001) is presented alongside commentary from 'real' trainers failing to acknowledge Booker's fictional status. According to Robert Miller and Rick Lamb in *The Revolution in Horsemanship and What It Means to Mankind*, natural horsemanship inaugurated nothing short of a revolution whose casualties were 'ignorance and injustice', which were replaced by 'new ways of thinking and acting informed by enlightenment and empowerment'. 'Child and wife beating,' they continue, 'once commonplace, are now illegal. So is animal beating' (Miller and Lamb 2005: 128). The faith that we 'can avoid the use of force, eliminate conflict, and establish a mutually beneficial relationship if *we know how*' situates natural horsemanship within a larger set of morally advanced practices of the self that could infiltrate every aspect of our lives both individually and collectively (Miller and Lamb 2005: 165).

The Horse Whisperer invites this exalted praise as the *ne plus ultra* tool of communication: the lives of a high-powered attorney and magazine editor (Robert and Annie MacLean, played by Sam Neill and Kristin Scott Thomas) are shattered after their daughter's tragic riding accident, which involves a nasty collision with a semi-trailer truck. Grace (Scarlett Johansson) loses her limb and her best friend; veterinarians repeatedly insist upon euthanising the severely injured Pilgrim. Convinced the horse's salvation is the key to her daughter's emotional recovery, Annie treks across the country, leaving Manhattan for Montana. A reluctant host, Booker

(Redford), eventually accepts the trio of lost souls and sets about teaching Pilgrim to behave like a horse again and restoring the fragile bond between mother and daughter. Months pass in Big Sky Country highlighting the gentle firmness that heals Pilgrim. What is most disturbing is how the film undoes the emphasis on gentle communication: when attempts at patience and kindness fail to heal the beleaguered Pilgrim, Tom Booker returns to extreme methods. In fact, the 'laying down' sequence in *The Horse Whisperer* complicates the ideological positioning of this international blockbuster about a mother, daughter and horse healed by a cowboy in the American West, which devolves into a cautionary tale for women and girls who stray from the *natural* functions of heterosexual romance and motherhood, with surprisingly Victorian echoes.

When Redford recreated Pilgrim's final encounter with Booker, the technique of nineteenth-century horse tamer John Solomon Rarey supplanted the methods of modern whisperers. Juxtaposing stills from Redford's film with illustrations from *The Complete Horse Tamer* (1862) reveals how closely he followed the nineteenth-century trainer:

Figure 1. Still from Redford's film compared with hobbling sequence from Rarey's The Complete Horse Tamer. *Courtesy of www.rarey.com.*

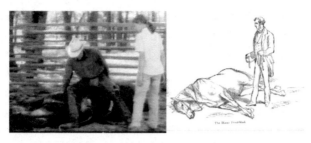

Figure 2. Still from Redford's film compared with laying down sequence from www.rarey.com.

The similarity is particularly striking in Redford's adaptation, which overtly sought to correct the misrepresentations in Evans's novel by seeking detailed technical advice from Brannaman on his own body position and manner of working with the horses playing Pilgrim. What is the significance that the auteur decided to 'rareyfy' rather than whisper?

Rarey's methods were so popular that his name became a verb in nineteenth-century dictionaries that meant 'to win by love, to mollify with oil of kindness, to reclaim a badly broken horse, to tame a horse by kindness' (Rarey n.d.), much as the term 'whisperer' has infiltrated contemporary parlance to mean someone who has an uncanny ability to communicate with anything from a dog to a ghost to a relationship. His meteoric rise occurred in 1858 after taming a horse for Queen Victoria that Prince Albert had deemed vicious. This resulted in an international tour attended by nobility from Emperor Louis-Napoleon to Baron Alexander von Humboldt to the Czar of Russia. Like today's superstar whisperers, whose stadium-filled clinics fall somewhere between a circus and a rock concert and may include spectators from Queen Elizabeth II to Cindy Crawford, Rarey staged exhibitions that attracted large crowds who contemplated a gentler way of treating horses. The prospect of humane treatment in a world of Dickensian cruelty encouraged many to reflect upon its possible impact on larger society. Ralph Waldo Emerson declared Rarey had 'turned a new leaf in civilization' and, in *Le Moniteur Universel*, Théophile Gautier proclaimed the methods of this American 'a moral victory'. Prominent abolitionist William Lloyd Garrison saw in Rarey a 'fitness to teach the world a great and everywhere needed lesson of humanity' (Brown 1916). Given such praise, why would John Lyons, often referred to as 'America's Most Trusted Horseman', denounce Rarey's technique?

'Mixed Messages from the Movie *The Horse Whisperer*' condemns the abrupt change in handling Pilgrim:

> *While we know that the story of Pilgrim, the movie's equine star, is supposed to be reflective of Grace – his traumatized, emotionally hobbled and finally free young owner – the activities undertaken by Tom Booker, played by Robert Redford, in training Pilgrim are dangerous.* (Lyons 1998: 32)

Dangerous to whom? In his monthly magazine *Perfect Horse*, Lyons exposes the implications for the actual horse in great detail, but the old cowboy's warnings about Pilgrim's metaphorical status being 'reflective of Grace' suggest that the danger extends beyond the barn into the world of gender politics. In fact, comparing the literal and symbolic significance of the 'laying down' sequence with Victorian and modern 'riding lessons' complicates the mythic connection between women and horses, exposing natural horsemanship as a technology of domestication. It also highlights a key problem for scholars of animal studies – struggling with the literal versus symbolic status of the animal body. This is further complicated by a radical shift in equine culture, which, except in extreme disciplines like steer wrestling and thoroughbred racing, has become increasingly feminised over the last few decades.

The success of *The Horse Whisperer* accelerated the consciousness-raising associated with the global phenomenon of natural horsemanship – particularly among women. Communication, partnership and unity are characteristic terms to describe these idealised interspecies connections, and modern equestriennes subscribe to this methodology with a religious zeal. Unlike most disciplines, where instruction focuses on perfecting a specific task (e.g. clearing a higher jump or attaining clean flying lead changes), natural horsemanship emphasises the relationship as the end product: 'Possibly the most significant factor in the speed with which this revolution has spread is the fact that, for the first time in human history, women dominate the horse industry' (Miller and Lamb 2005: 80). Miller and Lamb feel that 'if this has been fortuitous for the equine industry [...] it has been a blessing to the horse', because women 'are nurturing by nature and try to avoid conflict'. The downside is that these qualities, 'which are less intimidating to the horse [...] can also cause the horse to be less respectful and to feel dominant to the woman'. They speculate that perhaps 'this is the reason that the clinicians who began this technique were all men' (2005: 81).

In spite of natural horsemanship's claims to promote justice across national boundaries, its gender politics remain problematic: as Linda Kohanov suggests, 'One of the most interesting, and frustrating, aspects of the 'horse whispering' phenomenon is its blatant disregard for the innovations of female trainers, and its ambiguous relationship with women in general' (2001: 178). Kohanov, author of *The Tao of Equus*, is critical of both the film and the novel on the grounds that '[when] both discuss the horse whisperer legacy, these innovative trainers are characterized exclusively as *men* who bucked convention – *men* who brought a new era of gentleness, respect, and cooperation to a grossly inhumane equestrian tradition' (2001: 178). The contributions of horse women like Sally Swift, Julie Goodnight and Sylvia Loch rarely merit a footnote: the revolution in horsemanship is unequivocally attributed to 'just a bunch of cowboys' (Miller and Lamb 2005: 165).

Contemporary society has so fully embraced the riding female that it is surprising to realise that this archetype was once fraught with anxiety. Jane Austen's uneasiness about Marianne Dashwood's desire to gallop recklessly on Queen Mab erupted into a full-blown phobia during the Victoria era, which was characterised by a simultaneous fear of and reverence for the *amazone*. Gustav Flaubert's Emma Bovary, Charlotte Brontë's Blanche Ingram, Anthony Trollope's Julia Brabazon, George Eliot's Gwendolyn Grandcourt and M. E. Braddon's Aurora Floyd articulate the instability of femininity in the presence of horses: these questionable heroines desire the horse as a symbol of autonomous sensuality in defiance of cultural pressures that maintain that 'the best mothers, wives, and managers of households, know little or are careless about sexual indulgences' (Acton 1888: 209).

Simply put, to quote Margaret Oliphant (the Victorian equivalent of Anne Coulter), when related to women the adjective 'horsey' was 'akin to immoral' (1867: 272). In fact, those who challenged the heterosexual norms via equestrianism faced severe punishment, the most characteristic being the loss of a child. For example, *Middlemarch*'s Rosamond Vincy miscarries after defying her husband's command that she stop vigorous gallops. In *The Rainbow*, Ursula miscarries from mere contact with wild horses. In Clarence Brown's *National Velvet*, Mrs Brown warns young Velvet just after she wins the Grand National that it is now 'time to put away childish things', clearly an admonition that once she enters puberty her intense relationship with The Pi (her horse) must be significantly altered. Unfortunately, Velvet does not heed the warning. Decades later, *International Velvet*, the sequel to the popular film adaptation of the children's classic, follows the standard line of retribution. We learn from her young niece that Velvet did not renounce riding until after she miscarried and became unable to ever have children.

The challenge these horsey heroines from the Regency to Reagan present to the dominant domestic ideology of Anglo-American motherhood illustrates the fundamental paradox of the state of the 'natural' woman. If the 'ideal of true womanhood' embodied in 'the literatures of surveillance, from conduct books to novels' was 'written on the assumption that a woman's nature is fixed and given', writes Jeni Curtis, 'what then could be the need for books that also assume that women can be produced, shaped, and trained?' (2000: 79). In *The Horse Whisperer* there is a disturbing conflation of the female and equine body that is a persistently troubling subtext of patriarchal power that will not yield. Metaphorical use of the equine body solved this contradiction. The spectacle of horse-breaking reasserted the primacy of the natural body while simultaneously 'breaking' it to the conventions of normative femininity. As Boyd Tonkin writes, *The Horse Whisperer* is 'less about taming troubled horses than the breaking-in of restless minds – most of all, uppity female minds' (1995: 56). Breeding and heterosexual reproduction in service of empire deceptively appear too anachronistic to be relevant to modern America, as feminism and multiculturalism have ostensibly undermined the imperial Victorian vestiges, yet *The Horse Whisperer* reveals an uncanny commonality with nineteenth-century attitudes by seeking to place women back in the saddle, back into an arena largely defined through motherhood and other duties of the domestic sphere.

This manoeuvre has great symbolic value in *The Horse Whisperer*, which becomes the medium for mother and daughter to exorcise the demons of modern civilisation. Annie and Grace's tutelage under Tom Booker replays central nineteenth-century discourses on horsemanship as a means to self-management that ironically results in individual freedom in texts like *The Wide, Wide World* and *Aurora Floyd*. Lynda Birke notes that this paradox also exists in contemporary 'popular horsey culture', where 'contributors to equestrian websites write enthusiastically about the liberty of the horse, while at the same time asking questions about how better to ride (and thus control) their animal' (2007: 107). Although, as Erlich states in *The Horse Whisperer: An Illustrated Companion*, there 'are no more frontiers', she finds that there 'is a fundamental need in all of us to move out from under tyrannies, whether political, emotional, economic, imposed from the outside or from within' (1998: 17). In *The Horse Whisperer*, the female mind is the final territory to conquer. The body of the horse provides the blank slate upon which to play out the irreconcilable drama between the wild and the tame that characterises the inherent contradictions of the training process. The natural horseman is the guide to negotiate the woman's spiritual journey into the West.

The *Illustrated Companion* excises the more disturbing scenes from its seven-page spread. Only one caption under a medium close-up of Annie and Robert as disturbed onlookers obliquely alludes to the shift in training techniques: 'It is difficult to watch, but Tom assures them the horse is not in any pain' (Erlich 1998: 100). The film, however, depicts the scene with a dramatic intensity not easily done away with by simple disclaimers. The long sequence mirrors the initial saddling sequence at the film's beginning. Close-ups of saddle blankets, Pilgrim's interested eyes, his inquiring ears, and girths are intercut with a pan of onlookers: Frank, Smokey, Joe and Diane. The camera is then positioned behind Grace's shoulder; the spectator's gaze is aligned with hers as Tom Booker approaches, leading an increasingly reluctant Pilgrim. As he comes towards Grace, Pilgrim's discomfort quickly escalates. A close-up of a stamping foot is quickly replaced by a distorted, anxious POV shot from Pilgrim. Extreme silence from all present, except for brief, encouraging words from Frank Booker that 'Tom will get him all right', further underscores Pilgrim's panic. His frightened snorts and pants accentuate his terror; a tilted, low-angle shot of wild eyes reminds the spectator of his tragic, savage state. An almost imperceptible yet significantly knowing look between Tom and his hand Smokey indicates that tactics have changed. Grace watches them loop a rope around Pilgrim's foot with horror. 'It's not going to hurt him?' she asks Tom. 'Nothing we've done has hurt him', he replies. 'This is Pilgrim's chance, and it's your chance, too.'

Close-ups of Pilgrim's violent reaction to his restraint are intercut with overhead shots as well as frequent flashed images of his wild eyes. The animal's panic discomforts the entire MacLean family. The father, Robert MacLean, simply turns his back while mother and daughter are united in a horrified embrace as the gentle cowboy roughly handles the horse.

Intervals of slow motion intensify the representation of the animal's fear. When Grace screams 'That's enough, stop!' she clearly echoes the spectator's sentiments. Repeated close-

Figure 3. Annie MacLean (Kristin Scott Thomas) and Grace MacLean (Scarlett Johansson) gaze in horror at Tom Booker laying Pilgrim down.

ups of Booker's hand on the rope remind the viewer who is master, and Pilgrim ultimately submits and lies down. At this point, the rough hands lovingly caress the exhausted animal now ready to accept Grace. 'There's a point where neither of you is gonna need me, and we're there', Tom exclaims. The camera then cuts between dissolves of happy onlookers and shots of Grace and Pilgrim cantering effortlessly. She comes to a halt, releasing the reins in absolute joy. When gentle tactics no longer work, violent means will be used.

Technical advisor and prominent natural horseman Buck Brannaman expresses ambivalence about the sequence and has subsequently refused to 'lay down' animals upon request. He suggests that Redford departed from authenticity for dramatic effects, wavering on his previous unqualified endorsement of this film as paying tribute to his way of life. John Lyons was more vocal in an article entitled 'Mixed Messages from the Movie *The Horse Whisperer*'.[1] Lyons finds it particularly

---

1   *John Lyons describes the considerable danger in using restraint as*

upsetting when, 'short of time to reach his goal, Booker ropes the horse [...] hobbles him then works him in the round pen'. He then lays the horse down. When the horse gets up, everything is perfect, 'implying that one exhausting session will cure a serious training problem'. Here Lyons identifies several dangerous messages of the film:

> **Dangerous message**: *The end justifies the means; or it's OK to compromise the safety of the trainer, owner and rider; or we can use out-of-control methods to establish control.*
>
> **Dangerous message**: *Forcing a horse to do something will show him who's boss.*
>
> **Dangerous message**: *Dominating the horse will cause the horse to obey.* (Lyons 1998: 34)

Lyons's words of caution and detailed analysis of training methodology underscore just how far this scene represents a rupture from the philosophy it ostensibly espoused. The idyllic images of Grace and Pilgrim cannot entirely contain the violence that riveted the once estranged mother and daughter in a tight embrace of horror.

---

a training tool: 'Relieving the pressure, like releasing the rein at the right time, is the most important message that we can give our horse. It tells him he's not trapped, that there is something he can do to get us to relieve the pressure he's feeling. It tells him that we are not unreasonable. Contrast that with the concept of roping a horse, shown in the movie. When a lariat tightens around the animal's neck, even a trained horse will want to fight [...] So he fights for his life – literally. The more he fights, the more frightened and frustrated he gets, and the more sore his neck gets from the lariat [...] He is increasingly distracted from anything we might be trying to teach him. He has one overriding concern – survival. The only thing he's learned is that he'd better not let himself get in that situation again' (Lyons 1998: 35).

The round pen may seem like an unlikely site to replay the debates relating to feminism and motherhood, yet *The Horse Whisperer* highlights an under-analysed tendency of these cowboy philosophers to reinstate conservative gender roles under the guise of the natural. While questions of whether women experience physical passion no longer trouble debates concerning contemporary motherhood in an era of sexual freedom, the strong desire to link this passage with reproduction through the discipline of the stable reasserts itself powerfully in natural horsemanship. This disturbance of the natural order occurs in the manège as well as the ménage. Brannaman finds that the insecurities of many modern horses go 'back to their separation from their mothers' when they have not been offered a 'replacement that they needed to become secure within themselves' (Brannaman 2001: 199). Grace figuratively did not have a mother. When her connection with riding is severed, so is her only connection to developing proper feminine qualities. Her plaintive wail 'who will ever want me' suggests she is missing more than just a lower limb.

The gender trouble associated with female acculturation becomes even more disconcerting when we examine the story of Grace. The tragedy of Grace and Pilgrim provides the narrative impetus; it is the singular motivation for the life-altering journey to Montana for the MacLeans. Without the horrific accident, life at the MacLeans' would probably have continued as usual – Annie obsessing over her career and Grace enjoying an intimacy with her father. Grace's accidental maiming, however, points to the absolutely unnatural instability of gender roles. Her tale appeals to a prelapsarian nostalgia symbolised by a return to the mythic West, where life is not out of kilter. It is an idyllic place – in spite of physical hardship – where each sex plays its role for mutual benefit.

Scarlett Johansson, the actress who plays Grace, understood the film in these 'feminine' terms: 'This film is about people building different relationships with each other and trying to heal a variety of wounds' (quoted in Erlich 1998: 118).

Cultural attitudes towards horses and their management are powerfully inflected by trends within Anglo-American civilisation firmly established in the nineteenth century. Like the human body, the equine body bears the indelible marks of the discursive strategies of patriarchal culture. Disturbingly, Annie and Grace MacLean learn that failure to submit to the gentle means proffered will necessitate increasingly harsh methods. Husband Robert MacLean must reassume the mantle of power under the tutelage of cowboy Tom Booker. The relationship between horse and rider proves to be an apt metaphor for evolving ideas of companionship and marriage that soften but do not ultimately challenge the deeply embedded structures of traditional masculine and feminine roles. While supporting increasing respect for the desire and well-being of the horse, no one would ultimately suggest that the mount usurp the rider's position – just as many would argue for increasing respect for women rather than their autonomy.

Gail Cunningham identifies the paradox that drives the girl-meets-horse story as an 'emotional yearning for a beautiful, powerful, and independent creature which nevertheless requires female nurturing'. She argues that this 'gives an implicit dynamic to much of the *I Wanted a Pony* type fiction'. For young girls, the 'intimate, quasi-domestic contact is as important as the riding', because horses are not admired 'simply for the power they confer on the rider, but also for the opportunity they provide for displays of physical and emotional intimacy' (Cunningham 1996: 69). The long textual history of this archetype requires only a few paragraphs for readers to get the idea. Redford too relies on this history, particularly in his fetishistic use of close-ups in the initial saddling sequence. The low-key lighting inside the stable adds a quasi-romantic sublimity to the rituals of leather and stirrups. Grace coos 'Hey babe' and 'Handsome boy' to the snorting, pawing, proud Pilgrim. Hints of their past unity are again revealed in a later scene where the maimed Grace sits in her darkened bedroom watching videotapes of their past performances at a Hunter Jumper show, but both novel and film markedly differ from traditional stories of a girl and her horse. Velvet Brown may have had her Mi Taylor, but he only helped her with the logistics of getting to the Grand National. Her relationship with The Pi needed no mediation because their bond goes deeper than training – it is the source of mystery and wonder that needs no outside intervention.

The shattered relationship to her horse mirrors Grace's shattered relationship to her unnatural world: the tragedy only makes the chasm more pressing. Before the accident, Pilgrim fulfilled both her budding maternal instincts and her desire for intimacy: we can guess that Grace can only approximate such a role when the model in her own life is absent. Once Annie takes the job as an editor, she and her daughter are no longer close. The brittle bond between mother and daughter highlights the reactionary meaning of horsemanship that operates in this film. When the tenuous link of show jumping vanishes between mother and daughter, only open hostility remains. Grace's sarcasm makes her frequently unlikeable: her maimed body represents her maimed soul. Redford underscores her inner hostility not only through close-ups of her angry face, but also through an intriguing use of sound when her Walkman fades in and out: from a diegetic to a non-diegetic representation of a state of mind. Being raised by a woman who has entirely abandoned all traditional roles, Grace – according to the ideological conventions of the sentimental blockbuster – is damaged goods, literally and figuratively. Culture has perverted her natural instincts – only Tom Booker and the West can put them right.

The stable becomes a stabilising metaphor for the return of that which has been most repressed over the last several decades: nature. Although sociobiology and neuroscience radically undermine the sway of poststructuralist approaches to the gender/sex debate, reducing concepts like free will and consciousness to synapses, proverbial common sense requires a middle way. In much of American popular culture, the horse represents that delicate balance. Identification with the horse is the wish to hold onto an unchanging certainty somewhere outside our own inauthentic experience, a move that facilitates imagining a self that precedes socialisation. Psychoanalysis insists upon the role of nostalgia as essential to identity and the desire to articulate ever-changing identifications.[2] Although both Jacques Lacan and Julia Kristeva carefully maintain that no return to an idealised state of nature before the fall into culture is possible, the wish to ignore such warnings is often too powerful. The majesty of the horse, not to mention its beauty, is further fuelled by its representation of something real: the illusory yet alluring belief in the authenticity of nature.

Redford essentially unravels the respectful, patient approach embraced by Brannaman in favour of a more

---

2   *Significantly, both the Lacanian Real and Kristeva's Semiotic suggest an impossible nostalgia for a prelapsarian wholeness that precedes entry into the symbolic. Lacan mused that it could be thought of as a state of nature before the 'fall' into the Symbolic (1982); for Kristeva, it is an ineffable totality of the drives that is responsible for articulating the chora, a mythic space that precedes evidence, verisimilitude, spatiality and temporality (1986).*

immediate, physical one. Lyons's plea to not 'whisper' to your horses the way Hollywood does resonates profoundly, but it is illuminating that he is one of the very few critical voices questioning the horsemanship practised in this film. Ultimately, *The Horse Whisperer*, in spite of its embrace of New Age metaphors of kindness and unity with animals for the bulk of the running time, proves to be rather reactionary at the conclusion: Tom Booker reveals the iron fist beneath the velvet glove. Patience and kindness are an option; however, if they are not accepted, force will be used. This regression to a hierarchical construction of the natural appeals to a society that wants to embrace kindness but resents radical attacks on patriarchal authority. The American man epitomised by the cowboy assumes his leadership role; the equine body legitimates his position. The implications of this symbol prove even more troubling as we move from the stable into the drawing room.

Jane Tompkins writes that horses are there 'to galvanize us' by symbolising 'the desire to recuperate some lost connection to life' (1992: 94). They seduce us through the allure of the natural. Like the Victorians, contemporary audiences simultaneously fear and revere the horsey heroine. After several decades dominated by anti-essentialist thought, animal metaphors reassert the futility of such trivial concepts as gender that hinder romantic possibilities. Common sense, legitimised in the animal body, trumps liberal ideology – in the mass-market aesthetic terrain where these horsey movies are situated – by appealing to the legacy of Victorian progressiveness. The celebration of natural horsemanship as a training methodology and symbol of ideal gender relations proves to have its darker side. As a paradoxical symbol of both the untameable and the well-trained, the archetype of the woman and horse that dominates contemporary culture seduces by its rhetoric of freedom, which is as illusory as gender equality as we move into the new millennium.

References

Acton, William (1888) *Functions and Disorders of the Reproductive Organs in Childhood, Youth, Adult Age and Advanced Life Considered in Their Physiological, Social, and Moral Relations*, Philadelphia: P. Blakiston, Son, and Company.

Anon. (2001) 'Horse Whispering: Method or Myth? Montana Native Tom Booker Carries on Ancient Tradition', *Equisearch* (www.equisearch.com), 2 June.

Birke, Lynda (2007) 'Learning to Speak Horse', *Society and Animals*, 15(3), pp. 217–239.

Brannaman, Buck (2001) *The Faraway Horses*, Guilford, CT: The Lyons Press.

Brown, Sara Lowe (1916) *Rarey, the Horse's Master and Friend*, Columbus, OH: F. J. Herr Printing Co. (available at http://thompsonrarey.com/jsrarey/index.html).

Cunningham, Gail (1996) 'Seizing the Reins: Women, Girls, and Horses', in Gail Cunningham and Sarah Sceats (eds) *Image and Power: Women in Fiction in the Twentieth Century*, London: Longman Press.

Curtis, Jeni (2000) 'The Espaliered Girl: Pruning the Docile Body in *Aurora Floyd*', in Marlene Tromp, Pamela K. Gilbert and Aeron Haynie (eds) *Beyond Sensation: Mary Elizabeth Braddon in Context*, Albany, NY: State University of New York Press, pp. 77–92.

Deterding, Diana (n.d.) 'Behind the Whispers: The Horse Whisperer Advocates Gentle Training', *International Arabian Horse* (available at http://members.tripod.com/dorians_chalet/whisperer.html).

Erlich, Gretel (1998) *The Horse Whisperer: An Illustrated Companion to the Major Motion Picture*, New York: Dell Publishing.

Evans, Nicholas (1998) *The Horse Whisperer*, New York: Dell Publishing.

Kilby, Emily (2003) 'Causes for Concern', *Equus*, 290, pp. 32–49.

Kohanov, Linda (2001) *The Tao of Equus: A Woman's Journey of Healing and Transformation Through the Way of Horse*, Novato, CA: New World Library.

Kristeva, Julia (1986) *The Kristeva Reader*, ed. Toril Moi, Oxford: Blackwell.

Lacan, Jacques (1982) *Feminine Sexuality*, ed. Juliet Mitchell and Jacqueline Rose, London: Macmillan.

Lyons, John (1998) 'Mixed Messages from the Movie *The Horse Whisperer*', *John Lyons's Perfect Horse*, 3, pp. 32–35.

Miller, Robert and Rick Lamb (2005) *The Revolution in Horsemanship and What It Means to Mankind,* Guilford, CT: Lyons Press.

Oliphant, Margaret (1867) 'Novels', *Blackwood's*, 102, p. 272.

Rarey, Damon (n.d.) 'The Original Horse Whisperer' (available at http://www.rarey.com/sites/jsrarey/).

Rarey, John Solomon (1862) *The Complete Horse Tamer* (available at www.rarey.com/sites/jsrarey/jsrbook.html).

Tompkins, Jane (1992) *West of Everything: The Inner Life of Westerns*, New York: Oxford University Press.

Tonkin, Boyd (1995) 'The Scolds Bridled', *New Statesmen and Society*, 8, pp. 56.

CAROL FREEMAN

☙

Blurring the Boundaries: Big Cat Diary

In the last paragraph of *Reel Nature* (1999), Gregg Mitman points out that, despite contrasts in framing and interpretation, in wildlife films, human and animal worlds are separate. Mitman observes that every effort is made to eliminate human presence and settings from a scene. Viewers want their nature intimate and pure, and the artifice of filmmaking, and indeed civilisation, hidden. Any sign of artificiality would destroy the illusion of nature as 'God's place of grace'. In an edition of his book published ten years later, Mitman admits in a new afterword that profound changes have occurred in wildlife filmmaking in the intervening years, but, strangely, he doesn't mention the popular BBC TV series *Big Cat Diary*[1] in either edition. This series of programmes, which includes *Big Cat Week*, *Big Cat Live* and *Big Cat Raw*, was broadcast from 1996 to 2008 and stunningly challenges Mitman's original statement. It shows just how far wildlife film can go in including humans and their technologies in the visual field and, later, interactions with its audience.

To put the series into context... Over the last two decades wildlife documentaries have evolved into a major presence in global media such as television, video and the internet, becoming a syndicated phenomenon in the 1990s. NBC contracted with National Geographic for natural history specials, CBS began to broadcast wildlife films on their Discovery cable channel, and Discovery's sister network Animal Planet was launched, with the catch cry 'All animals, all the time'. At PBS there was a thirty per cent surge in viewing nature series; meanwhile, in Britain, the BBC's *The Trials of Life*, a series that exemplifies Mitman's statement, generated over $100 million in sales. Now, wildlife films compete for audiences in a global marketplace based on a belief among producers that wildlife is universally appealing and that wildlife series move easily from country to country.

Over these decades, of course, there have been changes in presentation. Cynthia Chris summarises these in terms of a shift from frameworks in which the animal appears as the object of human action (e.g. as game), to an anthropomorphic framework in which human characteristics are mapped onto animal subjects, and then finally to a zoomorphic framework where knowledge about animals is used to explain human behaviour (Chris 2006: x). *Big Cat Diary* does not conform to the second and third generalisations, because, although the series deliberately segues into human dramas, its concerns

_____

[1]   Big Cat Diary, *BBC Natural History Unit, Bristol, UK, 1996–2008.*

are primarily focused on the wildlife itself. The series does fit to *some degree* with the first three requirements of the 'Blue Chip' documentary as defined by media scholar Derek Bousé: it features depictions of megafauna; it dwells on visual splendour, especially stunning scenery; and it relies on dramatic narrative or 'family romance' (1998: 134). But what this series overwhelmingly adds to these elements – so contesting all the above observations – is an almost constant human presence in the visual frame and an auditory presence that introduces an intimate and conversational overlay which consistently spoils the 'natural' picture and blurs the human/animal boundary.

The series blurs other boundaries associated with traditional wildlife documentaries as well, including the boundaries between authenticity and artifice, and between documentary and drama; it also narrows the spaces between location, film and global audience. It was the first of a new category of wildlife film dubbed the docusoap, defined by Wiktionary as 'a genre of reality television in the style of a documentary in which an apparent plot is constructed by intention or editing in order to make programmes in this genre resemble soap operas'.[2] It also has connections with reality TV. In breaking the rules that governed wildlife filmmaking for decades, *Big Cat Diary* presents multiple issues for discussion. The one I focus on in this essay is: does this approach to visualising wildlife promote the welfare of non-human animals, or does the series merely exploit them?

---

2   *The series spawned other programmes using the diary format, for instance* Elephant Diaries *(2005, 2008),* Chimp Week *(2005) and* Orangutan Diary *(2007).*

Big Cat Diary concentrates on the experiences of cheetahs, leopards and lions in the Maasai Mara, a large, unfenced reserve in south-western Kenya where it was filmed during the annual wildebeest migration. When the BBC Natural History Unit launched the series in 1996, it was advertised as 'a revolution in wildlife documentary making' and 'the truest portrait of these animals' lives to date'. It challenges what Mitman identified as a single continuity in wildlife films, as well as suggestions in Ralph Lutt's book *The Nature Fakers* that the viewer is not aware of 'the days and weeks that the filmmaker waited to capture a single scene, because the tedium has been edited out of the show' (Lutt 1990: 193). This series was shot for fourteen hours a day, seven days a week, with six camera teams, and this is frequently referred to in the series. While there is some explanation of subjects such as migration, drinking habits and the food sources of the animals involved, the blurring of boundaries between documentary and drama is nowhere more evident than in publicity that seems to undermine these informative aspects of the show. Necessitated by a highly competitive market, advertising, trailers and introductions to episodes mix genre codes and conventions. The blurb on the DVD cover of the 2006 series uses a quote from *The Guardian*, 'Who wants to watch soaps when there's this? Believable characters you can actually care about', and stresses the 'constant life-or-death drama' resulting from the animals' 'struggle for survival'.

The series was also publicised as a 'diary' – a recording of the ups and downs in the lives of named individuals and families followed over months and updated over years. The second series of episodes, *Big Cat Week*, was broadcast on a daily basis in the UK and achieved the status of a news report, with video footage sent back to Britain via Nairobi as events happened. It fulfils a mainstream audience's desire for unpredictability and personal involvement with a series' subjects, and fosters familiarity with particular animals. The presenter constantly invites the viewer to understand or empathise with animal behaviour, saying 'You try it!', 'What is she thinking of?' and 'The game's up and Shadow knows it', and then, from the wildebeest's point of view, 'How would it feel to be grasped by her teeth?' In the UK this series averaged audiences of 6.5 million viewers from 2004 to 2006, significantly rivalling human soaps like *EastEnders* and *Neighbours*. In 2005, another series, *Meerkat Manor*, followed the lives of animals in the Kalahari Meerkat Project conducted by the Department of Zoology at the University of Cambridge. This Discovery Channel series aired for four years and covered fifty-two half-hour episodes. In a similar vein to *Big Cat Diary*, it draws on 'the style and language of the soap opera genre, singling out heroes and villains, developing characters through time, making use of cliff-hangers at the end of episodes and before commercial breaks' (Candea 2010: 242).

Big Cat Diary brings humans and wildlife together in a number of ways. While the series reveals the day-to-day lives of the animals it features, the physical presence of camera crew, vehicles and radio equipment is a part of almost every scene. Some early episodes included scenes inside tents crowded with computers where footage was edited on site before being sent back to Bristol. The series shows the 'personal' relationships that develop between filmmakers and animals. It was filmed like an amateur documentary, with often shaky camerawork and tilted shots resulting from filming in a fast-moving vehicle responding to sudden events. Morgan Richards outlines the antecedents of the series and why and how this type of wildlife film emerged as a response to wider changes in the television marketplace, such as the rise of reality TV shows such as *Big Brother* and factual entertainment. She discloses that the *Big Cat* filmmakers were consciously looking for new technologies and formats, and shows how the series transformed and developed, pointing out that, with budget restraints, this kind of series could be produced cheaply and easily.

While in some ways it looks familiar, one of the most important elements that differentiates this wildlife series from others is the particular mix of named individuals of a species and the constant presence of humans and animals in the same visual frame. There is a predictable focus on danger and adventure, with the perils of 'raising cubs with predators all around' and battles over territory portrayed as 'high-octane action', accentuated by the theme music featuring African drums and Maasai chants, that repeatedly plays during the series. Opening sequences of episodes contain cuts of lions pursuing and attacking and camera crews in pursuit of their prey. However, while killing and death are a significant part of *Big Cat Diary*, the camera and presenters consistently construct animals in subjective or family terms. With the animals often very close to the narrator, an involved commentary encourages audience identification, or an intense interest in the outcome of a scene. There is a sense, then, in which human and non-human animals interact physically and emotionally to produce stories. Filmmakers and the series' presenters build on the cats' behaviour and the events in their lives that the camera observes, weaving them into dramatic 'everyday' tales articulated and explained by on-the-spot narrators. The camera constantly focuses on instances where animals interact with the film crew; it shows cheetahs jumping on and 'marking' vehicles (and sometimes the humans inside them) as moveable parts of their territory, and using them as vantage points or as shelter. In one memorable scene in the first series of *Big Cat Week* in 2004, a cheetah called Kike who has caught a topi calf escapes the animal's irate mother by jumping onto a jeep, just above its open roof and presenter Jonathan Scott's head. Kike drops the baby when the pursuit begins, and now the sound of her panting breath and Scott's amazement and excitement is palpable. He says 'Did you hear the noise of that topi? Did you see the look on Kike's face? Here – listen, listen! Turn the car off!'

'Did you see the look on Kike's face?' Jonathan Scott and Kike, who has just escaped an irate topi mother in Big Cat Week, *episode I.*

In the flat African landscape, jeeps are like mobile termite mounds to the cheetahs, they also provide lookouts for spotting prey or keeping an eye on other predators. Many of the animals in *Big Cat Diary* become accustomed to humans, intentionally approaching them and absorbing their technologies into their lives. Warthogs are shown chewing through computer cables, banded mongooses investigate equipment boxes and young lions make off with a jeep's spotlight.

A lion cub, habituated to the presence of vehicles and camera equipment, has stolen a spotlight cover from one of the jeeps. Other cubs crowd round to see.

Big Cat Live showed that film equipment fascinates curious young hyenas, who spend hours trying to dismantle the remote cameras by pulling forcefully on the cables with their teeth.[3] Similarly, in *Meerkat Manor*, the animals investigate shoes and climb onto human backs. Closing the physical gap between human and animal has obvious limitations: the instance where a cub leaned forward and licked a narrator's head was edited out of *Big Cat Diary*, according to presenter Jonathan Scott, because the BBC didn't want viewers to 'misunderstand' his

3 *Interactions like this have become a feature of some of David Attenborough's films over the last decade too. He narrates a film about grizzly bears entering townships in Alaska to raid rubbish bins; another called* The Cats of Rome *focuses on the lives of feral cats; another shows how monkeys in Thailand are integrated into human lives. These films do not adhere to elements of his usual Blue Chip documentaries.*

relationship with the animals. He writes in his book *Cheetah*, 'It is imperative to preserve the natural divide between us and the big cats', and he points out that his familiarity with Kike would not happen with a lion or leopard. Scott continues: 'these are not pets, they are wild creatures, and the golden rule is not to touch them, however tempting it might be' (2004: 70). The animals' ability to accommodate humans into their lives or even exploit the presence of humans and their objects can be seen in terms of their *agency*.

On a technical level, *Big Cat Diary* deliberately breaks down barriers between authenticity and artifice that are stringently maintained in traditional wildlife documentaries. From 2004 to 2007, *Big Cat Week* was broadcast in prime time four days a week on BBC One, with a deliberate focus on the processes of filmmaking – the narrators' voice and visual presence in a scene, behind-the-scenes videos on the website and, eventually, film of the lives of the Maasai off-screen. In the constant commentary there is also frequent mention of the long and tiring search for particular individuals, hours spent obtaining film footage, and the work of spotters, camera crew and presenters in achieving a sequence. The camera crew often arrive as an event is in progress, or the action moves into focus in front of a stationary vehicle, as animals travel into and out of view. This is transparent filmmaking that does little to hide the tedium and difficulties behind the 'art'. Rather, it foregrounds the idea of constructedness.

The artifice of film is also highlighted in the constant presence of camera equipment, the deliberate focus on the process of driving and the sound of car engines behind a presenter's voice. One of the ways the show persuades the audience to test the claim of authenticity is by informing them how to recognise individual animals – for instance, by

Lion presenter Simon King – vehicles and cameras are part of almost every scene in Big Cat Diary.

pointing out different tail tufts on cheetahs and whisker spots on lions – making composite constructions or the substitution of one animal for another more difficult. However, this was apparently not so in *Meerkat Manor*, where researchers noticed discrepant markings that indicated the programme had substituted one individual for another in some shots (Candea 2010: 251).

A more concerted effort to achieve authenticity appears in multiplatform aspects of the show. *Big Cat Uncut* and *Big Cat Live* – a three-week-long webcam recording involving seven remote mini cameras, thermal imaging and twenty-four-hour filming – premiered in 2008. During the final episode, the team of presenters sent text message updates to the website throughout the day. This online video is a *Big Brother*-like look into the lives of animals, including hyenas, baboons and aardvarks, that reveals how nothing happens for long periods of time. After these live broadcasts, *Big Cat Raw* was aired. In this ten-minute web special an interactive website invited the audience to 'share the logistics and field craft required to launch such a bold project' with the filmmakers. The entire film crew were introduced, their camp was shown in relation to the animals they were filming, and camera techniques like zooming and panning were discussed and demonstrated. This was an almost over-determined attempt to expose the artifice of filmmaking. The connection and interconnections between humans, animals and film were deliberately exposed, however uncomfortable it was for viewers and for presenters, who stumbled on their words, displayed embarrassment and were obviously off-balance without animal bodies to focus on and the editing they usually relied on. Sceptical viewers had the opportunity to ask the filmmakers a range of questions which they posted online, including those relating to fakery or deception. The message boards registered thousands of posts.

The most profound difference between *Big Cat Diary* and traditional or Blue Chip series, however, is the narrowing of the space between the film's narrative, the global audience and the actual situation of the animals involved. Outside the film space, books by presenter Jonathan Scott and his wife Angela Scott contain extensive information about the biology, history and conservation of the three species, and discuss aspects of filming. Of course, books about series are common, but since 2007, *Big Cat Diary* has melded the film stories with website-driven interactivity and community building. The BBC and Mara Conservancy websites provide regular news bulletins, updates and blogs, as well as video material about the animal 'stars' for Twitter, MySpace and Facebook, and information about conservation efforts in the area. Currently, a blog continued by Maasai guide Jackson Looseyia keeps followers up to date with events in the lives of the animal stars and the Maasai Mara Reserve.

'It's such a magical place... the Mara always delivers for us.' Jonathan Scott muses on the filmic qualities of the Maasai Mara at the end of episode 5 of Big Cat Week.

Similarly, the series *Meerkat Manor* gathered a huge fan base, numerous blogs and web pages, and a Friends of the Kalahari Meerkat Project Society was set up. This, indeed, is wildlife colonising global media space.

ANIMAL AND HUMAN COMMUNITIES

So how does the series actually affect the animals involved, both directly and generally?

Cheetahs are classified by the International Union for Conservation of Nature (IUCN) as vulnerable, with only an estimated 7,500 believed to remain in Africa, and leopards are near-threatened. The major threats to the survival of both these species in Africa are competition for prey and conflict with humans over livestock. In some areas, trophy hunting and poaching are also dangers. In others, habitat destruction. Cheetahs also have very low genetic diversity, so are sensitive

132

to ecological changes. The Maasai Mara Reserve is designated a Category II National Park: a protected area managed mainly for ecosystem protection and recreation, which must be environmentally and culturally compatible.[4] A local non-profit cooperative established in 2001 by the Trans-Mara County Council, the Mara Conservancy, manages a third of the reserve and was claimed to be a model organisation that has effected a number of dramatic improvements in this less-visited area, including clamping down on poaching; establishing a more transparent revenue collection system, with a percentage going directly into conservation; strengthening incentives for local Maasai people to tolerate wildlife; and encouraging conservation professionals to implement sound ecotourism principles. The BBC's *Big Cat Diary* website (now reduced in content) raised awareness of many of these issues during and just after the series was aired, and supported an anti-poaching patrol set up by the Anne Kent Taylor Fund. An online video on the website claimed that the de-snaring patrol has saved the lives of countless animals – leopards, lions and elephants, as well as smaller species.

In addition to this kind of support offered to conservation projects by the BBC, the global audience's involvement with the animals has functioned as a regulator. When news broke that Honey, one of the stars of the series, had died as a result of a tranquilliser dart administered by a Kenya Wildlife Service vet, viewers were incensed not only about the blunder, but

---

4   *The Maasai Mara National Reserve is surrounded by conservancies of varying sizes, and with varying conservation aims and regulations: Ol-Chorro, Lemek, Olare Orok, Olkinyei, Motorogi, Mara North, Naboisho and Oloisukut. The area they cover is referred to as the greater Mara, or the Maasai Mara ecosystem. Details are available on the reserve's website and the Mara Conservancy website,* The Mara Triangle: *http://maratriangle.org/*

also that the BBC had not informed them in episodes that were broadcast after the incident. The reaction of viewers is an example of how the existence of a global audience with access to websites can help encourage good practice (Behr and Sanderson 2008). This was not so clear-cut in a similar instance associated with *Meerkat Manor*, where online criticisms focused on the attitude of Meerkat Project researchers, which was seen as cruel. In turn, questions emerged about whether audience members had a 'distorted and overly romantic image of animals' and viewed meerkats as if they were 'pets'. One viewer asked whether researchers had a responsibility to the animals they got to know so well – that is, did intimate involvement in the lives of these animals produce a relationship that demanded a less 'detached' response (Candea 2010: 242, 251)?[5]

The online focus on local people and projects reinforces how the lives of humans and animals are constantly intertwined, not only in the filming of the series where camera crew intermingled with the cats, but also on the ground in the everyday lives of animals in the reserve. On the *Big Cat Diary* website, two Maasai guides provided blogs about their experiences and a video showed a Guiding School in the Mara that trains local people to understand wildlife and the ethics of conservation. At one stage, guide Looseyia was asked to dub his audio response to filmed sequences – called 'a visual and audio safari' – onto visuals in the computer tent. His local knowledge was reported to have been a massive hit with the viewing audience. He said learning about and understanding their environment meant local communities would care

---

5   *See Candea's thoughtful article on anthropological relationships with wild animals, which proposes seeing engagement and detachment as symbiotic rather than dichotomous: 'a vital, ever-changing, and often microscopic co-implication of two profoundly different forms' (2010: 255).*

for animals, including predators traditionally considered a nuisance or a danger.

However, presenter Jonathan Scott suggests that tour guides bend rules to keep visitors happy, that tourism can be a stress factor that encourages disease, that cubs have been run over by vehicles in long grass, that the presence of more than six vehicles reduces hunting ability, that sometimes thirty vehicles can surround an animal, and that off-road driving, discouraged in many game parks, is a major problem in the Mara Reserve (2004: 63–65). The film crew itself could number up to sixty people, with ninety-four for *Big Cat Live*, while the Maasai Mara's website currently claims that 'The Mara has several conservancies surrounding it, that have restricted number *[sic]* of vehicles allowing a more private game viewing.' Scott also admits that the kind of human–animal intimacy the series encourages could be a problem. He writes: 'If the animals start to feel that it is safe to make more intimate contact with human beings, they might run into trouble when they wander outside the Reserve and encounter herdsmen who might harm them' (2004: 70).

Paul Omondi's thesis (1994) on conservation and human needs in the Maasai Mara concludes that the ideal programme for conservation is the integration of education, wildlife damage control and local participation in policy-making. But in the 2009 edition of *Reel Nature*, Mitman implies that the entertainment industry faces a difficult challenge if it seeks to encourage community-based conservation. This difficulty is exemplified by one of the expensive, luxury private safari camps within the Mara Reserve, called Governor's Camp, where the *Big Cat Diary* crew stays when filming, a detail not advertised by the BBC, which instead stresses the deprivations endured by the presenters and crew. In its format and production – people in vehicles searching for and filming animals on a daily basis – the *Big Cat Diary* series mimics a wildlife safari. At the end of one week's episodes, Scott's statements sound like publicity for Governor's Camp, or the photographic safari tours he runs with his wife in Kenya. But Governor's Camp is also involved in community support, and its website says it takes an active role in conserving the wildlife it depends on by providing such things as free accommodation for volunteer vets (see http://www.governorscamp.com). In a conversation I had in 2007 with Jonathan Ledgard, former Africa correspondent for *The Economist* and author of *Giraffe*, the heart-breaking novel based on the true story of a massacre of animals in a Czechoslovakian zoo, he suggested that camps like this, with well-heeled guests may, indeed, be the ones that ensure the future of Kenya's wildlife – their footprint-to-dollar ratio is far more generous too. That is, they spend money on establishing facilities that tend to conserve species, such as wildlife camps and safaris.

The impact of tourism on the lives of the animals in the Maasai Mara, then, has the potential to be dramatic. Tourism in wildlife parks is a major source of hard currency for Kenya: visitors' fees fund the Mara Conservancy's initiatives and pay pastoralists compensation for cattle killed by lions or leopards. Sanette Ferreira (2006) and Ben Gardner (Gardner et al. 2008) agree that conservation and tourism are mutually interdependent in Africa – conservation must pay for itself where people may be starving. Studies in the Okavango Delta in Botswana have shown that the economic benefits of ecotourism have resulted in positive attitudes in local communities, which have led to a stabilisation or increase in numbers of some endangered species (see also Anon. 2008). However, there is an inevitable tension between getting more tourists, stimulating the economy and sustaining damage to habitat. As Joseph Ogutu, Nina Bhola and Robin Reid suggest, when wildlife becomes a commodity, international tourist companies, traders in wildlife, pastoralists and poor communities all want to exploit the 'product'. Their research also shows that money from tourism paid to local farmers can ultimately mean more land being bought up and turned over to cattle, destroying habitats, blocking annual migration routes and increasing the likelihood of predator losses and reprisals (2006).

IS THIS FILMMAKING ETHICAL?

Some of the ethics of wildlife filmmaking identified by Charles Jonkel at a symposium on the subject held in Bath in 1982 were the need to generate a better understanding of animals and improve their status, to help prevent elements that threaten species, to encourage the interaction of local people in animal welfare and conservation, and to assert the value of wildlife (Boswall 1982: 12). *Big Cat Diary* is a wildlife docusoap that sets out to appeal to human emotions in its exposé of the everyday lives of non-human animals in Africa. It certainly asserts the value of wildlife to Kenya and tourism to the reserve, but Derek Bousé also points out the unique set of theoretical problems that arise from the different kind of interaction that exists between filmmaker and subject when the subject is animals. This is a case that demands special responsibilities and produces different results. Among these problems are the following (I've added to them): since animals are unlikely to suffer embarrassment from disclosure of their 'secrets', it is held that they should have none; animals don't have the right to privacy or any rights that might protect them from invasive filming practices; consent is impossible to obtain (are animals willing subjects of films of their intimate lives?); camera angles, close-ups and voiceover narration impose meaning onto their behaviour that may well be completely off-mark, as the animals have no way of explaining; actual evidence is therefore suspect; and there is ample possibility for substitution and construction of composite actions and fakery (Bousé 1998: 120–121). Even if fakery does not occur, such a close focus on individual animals means the intimate details of their lives are exploited for commercial purposes. Richards suggests that wildlife documentary makers have a responsibility to 'accurately and truthfully convey the realities of wild animals and the issues they face' (2012: 13). But in respect of documentaries, these realities are always mediated through the camera and the voiceover, and 'truth' is often defined by the context of a character or an event in a film or series. As Simon King says at one point, 'For *Big Cat Week*, Simba [the name given to one of the lions] is a key character'.

Films and TV series shown on global networks often act as virtual brochures to feed a growing trend towards ethical consumption and shape would-be tourists' desire for an authentic, eco-friendly experience. TV programmes like *Big Cat Diary* are key drivers in influencing attitudes towards animals and, in turn, generating interest in conservation projects and information about the future of the world's animals. As Mitman comments in his 2009 edition of *Reel Nature*: 'a concerted effort is needed to strengthen the connections between filmmaking and community activism already underway'. He also says that 'New media technologies have opened up possibilities for new material, new voices, and new points of view' (2009: 220). In the *Big Cat* series, a new style of wildlife filmmaking encourages viewer empathy and new insights into human–animal interactions. In *Big Cat Raw*, Joseph Looseyia and presenters Simon King and Jonathan Scott talk about the emotional impact of seeing wild animals and quickly coming to care about them, as well as the relationships that form, saying 'we mean nothing to them, but they mean so much to us'. The local point of view expressed by Looseyia is anything but detached, as he refers to 'baby baboons, testing their strength' and imagines the little baboon saying 'alright Grandpa, where will we go today?' And while the observation 'It's more their home than ours' is perhaps obvious to us, it sends an important message to a global audience.

The series therefore foregrounds the differences and the similarities between human and non-human animals, as well as enabling an appreciation of the animals' otherness and the need to respect their space. But a factor increasingly taken into consideration by academics and practitioners when dealing with non-human animals is their ability to accommodate, interact with and exploit the presence and practices of humans. However, as Donna Haraway notes in her essay on *Crittercam* (2006), animals are not completely symmetrical actors whose agency and intentionality are merely variants of those that humans possess. We must adapt to them as they adapt to us. Indeed, in *Big Cat Diary* it's a neat reversal when vehicles colonised by cheetahs place filmmakers in the role of nervous 'observers', and when one presenter, peed on through the open roof, is forced into the position of passive victim.

A cheetah licks the window of a jeep: closing credits of Big Cat Week.

References

Anon. (2008) 'Tourism Crash Threatens Big Cats', *BBC News* (online), 29 April, http://news.bbc.co.uk/1/hi/sci/tech/7372298.stm.

Behr, Mike and Elizabeth Sanderson (2013) 'Honey, Star of Big Cat Diary, Killed by Vet's Blunder', *Daily Mail*, 2 February, www.dailymail.co.uk/news/article-511955/Honey-star-Big-Cat-Diary-killed-vets-blunder.html (accessed 4 August 2013).

Boswall, Jeffrey (1982) 'The Ethics of Wildlife Film-Making: A Discussion', *BKSTS Journal*, January 1982, pp. 12–13.

Bousé, Derek (1998) 'Are Wildlife Films Really "Nature Documentaries"?', *Critical Studies in Mass Communication*, 15, pp. 116–140.

Burt, Jonathan (2002) *Animals in Film*, London: Reaktion Books.

Candea, Matei (2010) '"I fell in love with Carlos the meerkat": Engagement and Detachment in Human–Animal Relations', *American Ethnologist*, 37(2), pp. 241–258.

Chris, Cynthia (2006) *Watching Wildlife*, Minneapolis: University of Minnesota Press.

Ferreira, S. L. A. (2006) 'Communities and Transfrontier Parks in the Southern African Development Community: The Case of Limpopo National Park, Mozambique', *South African Geographical Journal*, 88(2), pp. 166–176.

Gardner, Ben, J. Igoe, F. Nelson and A. Williams (2008) 'Community-

141

Based Conservation and Maasai Livelihoods in Tanzania', in K. Homewood, P. Kristjanson and P. C. Trench (eds) *Staying Maasai? Livelihoods, Conservation and Development in East African Rangelands*, New York: Springer Press.

Haraway, Donna J. (2006) 'Crittercam: Compounding Eyes in NatureCulture', in Evan Selinger (ed.) *Postphenomenology: A Critical Companion to Ihde*, New York: SUNY Press, pp. 175–188.

Ledgard, J. M. (2006) *Giraffe*, London: Jonathan Cape.

Lutts, Ralph H. (1990) *The Nature Fakers: Wildlife, Science & Sentiment*, Charlottesville, VA: University of Virginia Press.

Mitman, G. (1999) *Reel Nature: America's Romance with Wildlife on Film*, Cambridge, MA: Harvard University Press.

— (2009) *Reel Nature: America's Romance with Wildlife on Film*, Seattle, WA: University of Washington Press.

Ogutu, Joseph O., Nina Bhola and Robin Reid (2006) 'The Effects of Pastoralism and Protection on the Density and Distribution of Carnivores and Their Prey in the Mara Ecosystem of Kenya', *Journal of Zoology*, 265(3), pp. 281–293.

Omondi, Paul (1994) 'Wildlife–Human Conflict in Kenya: Integrating Wildlife Conservation with Human Needs in the Masai Mara Region', thesis, Montreal: McGill University.

Richards, Morgan (2012) 'The Wildlife Docusoap: A New Ethical Practice for Wildlife Documentary?', *Television and News Media*, 22 November, pp. 1–15.

Scott, Jonathan (2004) *Big Cat Diary: Cheetah*, London: Collins.

SAMUEL PRINCE

ॐ

Bear #141

After Werner Herzog's Grizzly Man

Estimates are all we have: it was you, the male,
28 years, filmed so starved diving for cub carcasses
and immature chum in the lake, flumped
and panting, that cumbrous, creosote-brown
coat sodden and mangy.

Not for you the cutesy nose-to-fireweed routine;
the Nat Geo trophy shot backlit by alpenglow,
snout to sky on the ridgeline; not for you
the japery of the Yellowstone Yogis, the Lindy Hop
and Charleston on floating lumber logs.

If the history of the west tells us anything,
it's that the hard-bitten loner who skulks into town
tends to mean turmoil. Stay chary; don't sidle to him
at the taproom bar, demand to know his business,
where he got that laceration.

The one they tagged 141, the number inked
on your inner lip during anaesthesia, hellbender
from the Alaska interior near-playful in your desperation
– the type that's seen a sow swipe at her plumpest young
for a mercy feed by the kecking streams.

Estimates: your gut spilled for those four garbage sacks
of human remains; for you those eleven Remington rounds
as you crossed the line from *why won't you die*
to *you're one tough son of a*. . . it didn't need that many,
though that's what you took. And even then.

JON STONE

❧

BEAR INTERVENTION!

In Luis Buñuel's *Exterminating Angel*, the bear is a minor character with an ambiguous role. Lucîa de Nobile has planned some sort of comic spectacle for her dinner guests, in which the bear will play a part, but decides to abandon the idea when she learns that one of the assembled, Señor Russell, does not like jokes. Excusing herself, she exits the dining room and instructs the majordomo to 'put him in the garden'. Thereafter the bear waits backstage to give his performance, which in the end is for us, the film's audience, while Lucîa's coterie lie stranded and starving in the music room.

In a few brief shots, the animal is seen roaming the mansion, unhurriedly, as if marvelling at the eccentricity of civilisation. His bestial lope in the dark is Buñuel's one visual concession to the mass delusion suffered by the guests, who find themselves trapped in Señor Nobile's 'Paradise of Thebes', reduced to drinking water from smashed pipes and breaking up cellos for firewood, despite it seeming to the audience as if nothing prevents them from leaving the room. The bear on the gloomy landing, casting a shadow twice its size, reminds us of the dangerous night-time wilderness surrounding an explorers' encampment, momentarily showing their predicament in a less absurd light. The effect is repeated once more, when the guests gather on the periphery of their prison, staring out into the shadowed dining room as the animal softly croons to itself.

What is the purpose of the bear? He seems to serve as counterpoint to the guests in two ways. In spite of his collar and chain, and his being far from his natural habitat, he is free to wander, while they, the wealthiest class of the all-conquering human race, suffer in confinement, in the very place they ought to feel most at large. And while the guests are soon stealing from one another and plotting murder, the animal, conspicuously, does no harm. When he finds his way onto the driveway outside, standing on his hind legs to get a better look at the assembled crowd, a servant tells the police: 'Don't shoot! No, don't kill it, please! It's quite tame.' The bear isn't even aggressive enough to kill and eat the sheep (also loose in the house); that brutality is left to the human characters.

There's a rich history of animals making monsters and fools of men in film, one that is in part inherited from folklore, where rabbits, foxes and monkeys

BEAR INTERVENTION 1
(Cabaret, 1972)

SALLY

Why don't you just come out with it? You can't stand Maximilian because he's everything you're not! He doesn't have to give English lessons for three marks an hour. He's rich!

148

And he knows about life. He doesn't read about
it in books!
He's suave...
...and he's divinely sexy...
...and he really appreciates a woman.

> BRIAN

Oh, screw Maximilian!

> SALLY

> (shouts)

I do.

> BRIAN

So do I.

THE BEAR enters Sally's room, and immediately breaks into
the sweet melody of "<u>SEXUAL BETRAYAL</u>".

> BEAR

Well, losing at cards leaves one spent
and debt gives one much to lament
and being thrown out on one's ear -
> that's a terrible tale!
But nothing, my girl, makes a rent
> like sexual betrayal.

> BRIAN

Wherever did you get a singing bear?

> SALLY

I've never seen it before in my life!

> BEAR

Well, the patter of awkward applause

149

is a sound like the tearing of claws
and the silence that roars when one bombs
      puts a hole through the sail.
But nothing, my boy, nothing gores
      like sexual betrayal.

How it howls like a gale
through the desolate vale
and it rips like a flail
through one's layers of mail.
It's as dumb as a nail
and it comes on like hail
and it ties up your chest
till it's tight as a bale.

        SALLY
I'm calling the police.

        BRIAN
Wait. I think it's almost over.

        BEAR
Well, an earthquake is bound to cause stress,
just as hurricanes vex and depress
and a landslide is likely to leave one
      depleted and frail.
But nothing, my dear, makes a mess
      like sexual betrayal!

THE BEAR exits, pursued by a stagehand.

There's a rich history of animals making monsters and fools of men in film, one that is in part inherited from folklore, where rabbits, foxes and monkeys play the part of trickster figures. Hence Bugs Bunny is perennially at least three steps ahead of Elmer Fudd or Yosemite Sam, while long-suffering Gromit frowns and rolls his eyes at his befuddled master in Nick Park's stop-motion *Wallace and Gromit* films. Wes Anderson's *Fantastic Mr Fox* (2009), based on the Roald Dahl story about a fox who joyfully ransacks the larders of his would-be killers, goes as far as concentrating all its character development in its cast of animal puppets, while the human antagonists goon about cartoonishly. Smaller animals can also be found routinely outsmarting cruel or imbecilic humans, from the mice Bernard and Bianca of Disney's *The Rescuers* and *The Rescuers Down Under*, to the star of *MouseHunt*, who bests even a tooled-up, typically intense Christopher Walken ('If you can think like a mouse, you can anticipate their moves. Then boom').

This type of narrative draws attention to our hubris as a species, often pitting animals against technology, the call sign of our evolutionary superiority (Walken's character's array of gadgets; McLeach's juggernaut in *The Rescuers Down Under*; the guns, traps and dynamite of various farmers and hunters). It's a morality tale that we've inherited from an age where animals were, if not better respected, at least viewed as worthy adversaries and potential alternative (rather than inferior) forms of intelligence.

As demonstrated in *Exterminating Angel*, however, bears do not readily conform to the trickster archetype, even when they get the better of us. The obvious explanation for this is that while foxes, rabbits and mice co-exist in the same environments as humans and pose no direct threat, real-life bears are large, dangerous animals whose encroachment into towns is a serious matter[1]. This should place them in the same broad category as tigers and wolves, who typically appear as antagonists, evil minions or obstructive agents, but while bears have certainly made the B-list in the natural horror genre (*Bear*, *Grizzly*, *Grizzly Park*, *Grizzly Rage*), they also tend to be portrayed sympathetically, often as friends or allies. Perhaps because they're physically slow-moving and powerful, they're frequently characterised as mentally ponderous or comically unsophisticated – traits befitting a clown but not a mischief.

The CBS series *Gentle Ben* exemplifies the problem with finding a place for bears in the modern fable. Its producer, Ivan Tors, had previously made a star of Flipper the bottlenose dolphin – rescuer, babysitter and general do-gooder – and reprised the same formula with a terranean mammal in 1967. But Bruno the Bear, playing Ben the bodyguard, spent most of the series affecting bored bemusement or being hauled along on the end of a chain while the human actors postured their way through various life lessons. Nothing about the character suggests a natural relationship with humans, whether collaborative or adversarial. Even the parent bear, chasing a young Clint Howard up a tree in the series' feature-length opener, seems more distracted than aggressive.

Often the power or stature of a bear character is foregrounded, as with Iorek Byrnison, the armoured polar bear in 2007's *The Golden Compass*, or the adult male of Jean-Jacques Annaud's *The Bear*, who discourages a hunter through a display of towering physical presence. Neither has to have particular recourse to his wits, and both rely on human trepidation and

---

[1]   *This is a particular concern with regards to polar bears, whose migratory habits are shifting as the Arctic ice shelf melts. See Jeff Tietz, 'Siege of the Polar Bears', Men's Journal, November 2013, http://www.mensjournal.com/ magazine/siege-of-the-polar-bears-20131101.*

their own isolation to avoid conflict with us and our technology. We're safe from these bears and any humblings they have in store for us, so long as we keep to our own territory.

But then there are examples of bears that cross paths with humankind more decisively, and so have to take on

BEAR INTERVENTION 2

(The Golden Compass, 2007)

SERAFINA PEKKALA

So many worlds. But connecting them all is Dust. Dust was here before the witches of the air, the Gyptians of the water, and the bears of the ice. In my world, scholars invented an alethiometer - a golden compass...

POLAR BEAR

Golden ... compass?

POLAR BEAR in pigtails, pillow-fighting with other pigtailed bears next to a sign saying 'No Boys Allowed'.

SERAFINA PEKKALA

That is a girl-den rumpus.

POLAR BEAR dressed in hoofish heels with a goat mask, sack over his shoulder, half-sunk in coloured spheres.

SERAFINA PEKKALA

That is a ball-pen Krampus.

POLAR BEAR in a corset stiffened with iron, a petticoat,

a farthingale, gown and sleeves with lace ruffs at his
neck and wrists. He is brandishing a rapier.

<blockquote>
SERAFINA PEKKALA
That is a duelling empress.
</blockquote>

But then there are examples of bears that cross paths with
humankind more decisively, and so have to take on a more
nuanced role. In 1967's *The Jungle Book*, Baloo, 'that shiftless
stupid jungle bum', becomes a parental figure to Mowgli, his
lesson in fighting 'like a bear' segueing into a street-smart
philosophy lecture, replete with practical tips ('Don't pick the
prickly pear with the paw; when you pick the pear try to use the
claw'). Notably, brute force fails 'Old Iron Paws' in the climactic
battle with Shere Khan the tiger. He's tough, but no sentinel,
and he's buffoonish enough to abandon a rescue mission
for the chance to boogie with the enemy. There are echoes,
however, of the trickster persona in both his relationship with
straight-laced Bagheera and his mastery of disguise.

At the other end of the scale, Pooh Bear – who, despite being
a stuffed toy animal, lives in the woods, climbs trees and braves
the vengeance of bees for a taste of honey just like a real bear[2]
– is looked on with fatherly indulgence by his boy master,
Christopher Robin, and must repeat the mantra 'Think, think,
think' in order to approach simple problems. Despite being
of too limited intelligence to show up his human companion,
his gently investigative, enquiring nature seems to provoke
unlikely adventures in a manner reminiscent of belligerent
trickster heroes like Monkey/Sun Wukong in *Journey to the West*.

Michael Bond's Paddington, hailing from the jungles of
'darkest Peru' and starring in a 1975 FilmFair TV series, as well

---

2   *The character was also named after a real black bear.*

as a 2014 cinematic feature, is a charming ingénu who ends up bidding high at an auction because he thinks the other people in the room are waving to him. But he's also intelligent, impertinent and a catalyst for disruption in the human world he has ensconced himself in, usually emerging unscathed from the chaos he instigates.

Hanna-Barbera's Yogi Bear is a picnic basket thief with a nemesis in the form of easily bamboozled Ranger Smith. His frequent use of rhyming and punnery, along with the considerable investment he places in his own cunning ('I'm smarter than the average bear!'), are characteristic traits of wood imps and mischief spirits, but like Pooh and Paddington, he can also come across as something of a naïf – certainly not as smart as he thinks. In his 2010 live-action/CGI outing, he suffers a pie in the face, among other physical humiliations. His diminutive companion Boo-Boo Bear is disappointingly un-Puckish, acting as a foil to Yogi's clowning.

Shirokuma Café's Polar Bear, who debuted on Japanese television in 2012, offers us the clearest vision yet of the bear as a variant of the trickster. Something of a wise fool, his character integrates many of the traits listed above, shifting from clown to provocateur without ever forsaking his genial, slow manner or failing to exude power. The world of *Shirokuma Café* is one where animals and humans share the same space peacefully, with the semi-anthropomorphic animals retaining the physical proportions of their real-life counterparts, as well as a few of their behavioural characteristics. Polar Bear, the proprietor of the titular café, looms over the humans and other animals, his teeth and claws unshorn, his eyes small black coals. He creates, serves and enjoys human food but is barred from the seal pool in the local zoo, presumably for good reason. He's also a dedicated punster, pulling props out of thin air in order to create miniature tableaux. For example, in the first episode, when a customer asks for seconds (*okawari*), he produces first sunflowers (*himawari*), then the daily special (*higawari*), then an axe and firewood (splitting logs: *makiwari*). He delights in making up stories of his youth that play on human perceptions of bears, or teasingly hinting at his rougher side, and he frequents a bar for 'wild' animals, drinking with a lion, a tiger, a wolf, and his best friend, Grizzly-san, a biker bear not averse to 'springing' his claws as if they were a brace of flick-knives.

It's Polar Bear I think of when Dr Conde, one of Lucîa de Nobile's guests, remarks on the behaviour of one of the other guests: 'It's a Masonic call for help. They must go to each other's aid. But here … unless, of course, the bear …' Were the bear a fox, he might have been the one to trick the guests into entering the music room, or to convince them that they cannot leave it. Were he a tiger, the guests would be heroic figures in a tense thriller. Were he a dog, he would make for an invaluable ally, perhaps sent to get help. Being a bear

BEAR INTERVENTION 3

(The Limits of Control, 2009)

NUDE

So, you don't like mobiles, either.

Huh.

No guns...

...no mobiles...

...no sex...

LONE MAN

No ... suspicion.

THE BEAR enters the hotel room.
THE LONE MAN and THE NUDE shut themselves in the bathroom,
where he unbuttons his sharkskin
and sits on the rim of the bath.
His shoes do not croak.
THE NUDE begins to paint her lips.
THE BEAR approaches the window.
He touches the glass with his fine, hard fingers
making the sound of hailstones, or dice,
or haildice, and surveys the city of Seville
as if it were an expanse of river,
dark but filled with pulsing fish.
THE BEAR has never been to Spain before;
he loved the brochure's baubled orange trees
and packed up his appetite, the few beliefs he keeps.
Spanish is easier than English;
they roll their 'r's, the Spanish do.
And the parts he had elsewhere?
Limiting and overly demanding.
In truth, he likes the sense
of a building's weight on his back
when he lowers his head
and crushes through its narrow entrances.

THE LONE MAN puts a slit between door and frame.
Is this a mix-up? Is the room double-booked?

Being a bear, though, he remains enigmatic and beyond blame,
even as his presence teases and provokes the guests. He could
almost be saying, 'I like the decor well enough, but it's rather
gloomy. Oh, there you all are. Is this a game? How do you play?'

157

WALTER C. METZ

❧

The Avant-Garde among the Animals

WHILE ONE would suppose that the differences between humans and animals would be obvious (humans sometimes overcome their instinctual urges, while animals generally do not), much Western popular media (from 1950s Disney films to the present *Animal Planet* fare) anthropomorphises in such a way that animals come to embody only the extremes of human behaviour, either bellicose and violent or cuddly and friendly. Documenting that the natural history tradition in English-language media forwards a crucial misrepresentation of difference between animals and humans, I build a model for the development of an avant-garde natural history filmmaking tradition that would be equipped to engineer an intervention against these tropes. Using documentary theory, I critique the *Battlefield* series of wildlife films presented on the Discovery Channel in 2003–2004. This discussion results in a position that, while CGI techniques pretend to transform our scientific vision of animals, the aesthetics of the filmic avant-garde have the potential to really do so, as well as to convey the complex content demanded by scientists.

As is the case for narrative filmmaking, experimental cinema is a viable conduit for reinventing natural history filmmaking. This essay pursues that hypothesis through an intensive study of the 2003 BBC and Discovery co-produced series of *Battlefield* films – *Lion Battlefield*, *Shark Battlefield*, *Wolf Battlefield* and *Polar Bear Battlefield* – which employ computer-generated imaging (CGI) techniques to create narratives about animals. While these films use visual devices common to the experimental cinema – impossible views from beneath the animals, for example, similar to the view beneath the ballerina in Rene Clair's *Entr'Acte* (France, 1924) – at the ideological level, the films merely replicate our common assumptions as to what animals are like (anthropomorphically like humans, especially in their maternal and violent natures). In short, these films speak to a purportedly 'green' America and Earth in the language invented to describe the opposite of a bleak, industrialising nineteenth century.

Instead, I propose considering the narrative and ideological features of experimental cinema as a base for rebuilding natural history filmmaking within an art school context. That is to say, what is the proper natural history film equivalent of Michael Snow's *Wavelength* (1967), an intensive study of the filmic zoom which refuses narrative engagement (a man falls dead halfway through the film, but the camera refuses to stop its inexorable passage through the room)? If *Wavelength* was equipped to dismantle the authority of the Hollywood cinema, then a new generation of experimental wildlife filmmakers should be able to intervene against the status quo on television.

I choose the *Battlefield* films in particular because of their significance at an historical crossroads in nature filmmaking. At the time of first airing in the United States, Discovery was in the midst of transforming its business model. Founded by John Hendricks in 1985, DCI began as a basic cable venue for science and nature programming, a realm hitherto limited in the United States to public broadcasting (*Nature*) and one-off *National Geographic Specials*. Replicating the early history of American network television itself, Discovery was to the cable industry what Pat Weaver's NBC was to RCA in the early 1950s, a place to advertise the industry itself. In 'Back to Nature', *Broadcasting and Cable*'s expose of the shake-up at Discovery, John M. Higgins explains, 'Discovery's family-friendly, educational bent gave cable operators something upbeat to pitch to subscribers'. Discovery spawned seventeen networks, through expansion into digital technology (Discovery Health) and acquisition (The Learning Channel), and became 'one of the most successful brands in television, a $2.7 billion-a-year enterprise' (Higgins 2006).

Since that time, the network has all but abandoned its interest in science and nature, a process which began, ironically, with the phenomenally successful *Walking with Dinosaurs* (2001), a visually innovative yet scientifically specious CGI reconstruction of the prehistoric era, inspired by the technical and commercial success of *Jurassic Park* (Steven Spielberg, 1993). The commitment to narrative and CGI spectacle over scientific content continued unabated at Discovery, first with the *Battlefield* films, and then with an absurdist endgame, shows like *Dragons: A Fantasy Made Real* (2004) and *Alien Planet*

(2004). By this point, none of Discovery's roots remained, and its final shift towards shallow reality-based entertainment was completed with *Monster Garage*, *Dirty Jobs* and *American Chopper*. This gradual 'harming [of] the company's brands', as Bob Miron, a Discovery board of directors member, put it, was the dirty work of Billy Campbell, a business executive from Warner Bros. Television and ruthless film studio Miramax, who 'was hired in 2002 to inject an entertainment sensibility into DCI's U.S. networks' (Higgins 2006).

One of the best pieces devoted to science and film – Carl Gardner and Robert Young's 'Science on TV: A Critique' – was published in 1981. That essay's prescriptions for good science television are nicely developed, and have, of course, gone completely unheeded. Gardner and Young argue that science television presents science as closed, not open (1981: 171), and as a product rather than a process; that it deals exclusively in positivism (1981: 171); that it relies on a false binary between science and society (1981: 173); that it subordinates the labour process both in science and in the making of the documentary (1981: 190); that the scope of scientific inquiry is always limited; that it depicts science as inevitable rather than the result of social choices; and that it is conventional, relying on celebratory classical narrative (1981: 186). These critiques, of course, apply not only to *The Voyage of Charles Darwin*, Gardner and Young's case study, but equally to the *Battlefield* series of films.

All four films in the *Battlefield* series operate under the assumption that to be commercially successful, a traditional narrative about the animals must be offered. In fact, each film relies on nearly exactly the same moves in opening narration, despite the vast differences between sharks, lions and wolves (oh my!). All four films begin with an authoritative male voiceover narrator intoning, 'This is a story about …', the subject subsequently introduced being a hungry mother (*Shark Battlefield*), a pride of lions (*Lion Battlefield*) or 'one of nature's top predators' (*Wolf Battlefield*). Each film also establishes its dominant interest in storytelling under the shroud of science: all four films preface their imagery with the claim, 'This is a story, but everything you are about to see is based on fact'. Both *Shark Battlefield* and *Lion Battlefield* further claim that their images are 'modelled on fifty years of science', the identical claims being laughable, since shark and lion biology do not have remotely the same scientific research histories.

All four films underline the visual importance of CGI technology for the representation of animals. The films implicitly critique the limitations of traditional wildlife documentary techniques (sitting in a tree for months waiting for an animal to walk in front of the camera), appealing to the viewer's appreciation of the special privilege of intimate access to the secret natural world they are about to be granted. In *Wolf Battlefield*, for example, the narrator enthuses: 'For the first time, you'll have an extraordinary view of the wolf and the wolf's world, through the eyes of its leaders and their family.' The film then proceeds to deliver computer-enhanced close-ups of the wolves' paws as they walk across the Rocky Mountain snow.

Similarly, the narrator of *Shark Battlefield* informs us that 'We've now entered the shark's sensory world' as the CGI imagery delivers simulations of infrared, heat-sensitive film in order to allow us to 'see' the shark's ability to detect scents diffused in the ocean. The films thus market themselves as delivering an improved, transformed vision of animals, yet rather than delivering on this avant-garde promise, they merely replace scientific knowledge with easily-obtained CGI

163

spectacle. The *Battlefield* films, then, demonstrate the problem that science filmmaking poses for the academic study of documentary.

Both Michael Renov and John Grierson have passionately argued for the appreciation of the poetics of documentary. Grierson famously advocated for documentary as 'the creative treatment of actuality' (Rotha 1952: 70). In 'Toward a Poetics of Documentary', Renov argues:

That a work undertaking some manner of historical documentation renders that representation in a challenging or innovative manner should in no way disqualify it as nonfiction because the question of expressivity is, in all events, a matter of degree ... In the end, the aesthetic function can never be wholly divorced from the didactic one insofar as the aim remains 'pleasurable learning.' (1993: 35)

As a matter of assessing documentary generally, I agree wholeheartedly with Renov's plea for attention to films that are aesthetically inventive: I would much rather watch Buñuel's *Land Without Bread* (1932) than Ken Burns's traditionalist films. However, in the specific case of science filmmaking, we need to interrogate more carefully the differences between productive and problematic 'pleasurable learning' and how the actuality is being 'creatively treated'.

All science filmmakers, including those who made the *Battlefield* films, who market their wares to a mass audience, believe arrogantly that they are conveying important scientific information in a narratively and aesthetically palatable form. However, this belief that one can house the science pill in a sugary entertainment shell produces more problems than it solves. When the *Battlefield* films introduce CGI aesthetics and narrative interventions about pregnant sharks and bickering wolves, the science content all but disappears. Furthermore, if only the aesthetic techniques of the avant-garde are adopted, all of the ideological critique of that impulse is also left behind. Thus, the *Battlefield* films produce one kind of 'pleasurable learning' at the expense of another, an experimental nature film which could both maintain complex scientific content and critique the ideological impulses of the traditional anthropomorphic documentary.

The *Battlefield* scripts rely on remarkable visual metaphors to encourage us to experience the animal world. In *Shark Battlefield*, a dead turtle emits 'smells [that] broadcast news of the turtle's demise', smells that the narrator insists in a simile are 'like a book that's dissolved in the water'. Because, apparently, the shark has media savvy – the visual ability to watch television news and read books – she has entered 'the dead turtle's detection zone'. The film thus links the viewers' world (one of books and television) to the shark's (one of swimming and eating). As the segment ends, these worlds collapse together: due to the shark's 'reading' ability, she gets to eat. As the show cuts to its first commercial break, the narrator intones, 'Our turtle won't last long.'

The *Battlefield* films thus pitch themselves to their viewers as being able to deliver scientifically reliable information, and in a form that is unavailable to traditional wildlife cinema. In this way, the series is part of a new development in non-fiction film that Mark Wolf has labelled the 'subjunctive documentary'. Wolf begins his analysis:

> *Whereas most documentaries are concerned with documenting events that have happened in the past, and attempt to make photographic records of them, computer imaging and simulation*

are concerned with what could be, would be, or might have been;
they form a subgenre of documentary we might call subjunctive
documentary, following the use of the term subjunctive as a
grammatical tense. (Wolf 1999: 274)

The only actual documentary that Wolf discusses is *500 Nations* (1995), wherein 'computer animation is used to bring a reconstructed city of Tenochtitlan back to life' (1999: 282). However, Wolf's idea about the subjunctive mode of documentary helps to explain the overall programming development of the Discovery Channel in the past two decades. The *Battlefield* series is merely the application of the subjunctive mode to wildlife cinema – the films present merely a 'virtual' habitat sewn together through unannounced shifts between actual wildlife footage and artificially created and/or enhanced images – that was begun by the application of CGI techniques to dinosaurs, first in the fictional *Jurassic Park* films (1993 and later) and then in the Discovery Channel's phenomenally successful series of films devoted to prehistoric times (among others, *Walking with Dinosaurs*, 1999, and *Walking with Prehistoric Beasts*, 2001).

In the same documentary studies anthology in which Wolf's essay appears, James Moran, in his essay, 'A Bone of Contention: Documenting the Prehistoric Subject' (1999), more fully explores the subjunctive mode of dinosaur cinema that pre-dates the *Battlefield* series of wildlife films. Instead of discussing non-fiction films, Moran focuses on the relationship between science and *Jurassic Park*'s fictional representations of dinosaurs. Also calling these gestures 'documentary in the subjunctive mode', Moran analyses how the representation of dinosaurs allows for a world in which the *image* is fictional but the *content* is truthful, because it is based upon science.

The phenomenally successful CGI representation of dinosaurs has forced a trend in documentary cinema in which the image is no longer tied to the ontological belief in its reality. Furthermore, the palaeontologists implicated in this corruption of the visual are invoked by the films to buttress their method via appeals to scientific truth. For example, Moran cites palaeontologist Ian Tattersall's argument that 'speculation is inescapable in any attempt to depict extinct species and may not necessarily sacrifice reasonable scientific accuracy' (Moran 1999: 262).

This leads directly to Moran's focus on *Jurassic Park*, the premise of which is that 'dinosaurs may appear in fictional contexts, but they should always appear as non-fictional in and of themselves. Unlike creatures of a mythical past, such as the unicorn or phoenix, the T. Rex from the prehistoric past did exist, and therein lies its fascination and the desire for its accurate representation within the narrative' (1999: 264). Just as wildlife documentaries have their biology advisors, so did *Jurassic Park*. Moran explains: 'On the set, Jack Horner, a professional paleontologist, advised designers about "authentic" dinosaur behavior' (1999: 264). The currently indistinguishable boundary between natural history documentary and Hollywood's science-fiction spectaculars is sealed by Steven Spielberg's self-assessment of the sort of film he wanted to produce: 'kind of like *Nova* meets *Explorer*, with a little bit of *Raiders of the Lost Ark* and *Jaws* mixed in' (quoted in Moran 1999: 265).

The importance of the dinosaur, both to popular science and the natural history documentary, cannot be overstated. Because of prehistory's ability to capture the imagination of small boys, natural history museums are a booming business. In Bozeman, Montana, home of Montana State University, the cornerstone of the collection of the Museum of the Rockies is the fossil collection and its presentation as the work of palaeontologist Jack Horner. Docents incessantly inform the young visitors 'what Jack thinks' a particular fossil means. Similar museums are cropping up all over the American West, their popularity supported by the same factors which support the Discovery Channel: dinosaurs are seen in a conservative culture as both educational and non-ideological, not directly subject to the effects of our climate destabilisation as are, for instance, polar bears.

While all science suffers from an overreaching attempt to make broad claims of relevance from incredibly limited data, this is most offensively true in the field of palaeontology. From a small number of fossils, the dinosaur museums and their natural history film counterparts make grand claims about our 'knowledge' about the social behaviour of the dinosaurs. In *Walking with Dinosaurs*, Jack Horner gleefully 'speculates' unabashedly without ever acknowledging the ideological contamination from the present these gestures are subject to. Typically, these claims project what we know of the current world (both human and lizard behaviour are correlated to dinosaur behaviour) back onto prehistory. When humanists speculate on meaning, this is seen as a lesser form of knowledge. When museum workers engage in similar interpretation under the respectable umbrella of science, it is worthy of hundreds of hours of educational television programming.

Dinosaur documentaries came to dominate the Discovery Channel's line-up in the wake of the success of the *Jurassic Park* films. In particular, *Walking with Dinosaurs* revolutionised the television industry. As Cynthia Chris explains, *Wild Discovery* was the network's flagship show by the mid-1990s because of the cheap production costs and the family-friendly content of its programming (2006: 86). *Walking with Dinosaurs* extended both of these industrial advantages. While animal filmmaking is much cheaper to produce than an hour-long drama – Chris quotes an article from *Forbes*, 'Animals without Agents', in which Robert LaFranco argues that 'The animals and plants are nonunion, not entitled to residual payments, and work for nothing' – there are still the costs associated with sending a film crew to Africa to gather images of lions. However, once the technicians who made *Jurassic Park* programmed the dinosaur CGI files, 'documentary' versions could be churned out at will for truly rock-bottom cost. Secondly, if animal films appeal to families, dinosaur films do so with a vengeance because of the enthusiasm young boys have for imagining the (reputedly) violent prehistoric beasts.

Faced with the ratings spikes the *Walking With* series produced for Discovery – between 2002 and 2004, DCI's revenues grew at the spectacular rate of 22% per year (Higgins 2006) – it was inevitable that the CGI imaging techniques would be directed elsewhere across the televisual landscape. The *Battlefield* films are the result of applying the technique to wildlife cinema, and it only got worse from there. By 2004, Discovery was airing shows like *Dragons: A Fantasy Made Real* and *Alien Planet*, in which CGI methods, and absurd interviews with scientists, are used to speculatively 'document' how dragons would fly if they actually existed or what life might look like on a fictional planet in a nearby solar system were it actually discovered. As *Anneke M. Metz* (2008) demonstrates, these films served as the limit case of the natural history subjunctive documentary. After that, Discovery had all but decimated its brand – bleeding the 'information' for the 'entertainment' in its previous 'edutainment' business model – and shifted towards conventional, non-educational reality programming such as *Monster Garage*.

The implication of Discovery's embrace of CGI in the past decade is profound. Wolf's analysis of the subjunctive documentary allows us to think about the dodgy relationship between science and narrative that has always dogged natural history filmmaking, from the safari films of the 1930s to the rabid anthropomorphism of the 1950s Disney 'True-Life Adventures'. As Wolf argues, 'In this era of computer simulation, there is a greater willingness to trade close indexical linkage for new knowledge that would otherwise be unattainable within the stricter requirements of indexical linkage that were once needed to validate knowledge empirically' (1999: 274). As the programming on the Discovery Channel engaged in more simulation and less indexical linkage, its status as science became more and more laughable.

Wolf's analysis of the subjunctive documentary allows a precise analysis of the *Battlefield* series of wildlife films. Wolf argues: 'Computer imaging and simulation represent a shift from the perceptual to the conceptual, a shift that underscores a willingness to exchange direct experience for abstractions that open up the wide vistas not directly available to the senses' (1999: 289). Each of the four films in the *Battlefield* series uses CGI to 'document' such 'wide vistas' of animal experience: in the shark's Pacific Ocean, the wolf's Rocky Mountains, the lion's African savannah and the polar bear's Arctic wasteland. The non-indexical visual representation of these improbably witnessed habitats is, however, linked to narratives, each of which is ideologically problematic. The invention of these shows, however, lies in their ability to outdo each other in their fascinatingly desperate attempts to engage the viewer with stories about the animals.

Polar Bear Battlefield is the least remarkable of the four films.

With the exception of the CGI images of surveillance and simulated infrared imagery of animal smells characteristic of all the films in the series, it is a conventional wildlife film. Cynthia Chris argues that the *Wild Discovery* series – her example is *Wild Dogs: A Tale of Two Sisters* (1990) – quickly adopted the normative, 'blue chip' techniques of wildlife cinema, through which the films 'follow members of a single species – usually a specific herd, pack, family, or other grouping – throughout a year-long cycle that includes mating, birth, raising young, and separation of mother and young' (Chris 2006: 87). *Polar Bear Battlefield* is produced directly from this mould: the film begins as a mother and her cub emerge from hibernation, and it follows them in their struggles for survival over the coming year. The film features an entrancing segment in which the young bear has to learn how to kill one of the beluga whales which is trying to survive the winter by breathing out of a small hole in the Arctic ice. While the film is conventional in its representation of nature, it is relatively innocuous.

The other three episodes in the series, however, are among the most disturbingly ideological presentations of wildlife ever offered on American television. The voiceover narrator of *Shark Battlefield* tells us that his story is 'about a hungry mother, a female tiger shark, and the extraordinary world in which she lives'. Throughout the episode, and ad nauseam, he reminds us that she is pregnant with fifty babies, and that if she does not eat, they will all die. The film is filled with rabid anthropomorphic gestures. After the first commercial break, we are encouraged to root for the shark as she follows a scent trail to possible food, but drama is created when the narrator tells us that other sharks have got to the prey first. 'There's no way she could know if she's following old news', the narrator sadly intones.

The film climaxes when the shark finally does eat. She comes across a colony of albatrosses and eats a few chicks learning how to fly. She has her babies, and the film ends with the narrator telling us that in five years, they will return to the shark battlefield, thus reassuring us that nature will continue in a cycle, naturalising the violence we have just witnessed and refusing commentary about the polluting human interventions which threaten habitat. In a final expression of how narrative trumps science on the Discovery Channel, the bumper to the next programme announces *Submarines: Sharks of Steel* as part of 'Warriors and Weapons Weekend'. Such metaphors of militarisation dominate the representation of the animal world in the other two films in the series, *Wolf Battlefield* and, the most egregious of the lot, *Lion Battlefield*.

If *Shark Battlefield* offers a story of a mother desperate to feed her unborn babies, *Wolf Battlefield* intertextually rescripts the musical *West Side Story* (Robert Wise, 1962) for the animal set. The film tells the story of a small wolf pack, which the narrator names the Jets! They are in competition with a much larger pack, the narrator's description of which reveals how deeply ideological nature films actually are:

Next door, they have the neighbours from hell ... There are problems with a pack this size ... [Their need for food] makes the big pack dangerous. Sooner or later, they could invade the Jets' living space. Our pack's best defence is to engage in chemical warfare. The agent they use is scent. It's a clear warning to outsiders to keep out. It's a signal all wolves recognise and ignore at their peril.

Thus, in the span of less than a minute, the film has endorsed both geopolitical and domestic conservatism. The wolves use 'chemical warfare', like Saddam Hussein. Therefore, the

West needs to be strong, like 'our' pack, and fight to the death. Similarly, the other pack is an invasive neighbour, 'from hell'! Thus, the destruction of the public space that is common to contemporary conservative America is also endorsed. Again, the wolf pack's life naturalises our own human space, making gated communities a perfectly normal response to our neighbour's imagined wolf-like aggression.

The two packs of wolves stake out their territory using their scent. The CGI image, simulating heat-sensitive film, shows a boundary between their two regions marked by red and green lines of scent trails oozing out of the Rocky Mountain snow. The film thus develops a World War I intertext, a sense that the wolves exist in a world of trench warfare. When 'our' small pack of wolves, out of desperation, chase a herd of elk out of their own marked territory, the narrator develops drama before the cut to the show's second commercial break: 'But will the wolves cross their own front line? They don't hesitate; the stakes are just too high. They are in no man's land now, and just a half a mile from the big pack's territory.'

For all of *Wolf Battlefield*'s engagement with violence and militarism, its ending drains the world of conflict, and climaxes with family-friendly harmony. The big pack dies from infighting. As we witness footage of wolves biting each other's necks, the narrator intones: 'The alpha sons and daughters challenge their parents' authority. But force alone isn't enough. Do any of them have the strength of character to be a leader? The big pack is in big trouble.' Only five adolescent wolves survive the battle. When they cannot fend off a young bear for an elk carcass, we know they are doomed. The narrator informs us: 'If this is the best they can do, these wolves will lose their battle to survive.' The film, however, leaves it there, sparing the young viewers the brutal denouement.

The film quickly cuts from this depressing outcome to its happy ending. 'Our' pack joins together to successfully protect its new-born cubs. The narrator attributes this success to 'the alpha pair's strong leadership'. Thus, *Wolf Battlefield*, while forwarding conservative messages of militarism and protecting one's own, strips its *West Side Story* intertext of its progressive tragic message. Whereas the Jets and the Sharks, reminding us of Shakespeare's *Romeo and Juliet*, cannot overcome their violence to protect Tony and Maria's love and lives, the wolf version of the Jets thrive and the Sharks die, as all evildoers must. Whereas *West Side Story* offers tragedy as an argument against human violence, *Wolf Battlefield* celebrates that violence as natural, inevitable and productive. The narrator frighteningly ends the film:

> *The alpha female and her mate now have another generation to defend their future. And with their neighbours decimated, ahead of the pack lies a land of opportunity. On the wolf battlefield, it's time for the Jets to draw a new front line.*

The ideological nature of the stories being told in *Wild Discovery* is clear from *Wolf Battlefield*. However, I would like to conclude with an analysis of *Lion Battlefield* that will point towards one possibility for the reinvention of this currently moribund wildlife cinema. My idea is to advocate the use of the avant-garde imagery of the *Battlefield* films as not just an aesthetic choice, but a political one. Ideologically, *Lion Battlefield* is the most problematic film in the series. In wall-to-wall voiceover, the authoritative male narrator leads us through an encounter with three lions. Not commenting on the film's first image, an aerial helicopter shot of the lions which looks more like a smart bomb graphic from the Gulf War than anything else, he proceeds to tell us: 'This is a story about a pride of lions and how they raise their cubs, and about its defence force of two brothers.' The film thus begins with a narrative that is oddly about both militarism and family. The greatest enemy of our heroes, he goes on to tell us, are nomadic males.

The film then tries, feebly, to retreat from its narrative base to introduce its science content: 'This is a story, but everything you are about to see is based on fact.' The film defends this assertion with an appeal to a new way of seeing: 'You're about to see the African savannah like never before … a virtual world, modelled on fifty years of science.' The film proposes to study the lions in their natural habitat, a virtual 100-square-mile grid of African plain, putting that entire space under what the narrator tells us is 'total surveillance'. Remarkably, in arguing for a poetics of documentary, Michael Renov predicts this development:

> *For indeed, the realm of filmic nonfiction is a continuum along which can be ranged work of great expressive variability – from that which attends little to the vehicle of expression (the not-so-distant apotheosis of cinema verité – surveillance technology – might serve as the limit case) to that which emphasizes the filtering of the represented object through the eye and mind of the artist.* (1993: 35)

Wildlife films are as culturally pressing as they have ever been in the history of cinema. *March of the Penguins* (2005) found spectacular success, but what do we make of a film whose main narrative is so banal – I saw this exact film when I was a kid in the 1970s: Mum Penguin goes off in search of food, Dad Penguin stays behind and freezes to death, we cry, the end – that its end credit sequence, when we see how the film was made, by cameramen bothering the penguins when they are at their most vulnerable, is by far the most interesting – if diabolical – part of the film?

Science studies, in this case the cultural analysis of wildlife biology, is a crucial component to the analysis of these films. However, the discipline of media studies – film and television history, theory and criticism – screams out its applicability to films like *Lion Battlefield* just as forcefully. In particular, the film announces its affinities with the avant-garde. The narrator tells us, 'You're about to see the African savannah like never before ... the way ordinary cameras cannot show.' The film thus announces its desire to have us see animals in a new way. The language for revolutionary seeing is, of course, the language of the avant-garde. At the moment when the lion walks over the camera, we have an 'impossible view', one where the camera cannot be in a conventional location because the lion would eat us were we actually there. This fascinates me because it engages some of the most basic theoretical questions about film that were asked by the historical avant-garde in the 1920s.

When Rene Clair mounted the camera beneath the ballerina dancing on a glass plate in *Entr'Acte*, a whole flurry of questions were raised about the status of film as it played between acts of a Surrealist ballet. The spectators of the ballet could not possibly see this view of the ballerina, because were she to actually dance on glass, it would break, thus killing us and her; because were we to actually see this, she would not look as beautiful as she would from the centre of the fifth row; and because bourgeois propriety would be assaulted.

Of course, when the *Lion Battlefield* narrator tells us that the film will make us see anew, he does not mean the same thing as the Surrealists did. He means merely that the film will give us yet another in a string of new aesthetic experiences. However, from a critical studies perspective, *Entr'Acte* is an ideal film with which to compare *Lion Battlefield*. Both films offer 'pleasurable learning' and the 'creative treatment of actuality', yet one is clearly more progressively engaged than the other. The latter film's militaristic metaphors are exactly what is under assault in Clair's film, which begins with two bourgeois gentlemen jumping absurdly around as a cannon also hops, out of human control. The camera looks down the cannon barrel until a shell comes out, in slow motion, and ends the shot. *Entr'Acte* is a bitter inter-war film about the repercussions of military technology run amuck over civilisation.

Lion Battlefield embraces that absurdity with a straight face. The second brother goes on 'border patrol'. The savannah is governed by nuclear *détente*: 'Every pride male knows exactly where the others are … a good way of avoiding volatile face-to-face encounters.' At one point the film celebrates the new, and much lamentable, if one believes in the importance of the freedom of the press, embedding of reporters into military units to control information: 'You are now on patrol with possibly the greatest animal defence force on earth.' Jackals and hyenas are introduced as the 'first wave of ground troops'. Vultures are 'the savannah's scavenging elite [who] arrive by air', later referred to as the 'vulture task force'.

So, in its failures to get us to see anew, ironically, *Lion Battlefield* offers a detailed pedagogy for what an avant-garde nature film might be. One path I believe media studies should take is the application of what it knows to these kinds of films. In the terms of my avant-garde argument, we should consider what canonical avant-garde films there are that could serve as models for a reinvented natural history and science filmmaking. When Snow's *Wavelength* isolated its structural analysis of the zoom shot, it did so by resolutely denying narrative significance. The continued zoom past the Hollis Frampton character's dead body in *Wavelength* is one of the most compelling cinematic encounters of my life. Should there not be equivalent gestures in natural history filmmaking? Would it not be nice, just once, to have the camera swing away from the lions, behind the filmmakers, to reveal the Third World labour which supports a contemporary film shoot on the plains of Africa? Remarkably, this technique lies at the heart of *Unsere Afrikareise* (Germany, Peter Kubelka, 1966), but lamentably, there is little chance of such a critique of colonialism airing on the Billy Campbell-controlled DCI networks.

The extent of the applicability of film to science does not end with the avant-garde, of course. Film's documentary ability to engage in participant ethnography seems another place to begin our work. In *Laboratory Life*, Bruno Latour settles into a lab, as an anthropologist would, to track the social life of scientists. The film camera, as with conventional anthropological cinema, would seem to be an ideal tool for performing such work. And in a world in which scientists are being interviewed on camera without end, it would seem there would be interest in this from the other of C. P. Snow's 'two cultures' (the sciences and the humanities) as well. I hope media educators in art schools will engage more thoroughly in the study of the relationship between the two cultures.

By way of conclusion, I would like to reflect upon the theoretical underpinnings of my pedagogical argument in this essay, a polemic for the creation of avant-garde wildlife films. On the film studies side, Bill Nichols argues for the reconsideration of our historical assumptions regarding the separation of documentary and avant-garde cinema: 'Our understanding of the relationship between documentary film and the modernist avant-garde requires revision' (2001: 580).

In a largely historical argument, Nichols traces the intertwined nature of the 1920s avant-garde and the simultaneous Grierson-influenced documentary tradition: 'Documentary, like avant-garde film, cast *[sic]* the familiar in a new light, not always that desired by the existing governments.... The modernist avant-garde of Man Ray [and] Rene Clair ... proposed alternative subjects and subjectivities' (2001: 583).

In the conclusion to *Watching Wildlife*, Cynthia Chris brilliantly analyses two Discovery Channel episodes of *Wild Discovery* – *Wild Jewels* and *Wild Treasures of the East*, both 1999 – that were shot partially in Iran. That same week, in late January 2002, George Bush had delivered his 'axis of evil' speech, positioning Iran as a demonic emitter of terrorism. Chris observes, 'I found something quite moving, and even a little bit subversive, in these admiring considerations of natural beauty, their fleetingly articulated antimilitarism, and their humane visions of a population then being vilified by much of the American press and by the U.S. administration' (Chris 2006: 199). Can we not, as art educators, teach to a world where such subversion is the result not of television's amazing, but clearly accidental, flow, but of deliberate artistic invention?

Of course, Nichols's evocation of the transformation in subjectivity authored by both documentary and the avant-garde cinema applies to traditional wildlife film in particular via the representation of animal subjectivity as it is made to ape humanity. The academic literature is flooded with books theorising the importance of the animal world for understanding the human one. However, there is no trace of this work in the films on the Discovery Channel. The startling deconstructive argument forwarded by Akira Lippit in *Electric Animal* (2000) has no place in Billy Campbell's fashioning of DCI as a neo-Miramax, that is, a money-making machine.

However, this does not mean that our filmmakers must submit to capitalist hegemony. Instead, we can train a new generation of filmmakers to embrace, not marginalise, Lippit's theory.

Happily for my project on the avant-garde potential of *Lion Battlefield*, Lippit ends his book with a brief discussion of the cinema. He does not discuss Jacques Cousteau and Marlin Perkins like everyone else who has ever written about wildlife cinema. Instead, he discusses the foundational filmmakers of the avant-garde tradition: Eisenstein, Vertov and Dulac:

> *A kind of origin of cinema, Eisenstein's assertion, like the writings of Dziga Vertov, Germaine Dulac, Antonin Artaud, and others who sought to discuss the new medium in ritual forms, bears the trace of organic metaphor, an attempt to describe technological animation in animist terms.* (2000: 193)

Moving at lightning speed through Freud and Derrida, Lippit concludes: 'the advent of cinema is thus haunted by the animal figure, driven, as it were, by the wildlife after death of the animal' (2000: 197).

Perhaps if we want our wildlife films to move beyond the facile anthropomorphism of seeing a pack of wolves as the Jets from *West Side Story*, we ought to begin teaching our filmmakers to parse Lippit's Metzian claim 'cinema is like an animal' (2000: 196), in addition to how to frame for high definition video or light yet another pointless interview with a palaeontologist. It is only under these conditions, I believe, that we can begin to imagine a more humane world in which both humans and animals are protected and nurtured.

The implications of this, of course, are profoundly important for understanding identity politics. The very same forces that produce ethnic and racial disparities in the world result in unequal access to environmental solutions to the global problem of climate change. It is no mistake that *Wolf Battlefield* invokes the 1960s liberal anti-racist framework of *West Side Story*, only to anthropomorphise the actions of the wolves as gang members, to naturalise human difference as a descriptor of animal difference. As Chris's conclusion indicates, the nexus of the human–animal interface offers status quo culture another sounding board for misrepresenting difference, ignoring the political context of Iran in depicting the lives of animals as independent of the consequences of the rhetoric of George Bush's 'axis of evil' speech. The avant-garde media-making tradition offers opportunities for media to represent difference in more productive registers than this.

References

Bouse, Derek (2000) *Wildlife Films*, Philadelphia: University of Pennsylvania Press.

Chris, Cynthia (2006) *Watching Wildlife*, Minneapolis and London: University of Minnesota Press.

Gardner, Carl and Robert Young (1981) 'Science on TV: A Critique', in Tony Bennett et al. (eds) *Popular Television and Film*, London: BFI, pp. 171–193.

Higgins, John M. (2006) 'Back to Nature', *Broadcasting and Cable*, 16 January.

LaFranco, Robert (1996) 'Animals without Agents', *Forbes*, 8 April.

Lippit, Akira Mizuta (2000) 'Animetaphors: Photography, Cryptonymy, Film', in *Electric Animal: Toward a Rhetoric of Wildlife*, Minneapolis and London: University of Minnesota Press.

Metz, Anneke M. (2008) 'A Fantasy Made Real: The Evolution of the Subjunctive Documentary on U.S. Cable Science Channels', *Television and New Media*, 9(4), pp. 333–347.

Mitman, Gregg (1999) *Reel Nature: America's Romance with Wildlife on Film*, Cambridge and London: Harvard University Press.

Moran, James M. (1999) 'A Bone of Contention: Documenting the Prehistoric Subject', in Jane M. Gaines and Michael Renov (eds) *Collecting Visible Evidence*, Minneapolis and London: University of Minnesota Press, 255–273.

Nichols, Bill (2001) 'Documentary Film and the Modernist Avant-Garde', *Critical Inquiry*, 27, pp. 580–610.

Renov, Michael (1993) 'Toward a Poetics of Documentary', in *Theorizing Documentary*, New York and London: Routledge, pp. 12–36.

Rotha, Paul (1952) *Documentary Film*, London: Faber and Faber.

Wolf, Mark J. P. (1999) 'Subjunctive Documentary: Computer Imaging and Simulation', in Jane M. Gaines and Michael Renov (eds) *Collecting Visible Evidence*, Minneapolis and London: University of Minnesota Press, pp. 274–291.

SOPHIE MAYER

৵

grrrrrrrrrrrrr

GIRLS GROW old in the bellies of whales
or their stories do riding outside in

dreaming of warm Bachelard & bone
needles burning fat of their fat in cupped

hands in abalone in *paua* fire/water they
leap into the gullet of the sea to get spit

out little fish sisterbrother tailing
hir nicotine rush it's alive to be other

where girls are horses: not love, one
flankflank you cannot come between

moor muscle that makes meaning
bracken is (a) skin a verb 'let's bracken!'

the whish of the moor where to *wuther* =
almost-silent scream pushed down

from the mouth through thighs & feet
of working & this warmhaired touch

unsidesaddled roan is *press* hipsay can-
ter can turn can run can race can rain

cant her cat(panion) how she externalises
(pussy as) prrrrrr can speak what she cant

can ask caresses can stretch clothesless
sheathless claws ring on his parry rip

to shreds the cage its lil twittypie
no is not me no *trammel* asshole no *thing*

for what is wild is grrrrrrrr is coming
for you riding the biggest fucking beast

you've ever seen

Films

Whale Rider (Niki Caro)
Before Tomorrow (Arnait Video Collective)
The Beaches of Agnès (Agnès Varda)
The Piano (Jane Campion)
XXY (Lucia Puenzo)
Wuthering Heights (Andrea Arnold)
I Am Nasrine (Tina Gharavi)
Bright Star (Jane Campion)
Diary of a Cat (Maya Deren)
The Two Towers (Peter Jackson)

NICOLAS PILLAI

࿓

Asta: The Screwball Dog and the Hollywood Crime Film

*T*HE THIN *Man* (1932) is an aberration in the career of Dashiell Hammett, the author who brought the hard-boiled detective story to maturity. Hammett's final novel reads like a drawing-room comedy spiced with murder, a swan song that combined tough-guy elements with the structure of an Agatha Christie whodunnit, introducing to the world protagonists who would take on a life of their own in movies, television and radio. Hammett's main character and narrator is Nick Charles, ex-private eye, now an elegant drunk living off the wealth of his wife, Nora. Over the course of the novel, the couple find themselves investigating a murder, he reluctantly, she enthusiastically.

Nick and Nora own a schnauzer bitch named Asta, described laconically in the first chapter:

Asta jumped up and punched me in the belly with her front feet. Nora, at the other end of the leash, said: 'She's had a swell afternoon – knocked over a table of toys at Lord & Taylor's, scared a fat woman silly by licking her leg in Saks's, and has been patted by three policemen.' (Hammett 1985: 8)

Hammett's publisher, Knopf, marketed the book cannily, playing up its sexual frankness with a one-page ad that stated, 'Twenty thousand people don't buy a book within three weeks to read a five word question' (Bruccolli and Layman 2002: 150). (The question, incidentally, was Nora quizzing her husband on his tussle with a *femme fatale*: 'Didn't you have an erection?') The book's healthy sales may explain its swift purchase by Metro-Goldwyn-Mayer. In 1933, a year later, Hammett was in Hollywood working on a movie treatment with seasoned screenwriters Albert Hackett and Frances Goodrich.

Directed by W. S. Van Dyke and released in 1934, the film adaptation had Nick and Nora played by William Powell and Myrna Loy, a screen couple formed some months earlier when they starred together in Van Dyke's *Manhattan Melodrama*. Known as 'One Take Woody', Van Dyke shot *The Thin Man* in an incredibly swift twelve days. Some credit for this is owed to the professionalism of the trained pooch that played Asta – a wirehaired terrier called Skippy. As well as changing the dog's breed and sex, the movie made Asta more prominent than in Hammett's novel. Indeed, the terrier became emblematic of the film and its sequels, a comedic canine whose cute tricks complemented the wise-cracking fun of his crime-solving owners (fig. 1).

Figure 1

Since the days of vaudeville, the performing dog had been a staple of American popular entertainment. Skippy was never short of work in Hollywood, appearing in eleven movies between 1934 and 1939. Responding to verbal commands and hand signals, Skippy was owned by animal trainers Henry and Gale East, and earned them no less than $250 a week. In Depression-era America, that bought a lot of dog biscuits. The success of the film *The Thin Man* prompted five sequels; by the third, *Another Thin Man* (1939), Skippy had retired, and so the remaining films feature different lookalike dogs playing Asta. In her autobiography, Myrna Loy recalled,

> *Several wirehaired terriers played our scene-stealing pet over the years, but we weren't allowed to make friends with any of them. Their trainer feared it would break the dogs' concentration. The first one, Skippy, bit me once, so our relationship was hardly idyllic.* (Kotsilibas-Davis and Loy 1987: 91)

In this chapter, I do not intend to give a detailed account of the career of Skippy or his replacements. My aim, rather, is to examine the narrative role of Asta in the Thin Man film series, and to argue that 'the screwball dog' is essential to their project.

HAPPINESS, HUMOUR AND HYDRANTS

In his study of the film star Cary Grant, Andrew Britton writes of another of Skippy's film roles, as the mischievous mutt George in *Bringing Up Baby* (Howard Hawks, RKO, 1938). Britton proposes that screwball dogs focus the comedy of repression, serving 'to express and to provide an occasion for a kind of childlikeness in the couple' (Britton 1986: 40–41). The screwball dog becomes symbolic of a happy couple's ability to make life together into a mutually enriching game – in Stanley Cavell's words, 'to make room for playfulness within the gravity of adulthood' (Cavell 1981: 60). Asta is an amusing dependant of Nick and Nora, not demanding excessive parental care, and able to follow his owners into spaces inappropriate for a child – swanky nightclubs, gambling saloons and seedy rooming-houses.

Figure 2

Asta serves primarily a comic function in the films. Sometimes he will sniff out a clue, but he is just as likely to hide or eat one. He barks at villains but bolts when he sees a cat. And when, at the conclusion of the first film, Nick and Nora fall into bed together, the film coyly cuts to Asta hiding his eyes behind a paw (fig. 2). This last example is characteristic of the way that the films complement sophisticated dialogue, wealth and glamour with bawdy or vulgar humour. One particularly accomplished sight gag in the first film has Nick taking Asta for a walk, and having to pause while the dog, off-screen, urinates at the sidewalk. When one examines the Breen Office's censorship notes for the series, one finds frequent instruction that the filmmakers refrain from depicting Asta's fondness for marking fire hydrants.

The first film's adaptation of Asta's entrance in the novel folds comedy and mystery into one another, introducing the dog as he pulls poor Nora into a smart hotel. He's tracking his master, who, characteristically, is propping up the bar. 'He's dragged me into every gin-mill on the block', scolds Nora. 'Sure', deadpans Nick. 'I had him out this morning.' It's a neat joke about deduction, with Asta methodically following a trail of martinis until he finds Nick.

In the second film, *After the Thin Man* (1936), Asta is given his own sub-plot involving Mrs Asta and a litter of puppies. Asta is forced to fend off a love rival, the dog next door who has been getting in under the fence. These rather silly scenes do serve a larger purpose, though, bluntly sketching a story of infidelity that reflects the film's main plot, told more obliquely. Again, Asta is used to communicate meaning that would otherwise be censored or obscured.

So Asta is not only a comic dog, just as the Thin Man films are not only comedies (they are also mysteries, and rare instances of stories about happy marriage). As much as the films ask us to enjoy the spectacle of Asta's vaudeville dog show – standing on his hind legs and pawing the air, or chasing his own tail – he's also important in the way that he progresses, reflects or subverts the main narrative. This is not to say that Asta functions as a chorus (he does not explicitly comment on the action in the manner of, say, Hergé's Snowy), rather that he non-verbally signals ways in which the films are asking to be read (a better comparison is to Cheetah in MGM's Tarzan series).

Production files for *After the Thin Man* held in the Margaret Herrick Library in Beverly Hills indicate that a musical tribute to the character was written which, mercifully, never made it to the screen. 'Asta's Love Song', dated 24 November 1936, with words and music by Bob Wright and Chet Forrest, begins, 'Bow-wow-wow, I love you', and goes downhill from there. However, the fact that such a thing was even written demonstrates the studio's awareness that Asta helped define the Thin Man films, contributing to what today would be called the series'

Figure 3

brand identity. It is notable that Asta is always credited in title sequences and trailers, and that the painted titles that open each film include the dog's silhouette alongside those of Nick and Nora (fig. 3). The success of the films prompted a slew of imitators, husband-and-wife detectives like the Bradfords, the Reardons and the Sloanes, all of whom seemed drab without a dog. Attempts to replicate the franchise's success in other media slavishly carried over Asta, regardless of his suitability for radio (*The Adventures of the Thin Man*, NBC/CBS, 1941–1950), television (*The Thin Man*, MGM Television/NBC, 1957–1959) or musical theatre (Arthur Laurents's ill-fated *Nick & Nora*, 1991).

Asta's family is not mentioned in subsequent films, and their inclusion in *After the Thin Man* can be seen as a by-product of the sequel format, the necessity to escalate while maintaining familiar series pleasures. At the end of the film, Nora announces her pregnancy, and the following four films will all, in their way, attempt to deal with the burden that a child imposes upon two carefree sleuths. A consideration of the relative functions of the Charles' son Nick Jr and Asta benefits from Britton's observation that 'in not being a child, but replacing one' the screwball dog 'dissociates the marriage from reproduction, or the prospect of it' (Britton 1986: 37). From *Another Thin Man* (1939) onwards, Asta's role changes as he becomes a kind of guard-dog for the child, articulating the films' anxiety over parental duty. As further sequels followed, and Nick Jr grew up, the necessity to give him dialogue scenes diminished Asta's role. Nick Jr could be cute (or horribly precocious, depending on your tolerance for smart kids), but he couldn't follow his parents into boozy nightclubs or criminal hang-outs. As a result, each film restricted Nick Jr to a domestic environment in which the films showed little interest.

The final entry in the series, *Song of the Thin Man* (1947), concludes with a shot of Asta crawling into the bed of the sleeping Nick Jr (fig. 4).

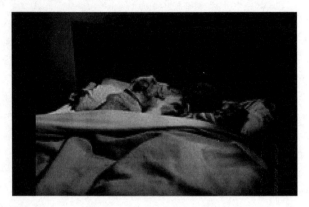

Figure 4

It is an odd way to wrap up the six films, failing to show us the family together or the star couple. Again, consultation of Breen Office reports shows that the scene as filmed was a hasty rewrite of an intended romantic moment between Nick and Nora, which the censor judged 'offensively sex suggestive' (Breen 1946). As it stands, the final shot of the child and his dog is a limp and cosy conclusion to a once subversive set of movies.

ASTA'S LEGACY

While Hammett's source novel is now rarely discussed, the Thin Man films continue to be remembered fondly, revived most recently by the cable channel TCM and a DVD boxed set. Even more celebrated are two films that prominently feature Skippy, the first dog to play Asta: *Bringing Up Baby* and *The Awful*

Truth (Leo McCarey, Columbia, 1937). One hesitates to claim too strong a connection between Asta and other canine stars of the time like Lassie and Rin-Tin-Tin, if only because the humans in those films were always secondary, while Asta is unthinkable without Nick and Nora. Perhaps a stronger line of inheritance could be traced to Eddie (the Jack Russell terrier Moose) and the Crane family in the NBC sitcom *Frasier* (1993–2004).

The screwball dog, a particularly assured kind of canine, seemed to have disappeared largely from cinema screens in the latter half of the twentieth century. In the twenty-first, however, there was to be one last hurrah. In 2011, Michel Hazanavicius's silent film *The Artist* garnered widespread acclaim, receiving multiple award nominations. A great deal of media attention focused on the film's trained dog, a Jack Russell named Uggie. Campaigns were launched petitioning for the award of honorary gongs to Uggie, and *The Guardian* website published a (silent) video featuring the dog visiting the newspaper's offices and sitting for a mock interview with columnist Xan Brooks. The delight with which *The Artist*'s screwball dog was met may give us some sense of the importance and popularity of Asta during the 1930s and 1940s, and his crucial role in the success of the Thin Man films. If Johnny Depp and Rob Marshall had been able to realize their planned *Thin Man* remake, one feels that Uggie would have been perfectly cast as Asta.

On 25 June 2012, Uggie became the first dog to place his pawprints in the cement outside Grauman's Chinese Theatre. Not too far away, side by side, are the handprints of William Powell and Myrna Loy. In a roundabout, tail-chasing kind of way, the memory of Asta was honoured.

References

Breen, Joseph I. (1946) Letter to Louis B. Mayer, 4 December. MPAA files for *Song of the Thin Man*, Special Collections, Margaret Herrick Library.

Britton, Andrew (1986) 'Cary Grant: Comedy and Male Desire', *CineAction!*, 7, pp. 37–51.

Bruccolli, Matthew J. and Richard Layman (2002) *Hardboiled Mystery Writers: Raymond Chandler, Dashiell Hammett, Ross Macdonald*, New York: Carroll & Graf.

Cavell, Stanley (1981) *Pursuits of Happiness: The Hollywood Comedy of Remarriage*, Cambridge, MA: Harvard University Press.

Hammett, Dashiell (1985) *The Thin Man*, Harmondsworth: Penguin.

Kotsilibas-Davis, James and Myrna Loy (1987) *Myrna Loy: Being and Becoming*, London: Bloomsbury.

Wright, Bob and Chet Forrest (1936) 'Asta's Love Song', 24 November. MPAA files for *After the Thin Man*, Special Collections, Margaret Herrick Library.

CHRISSY WILLIAMS

&

Ambrosius
from Labyrinth

S HEEPDOG steed for a fake fox terrier,
noble Ambrosius, who lost the battle,
lost the hierarchy, his sense of purpose,
wears a saddle for his sharp-fanged master.

Brother to Merlin, his soft eyes hidden,
long of fur and long of suffering,
chided for good sense, chided for running,
fails his first test of self-preservation.

Dark paws raised in pantomime horror,
dodging the claws of the fox who feeds him,
he flees in shame. He is not a good dog,
not like his wet-nosed, keen-smelling keeper.

He will not be there, should you need him.
He'll lock the door and be loyal to his stomach.
He will cower, quaking, bemused but kindly,
a true dog lost in the magic of beasts.

ANTHONY ADLER

❧

A Pirates of the Caribbean *Bestiary*

i. his Highness' dog

K<small>IDS CAN</small> be hanged so nobody needs a puppy
as an introductory memento mori.

This mutt has the keys in his mouth and can only
withhold them. Later he may well become a god.

ii. 'Dead men tell no tales'

She speaks for the old tongueless sailor
in rebuses and hieroglyphs.
Wind in your sails! mostly means yes and the rest
is punctuation for the weather.

iii. 'We named the monkey Jack'

Every captain needs an animal homunculus.
It must be named for his departed nemesis,
a rum libation raised for mutineers and debts.

iv. flotsam

How we mourned when the kraken
washed up on the beach
like an archeteuthic hairball.

v. the ocean unbound

The goddess turns into a tottering pile of crabs.

SIMON BARRACLOUGH

⌖

Les Chiens de Mon Oncle

For a few years now I've been 'collecting' dog performances in films (I also like to collect awkward or amusing dinner scenes, but that's for another essay). I count the following among my most prized pieces.

There's the terrifyingly persistent Doberman pinscher in Dario Argento's *Tenebre*, which clears an eight-foot fence with all the application and focus of an Olympian; and the similarly dogged American pit bull in *No Country for Old Men*, which pursues Josh Brolin at night over land and in water, meeting its gun-shot demise mid-leap.

Less menacingly, there are the half-dozen nocturnal hounds that caper around EUR in Antonioni's *L'Eclisse*. One of them, a black poodle, has the good grace to walk several steps on its hind legs for Monica Vitti, providing a rare moment of delight before a row of tinkling flag poles draws her back into existential sobriety. If I didn't know better, I'd say this same pack was hired by Bruce Weber for his Chet Baker documentary *Let's Get Lost*.

I've also enjoyed another striking Doberman, in Martin Scorsese's more recent *Hugo* (this one likes to share baths as well as sniff out ticket dodgers), and the beautifully coiffured, statuesque poodle in *Let the Right One In*, which stumbles upon a fresh victim of vampirism in a beautifully composed snowscape. And who could forget the weird slow-motion lick of the outwardly fearsome guard dog in Hitchcock's *Strangers on a Train*? A potent creature unexpectedly emasculated by cinematic technique and the exigencies of plot. There are dozens more, and I'm sure your own spring to mind. Oh – the huge preening pack wrangled out of the elevator by Jerry Lewis in *The Bellboy*, Stan and Ollie's pooch 'Laughing Gravy'; the list goes on.

I'm not so fond of scenes that humanise dogs too much. I never got on with Lassie – she's just too utilitarian and sensible – and I have no time for the antics of *Beethoven* or the lip-synced silliness of a *Marmaduke*. The thing about Jacques Tati is that he 'let a dog be a dog', to paraphrase Prince's hit 'Gett Off' ('Prince' being, of course, a popular dog's name).

Jacques Tati's films are unusually alive with remarkable and comical creatures and I could easily focus on the canine shenanigans that pepper *Les Vacances de Monsieur Hulot*. But *Mon Oncle* is the film that takes the 'Bonio'.

So *Mon Oncle* opens with a pack of comical stray dogs going about their doggy business. Or so I remembered until I watched it again recently and noticed that they don't appear straight away. The first things we see and hear are a construction crane, the unpleasant sound of drilling and the opening credits displayed on modern signs.

Modernity

The camera tracks down these signs, revealing two men working in the muddy brown ground: one drilling, one sliding a girder or some kind of foundational support into place. For just over a minute we endure the drilling and receive the requisite information, and then the picture and sound fade

[1] *The version of* Mon Oncle *I will be discussing is the French-language version (there are considerable differences between this and the re-dubbed, and in places re-shot, English version,* My Uncle*).*

before revealing an altogether more peaceful and cosier view.

The impeccably designed signs and rectilinear lines give way to hand-written chalk on the side of a higgledy-piggledy building on a charmingly unkempt street with antique lamppost, cobblestones and old-fashioned window shutters. After a beat or two, a small pack of neighbourhood dogs leap into view and set about the place, sniffing, playing and peeing, as dogs will.

Tradition

So the two symbolic worlds of *Mon Oncle* are introduced: the modern developing suburb and the ancient crumbling *quartiere*. The casually anarchic Monsieur Hulot (the 'oncle' of the title, played by writer and director Jacques Tati) lives in this latter world, and his nephew Gérard lives in the former world with his fastidious, rule-bound, upwardly mobile parents, the Arpels (Madame Arpel is Hulot's sister).

We stay with this little pack of dogs as they scamper through the neighbourhood upsetting dustbins and snaffling bits of discarded food. They seem to be leading the camera, lending the film an unusually natural feel.

It's hard to train a pack of dogs to do one's bidding, and, despite stories that Tati rubbed key points of their route with meat beforehand (Guillen 2010), the camera has no choice but to do its best to keep up. In some ways they are directing the film.

One of the dogs stands out: the pedigree miniature dachshund with its check-patterned coat. While it may look a little more refined than the mongrels in the pack, it certainly behaves the same as them: cocking its leg, sniffing in bins and licking from a discarded sardine tin.

The dogs eventually set off after the 'rag and bone man' who leaves the *quartiere* with his horse and cart, but they take a detour through a hole in a crumbling wall beyond which we see tall, grey, charmless concrete accommodation blocks. The dogs continue, following the smooth curve of a new road, until they reach the suburbs and the home of the little dachshund.

The dachshund, we soon learn, is 'Daki', the Arpels' pet dog, and it lives with them in their absurd, high-tech International Style house in the suburbs. Daki fits through the bars of their automatic gate, leaving his pals from the old part of town peering in, excluded.

So, within minutes the dogs have mapped out the terrain of the film for us: its geographical spaces and the poles of its political compass. But more interestingly, they embody the subtle switching and interference of these apparently separate spaces and positions.

Daki may seem privileged, but he behaves just like the rest of the pack. The other dogs are excluded, but the only thing

Daki's friends at the gate, artfully composed

keeping them out, ultimately, is the gate and its awkward dimensions. Later in the film, Monsieur Hulot accidentally pulls the gate from its hinges, suggesting that these barriers are more permeable than they seem at first (also, an outside dog does get into the garden later in the film, causing no little consternation).

In a similar way, Monsieur Hulot and nephew Gérard move between social strata and between modern and traditional ('antiseptic' and 'authentic') registers of behaviour throughout the film.

'They are, for me, marvellous comedians' (Tati 1977)

Jacques Tati loved dogs. He always kept one, always called 'Azor' for some reason (this repetitive naming places him more in the Arpel camp than the Hulot camp, it seems to me). He had a natural touch with dogs and had little trouble getting them to do what he wanted.

It was his crew and financial backers who struggled with the task of getting them to perform on camera: 'The fact that about 40 technicians have to wait patiently while a dog condescends to relieve himself on a lamp-post gives me great financial responsibilities' (Gilliatt 1976).

One of Tati's great tricks was to draw on their natural behaviour to create the comedy he wanted. In *Mon Oncle*, as Monsieur Hulot is drifting around the local market, Tati stages an encounter between one of the local dogs, sitting beneath a greengrocer's stall, and the gnarly, toothy fish that Hulot is carrying around in his bag.

As Hulot and the greengrocer argue over a couple of squashed tomatoes, knocked off the stall by a young girl earlier, Hulot's fish 'confronts' the dog beneath the table. The dog responds instinctively to the fish's gaping jaws.

Dog vs fish

There are many things that make this scene so funny and so typical of Tati's brilliant comedic imagination. The 'battle' between the living dog and the dead fish is comically futile. The fact that the dog only reacts when the fish comes within a certain 'exclusion zone' and relaxes once the fish has retreated is also amusing. To cap it all, neither Hulot nor the greengrocer has the faintest idea that this battle of the species is going on underneath their more 'civilised' altercation about who smashed these tomatoes.

What I love most is how Tati exploits the instincts of the dog to get his effects. Dogs are hard-wired to react defensively (or offensively) to the bared jaws of another dog, or animal. Indeed, it takes some adjustment on their part to accommodate the smiles of their human companions.[2]

The best example of Tati bending a dog's natural behaviour towards a dazzling joke comes later in the film, with Daki the dachshund and an automatic garage door.

OTHER CRITTERS

Mon Oncle contains many creatures in various states, serving several purposes. Tati came from a long line of accomplished

---

2   *When I was a little boy, we had a pet Scottish terrier called Sam (short for 'Samantha Black Beauty', her fancy kennel name), who surprised us all when my grandma bought my dad, for some bizarre reason, a genuine shark's jaw for Christmas. The moment Sam laid eyes upon this disembodied jaw, this bleached-clean threat floating in the air like the Cheshire Cat's smile, an almighty battle ensued that lasted for months and ultimately led to the destruction of the shark's jaw (but not until Sam had sustained many maddening pin-prick wounds to her soft black nose).*

horsemen,[3] and, as well as loving dogs, he clearly valued all animals for themselves and for their comedic potential. In addition to the confrontational fish discussed already, another fish dominates the film: the fish fountain in the Arpels' garden.

Ugly, preposterous and outsized, the garden's gurgling centrepiece is only switched on for 'deserving visitors' (not family or tradesmen). There is much awkward hilarity as the fountain is switched on and off repeatedly as visitors to the house are classified as 'fountain-worthy' or not. It is the proudly naff spindle around which their accumulated absurdities revolve.

Grocer bemused by the ridiculous fish fountain

As a parallel to this fountain, and as an example of the complex patterning and mirroring that runs throughout *Mon Oncle*, Gérard is glimpsed doing his homework, reading from a book

3 *If you'd like to know more about Tati's life, David Bellos's* Jacques Tati *(1999) is invaluable.*

about the natural sciences. However, instead of writing his assignment, he rigs up a rudimentary spout to spray water from the blowhole of the whale on the cover of his text book.

Homework

He may live with uptight, absurd parents, but in some ways their pretentions (like the fish fountain) contribute to Gérard's imaginative life in combination with the more relaxed and playful influence of his uncle.

Along with horses, the nearly ubiquitous dogs and the various representations of fish, *Mon Oncle* also contains a canary, which is played by Hulot using sunlight, as if it were some kind of feathered theremin or sentient instrument. On returning to his ramshackle home, Hulot adjusts his window and notices that as he moves it through various angles he hears birdsong, almost as if the hinge is chirruping rather than squeaking. He eventually realises that light deflected by the window is falling on his neighbour's caged canary. When the sunlight hits, the bird sings. Hulot finds the best angle for maximum birdsong and wedges the window in place to prolong the bird's cheer.

Playing the canary

Tati added all sounds in post-production (lending a subliminal layer of comedy to all proceedings), but this is another wonderful example of natural behaviour in service of the comedic imagination and in pursuit of daily delight over tedious routine or responsibility.

LEASHED/UNLEASHED

In contrast to the rambling pack of strays with whom the pampered Daki occasionally takes up, there are a couple of leashed dogs to be seen in *Mon Oncle*. They are glimpsed in the main square of Hulot's beloved *quartiere* and are clearly very unhappy with their lot, straining and tugging this way and that to break free.

Crucially, the men holding the leashes seem every bit as constrained as their dogs. In one scene, the wife of one of these dog-walkers leans out of her apartment window just as her husband is making his way to the local drinking hole 'Chez Margot'. She calls the dog's name and the dog drags its master away from this leisurely den of daytime drinking and back towards the house.

Later in the film, at an elaborately disastrous garden party presided over by the Arpels' giant metal fish, an unexpected guest (in full equestrian regalia for some reason) allows his black dog to get loose and chase Daki around the garden. Chaos ensues, and Hulot eventually manages to secure the reprobate hound. Except he accidentally attaches the leash to the necklace of the Arpels' neighbour instead. The fluidity of man and dog continues: which is free, which is tethered, and which stands the best chance of happiness?

In another scene, as Monsieur Arpel patrols the plastics factory – Plastac – where he is some kind of senior manager, he takes Daki along with him. The little dachshund, in its familiar checked waistcoat (which perfectly matches Arpel's smoking jacket at one point in the film), trots along the corridors alerting the slacking employees (both blue and white collar) that the boss is around.

As Daki passes, a fresh wave of concerted activity spreads through the building. In some way these humans are leashed to this little dog that has become a symbol of their boss, their responsibilities and their contract with repetitive, unfulfilling work.

Daki gets the secretaries working

Daki and the other dogs I've mentioned are not simple emblems of 'freedom' or 'nature': they have a fluid role, switching from master to rebel, from anarchic sprites to representatives of order and control.

Whenever I'm in danger of thinking Tati's symbolic or political template is rather crudely divided into the binaries of work/leisure, ancient/modern and free/enslaved, his dogs get involved with some business that blends and commingles these positions.

In another scene, Daki's doggy pals exhibit a spirit in contrast to his rather authoritarian presence in and around the workplace when they somehow get into the factory (notably before Hulot's hilarious job interview), and Daki is later drawn to the gigantic red 'sausage links' that Hulot accidentally manufactures in place of the long pipes the factory is supposed to produce. He may spur the employees to work, but he's happiest when they mess up and provide him with gigantic sausages to crave.

DAKI AND THE ELECTRONIC EYE

For me, the greatest gag in *Mon Oncle* (and goodness knows there are dozens and dozens to consider) involves all the themes discussed so far and is based squarely on Tati's understanding of dog instinct and, yes, dog *psychology*.

It is the Arpels' wedding anniversary, and Monsieur Arpel has treated them both to a gaudy new Chevrolet Bel Air that looks like a giant gelato on wheels. Unbeknownst to him, Madame Arpel has fitted a new automatic garage door operated by a knee-high electronic eye. Now Monsieur Arpel needn't get out of the car to open the garage door, he can simply drive in and out, saving time and inconvenience.

The Arpels are delighted with their new acquisitions, and while they are inspecting the garage together, Daki, excited and curious about all the new activity, skips through the beam of the electronic eye with his tail up.

The door slams the Arpels inside their grey tomb. This is comical and satirical enough, but what happens next is nothing short of genius.

The Arpels, in a state of mild panic, sternly call Daki back, hoping he will walk through the beam again and release them. Daki obeys, but, cowed by their harsh tones, his tail drops in fear or shame, so that when he walks back through the beam his body passes beneath it and his masters remain entombed.

Never did filmmaker, comedian, visionary and dog work so perfectly together to create such a resonant, multi-layered joke. Regard the Arpels: imprisoned in a world removed from

214

Daki with his tail up

Daki with his tail down

nature, instinct and caprice by the little animal they 'own' and which has entrapped them through its curiosity, alertness and fear.

If you know the film, you will see how this scene echoes the earlier one in which the Arpels, disturbed by the sounds of Hulot tinkering in the garden, peer through their house's round windows in the night, turning their home into one huge suspicious security guard.

The eyes of the Arpels' house

In both scenes, the Arpels peer from inside their carefully constructed domain at a world full of people and creatures they cannot control or fully understand.

Would it spoil it for you if I revealed that all the electronic gadgets in *Mon Oncle* were operated manually by hidden crew members? That there was no actual electronic beam connected to the garage door? It shouldn't. Tati's world is wonderfully fake, as is every cinematic world, and such artifice is necessary to create perfection.

You know, and I know, that the interaction between the Arpels, the electronic eye and Daki *is* real and genuine on its own faked terms.

FIN

So *Mon Oncle* spins many symbolic and satirical plates, playing off instinct and nature against artifice and control. Progress drills noisily into tradition and 'freedom' frolics around enslavement and responsibility. But all these notions and states of being chase each other's tails and become blurred.

If Tati has an axe to grind, it's a rubber axe with the sound of metal and impact dubbed on later by the Foley artist (the folly artist?). The dogs of *Mon Oncle*, in their openness, their lack of fixed meaning and their ability to morph from the leashed to the unleashed, and from figures of authority to spirits of liberation, embody the soul of the film and keep it from sliding into didacticism or despair.

What I take away from the film, along with some timeless jokes, is the sense that we have cultural choices to make and natural instincts to respect, and a gently melancholy environment in which to negotiate the two.

At the end of the film, Monsieur Hulot receives a kind of death sentence: his brother-in-law sends him to the provinces to work as a sales rep for Plastac. Arpel picks him up from his tottering, shambolic home in the dilapidated *quartiere* (the first time in the film that Arpel has made this trip) and drives him to the airport, where he bids farewell to Gérard and joins a throng of travellers.

But Hulot's expulsion is necessary for Gérard and his father to reconnect, and we see the two sharing a joke and holding hands and we know that things are going to change. Arpel will be less stiff and authoritarian and Gérard will be less resentful and distant, and (thanks to hindsight and film history) we know that Hulot will return magnificently in Tati's next masterpiece, *Playtime*.

The final shots of *Mon Oncle* belong to the pack of dogs we saw at the beginning. They erupt onto the screen again at the airport and run all the way back to town, ignoring road markings and evading traffic police. We see them, and Daki, sniffing around the square and jumping on carts.

But we see them through a window with a net curtain fluttering in the breeze. Eventually the wind draws this literal veil over proceedings and we are left hanging between the past and the present, nostalgia and hope.

Drawing a veil

References

Bellos, David (1999) *Jacques Tati*, London: Harvill.

Gilliatt, Penelope (1976) *Jacques Tati*, London: Woburn Press (excerpts available at http://kinoslang.blogspot.co.uk/2013/04/tati-speaks.html).

Guillen, Michael (2010) 'Tati & His Dogs', *Twitch* (online), 29 January, http://twitchfilm.com/2010/01/tati-his-dogs.html.

Tati, Jacques (1977) 'Lessons from Dogs' (interview), excerpt available at http://www.youtube.com/watch?v=nDzkromq368.

ALIEN vs JONESY by Angela Cleland

INT. UNDERCARRIAGE ROOM - "C" LEVEL

Jones the cat enters.
Slinks between boxes.
Searching.
Chains clank.
The Alien shifts in the darkness.

> ALIEN
> Treads another soft-shell - a nymph. Warm,
> mewing, incomplete. Wanting for the comfort
> of a host in which to moult, reform,
> become itself. Seeking chrysalis mother.
>
> Oh, saliva, acid-rush gullet.
> Lips, lips back, jaws all shudder
> and slaver - take your pleasure now, now -
>   skull it!

Brett enters.
Still looking for Jones.
Another yowl followed by a hiss.
Two eyes shining in the dark.
Jones.
Relieved, Brett moves toward the cat.

                    JONESY
        Fssst - a snapped flare, from my x-ray
        bones to whiskers I am stiff objection.
        Cut from hard dark you are, bad spirit -
        of the humans, but not one of them. Tell me,
        what is so good about growing inside them?
        Why all the fuss over your inept exit?

        I have seen your kind before, though
           smaller,
        a bruised squall, pink lungbag, screaming
        into life, seen the tides of its entrance,
        through endless mopping, swallow the
           familiar
        ground. I know you have come to eviscerate
        our cosy routines. And you rise, hungry
        crucifix wanting a thief. Well, praise me!
        I have come armed with your stop-gap Jesus.

Brett reaches for Jones.
Jones hisses.

                    ALIEN
        Spit and keratin! All voltage, this menace -
        born cruel, the colour of poison carapace,
        snare-snap pupils, pin-mawed mug,
        concentrated disdain for blood.
        Let it live - grow into a host as delicious,
        as cruel. See - it bears a kind gift,
        true to its kind, it bears a cruel gift.

An arm reaches for Brett.

[2nd, 3rd and 4th sets of screen directions taken from the shooting script for
Alien *by Walter Hill and David Giler, based on the screenplay by*
Dan O'Bannon.]

REBECCA WIGMORE

☙

The lion handler's advice to a young Melanie Griffith

Y OU WANT to share a bed, fine. I get the appeal,
that Serengeti jerk and sweat, the mystery of his sleep.

We can never really know if our animals love us.
All we can do is crush head into mane,

that sexy attic, and wear his paw as our heaviest hat.
Let me know when you want to swim with him

in your mother's pool. I can watch
for signs of cupidity, entitlement.

When you start spotting the mattress,
come cry to me; try to retain eye contact.

That blood is my business.
I gotta tell you,

once he owns something, all is lost.
But we're all better as hopeful little renters.

He don't even know that you all call him Neil.
And yet who's spooning your mom's soft, blonde head

as she scans the trades for threats? That's
my point babe – you grow into these things.

We can never really know if our animals love us.
Here's a list of things you're too old for: Narnia, everything.

CLIFF HAMMETT

ॐ

Analytic Animals: Agency at Some Interfaces within Chronophotography

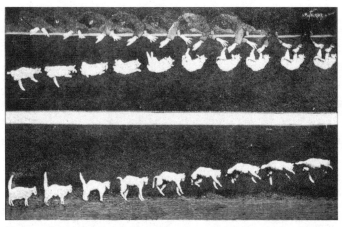

Figure 1: Chronophotographic sequence of a cat landing on its feet (sequence runs right to left).

IN 1894, an alliance was struck. An alliance between the stubborn agility of a white gardener's cat, a French human called Etienne-Jules Marey and an assemblage of instrumentation and practice that went under the name of 'chronophotography'. Together, they produced a temporally ordered sequence of images that appeared to contradict one of Newton's laws, which stated that once an object is in motion it can only change direction through external force (Braun 1994: 166–170). That is to say, the apparatus confirmed the garden cat as an apparent exception to this law – if it was dropped whilst upside-down, it seemed to spin itself and land on its feet.

This is not how such experiments are usually described. Hoisted from its hunting ground and suspended by its paws, the gardener's cat could equally be portrayed as a passive subject of experimentation. Were it not for the triviality of the consequences for the cat, we might want to say victim. Certainly the cat must have been indignant. How do we decide which accounts to accept? The question here is, in part, a question of agency: what is acting, and what is being acted upon? Speaking of the movement he conceived of as gravity, Newton was reputed to have said 'the apple draws the earth, as well as the earth draws the apple' – but as we will see, the entanglements of agency can be far more complex, with instruments and animals shaping each other and the direction of study.[1] Building upon this, there is a related but separate question of intentionality: according to whose plan does this

1   *This definition of agency draws heavily on the work of Andrew Pickering, principally* The Mangle of Practice *(1995). However, for this essay, I did not wish to enter into the theoretical considerations a full introduction of Pickering's concepts would inevitably entail.*

practice proceed, what, if anything, wants this to happen, and where does this desire and drive emanate from?

Finally, it is a question of belonging. Chronophotography opened up new worlds. The imagery it provided was radical – the bodies of the animals photographed were spliced, segmented, yet – unlike in later cinematography – they were arranged in an often overlapping montage, one continuous form moving in space. It provided the Futurists with 'the language and tools of kineticism; the rejection of still photography and inert representation, with the false realism of motionless detail' (Dagognet 1992: 148). It was integral to the consolidation of physiology, by making it 'possible to track life phenomena down into experimentally quantifiable and verifiable "units"' (Väliaho 2010: 34), and by doing so shaping scientific management and industrial modernity (Dagognet 1992: 170). To whom do these new worlds belong? Are they the product of a singular and innovative human genius, who went by the name of Etienne-Jules Marey, and those other humans (such as Demeny and Uexküll) who followed him?

It seems useless to even try to answer yes, or to attribute credit to one of the other nodes – the chronographic and chronophotographic instrumentation, the equipment and staff of the physiological station, or the many animals (including humans, but also bottom-hugging fish, fast-moving protozoa, tottering horses, luminous wasps and many others) whose movements had been recorded. So what are the other options? An alternative, which will be pursued here, is to map some of the movements of agency and contours of belonging – an effort that might be most productive along the different interfaces, both within chronophotography and to other bodies and practices. That is to say, we will examine some points of communication between the participants, seeing how they acted upon and changed one another and what desires were generated, and attempt to think afresh about what was produced in those worlds. This discussion of interfaces is highly selective; the focus is primarily on those needed to make sense of the chronophotography of animal bodies, and it does not extend to other areas of Marey's work such as studies of internal physiology and of the external movements of non-living objects.

INTERFACE A: IF THE MECHANISM FITS...

The practice that gathered around the early Marey constituted what is known as the 'graphic method'. Although his work crossed a number of disciplinary boundaries, he was a physiologist first and foremost, and his primary concern was to investigate the movements of living things. Marey's attempts to capture external movement built on his work on internal physiology, such as his development of the spymograph, which produced a graphical representation of the pulse. His practice, which tended to respect the integrity of each animal as a self-sustaining system, was informed by an opposition to vivisection. This was expressed not in terms of welfarist concerns but rather through a distaste that a scientist should use techniques which destroyed their object of study and – it must be added – doubts of the validity and effectiveness of such methods, as they often relied on the sense perceptions of the vivisectionist.

Through a variety of intricate instruments, methods were sought within Marey's practice by which the human observer could be removed, so that phenomena could be recorded solely through instrumentation. Studies of the gaits of horses provided a compelling justification for this. Attempts by sensory observation – through eye and ear – had failed to produce agreement on how the horse walked, ambled or ran (Marey 1879: 145).

Figure 2: Horse and rider furnished with Marey's chronographic instrumentation.

To solve this problem, an approach was taken from earlier work studying the human gait. This alone is not insignificant – human and horse gait were viewed together as nature spoilt by convention. The superior walking commanded by physiology was spoilt in humans by a desire to appear distinguished; in horses it was its representation in painting that was so often found lacking (Mayer 2010: 88–91). The experimental technique was to place rubber air balls under the shoe – in this case, the horse's – that when compressed would push air up to transmitting tubes through to a registering device held by a rider (figure 2). Each aspect of the instrumentation – such as the size of the rubber ball, the robust tubing designed to be 'not easily crushed' – was configured bespoke to the horse's physiology. François Albera gives the following example, from later experiments, of how in Marey's methodology instrumentation is generally adapted to animals, rather than animals to instrumentation: 'To imitate the *jerks* of horses' traction, it may be necessary to make *facets* and salient angles on the *drum* round which the rope is wound [Albera's italics]' (Albera 2010: 66).

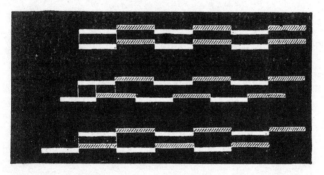

Figure 3: Graphical representation of three paces – amble, walk and trot.

The creators of the instrumentation thus responded to issues generated by interactions between horse physiology and components of instrumentation, and the system evolved in accordance with this. But the horse's agency within the system can be traced out a step further, into what Dagognet calls 'autography', writing by nature itself. On this account, we can see the horse-instrument assemblage as directly writing a record of its movements, enabled by the process of configuring the instrumentation to the body of the horse, in line with a desired end. This writing, however, is always structured by the instrumentation – which was in turn structured by the animal's body.

INTERFACE B: EQUI-DISTANT GRAPHING

The equine investigations did not finish here – far from it. Following the famous sequences of horse photographs shot by Eadweard Muybridge, Marey began using specially designed cameras to record the movements of animals. As is well known, the work carried out in Marey's practice made substantial contributions to the technologies of cinema, as 'the first to use a single camera to produce photographs on a strip of sensitized film in real time, rapidly enough for the illusion of movement to be constituted for more than a single viewer at once' (Braun 1994: 150). This has led to his work being seen by some as merely a precursor to cinema – an injustice argued against by both Dagognet and Braun, among others.

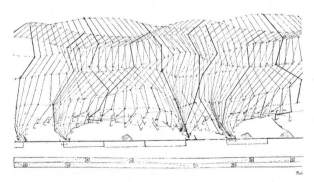

Figure 4: Diagram of a horse at walking pace.

We can see how the images produced by Marey's instrumentation are in some ways a continuation from the earlier graphic method and differ radically from that of later cinema. In some instances, the humans before the instrumentation were dressed in black with white stripes to create a form of 'graphing'. The environment was specially prepared – a black painted shed and black velvet curtains, to prevent any other physical object from acting on the film (Marey 1972: 71). This process was also used with horses – they were clothed, even painted, black and white points and stripes were attached to their limbs. Such considerations even extended to ensuring the track was moist so the horse would not kick up dust. Figure 4, taken from *Movement* (Marey 1972: 209), shows a particularly striking example of what could be achieved with this method. What does the body become when it is broken down into a succession of lines; what is this reproduction? The body disappears and yet continually reasserts itself through these analytics; it's removed, yet every line is the body – a different body, a line-painted, hoofed body. More than analysis, it fuses the rhythms of the horse and the chronophotographic instruments into a unique temporal tracing that belongs to neither machine nor animal, but also to both.

Chronophotography, it is often said, broke down the smooth movement into a succession of points which could be analysed and then synthesised into a new movement. Stephen Mamber argues that breaking down movement in this way in order to perform a capture of movement foreshadows a certain digitality (Mamber 2004). This is in line with a contention of Lev Manovich's, that an important break in the movement from the analogue to the digital was the creation of film as a series of discrete time states (Manovich 2002: 50). It can certainly be argued that this method of analysis, and perhaps most pointedly this method of production, foreshadows the use of motion capture within film. What's more, the being that is created through this horse-graphing feels strikingly reminiscent of 3D wireframing. Yet we must be very wary of capitulating to the paradigmatic error when dealing with Marey's work – viewing it as one or the other kind of mere 'proto'-cinema, and not, as Mamber says, an alternative system (Mamber 2004: 84).

INTERFACE C: CLOCKING THE IMAGE

Väliaho draws attention to an important aspect of chronophotography as practised under Marey. The practice that assembled around him did not just produce images, whether graphic or chronophotographic – it also produced mechanical models, or automata, which replicated the movements of living creatures such as insects and birds. These models were in part an expression of Marey's anti-vitalism – he held that both living and non-living things were subject to the same laws. They also provided verification of the abstract principles derived from chronographic and chronophotographic practice. Such contraptions, Väliaho argues, 'continue Vaucanson's "program" of attempting to simulate life functions experimentally' (2010: 40). Vaucanson for us is a stand-in for the practice of creating automata – the mechanical duck which digests bread and excretes it being the most famous example.

What should not be forgotten, however, is that the recording instrumentation itself shares a common lineage with attempts to simulate life. It was perceived as vital to regulate the temporal progress of the graphing needle, dry plate or film – the latter proving particularly challenging (Braun 1994: 55–58, 155). Such struggles put Marey's practice in the company of those investigations that led to the development of the first reliable clock mechanisms. Indeed, automata were developed together with clocks, which in their early instances were often magnificent spectacles but terrible timekeepers (Hillier 1988). As clocks developed, they succeeded in regularising the partition of time across space. What chronophotography achieved was twofold: the production of a regularised taxonomy of moving bodies in the form of the new science of physiology, and the splicing of those bodies along the axis of such metrical time and allowing for its resequencing.

A different temporality emerges from the serial photography of Eadweard Muybridge, who developed a series of cameras that were activated by the horse breaking the string triggers with their hooves (Newhall 1972: 83). In Muybridge's practice, as in the earlier horse experiments under Marey, the animals acted corporeally upon the instrumentation; in Marey's chronophotography, the instrumentation was redesigned to require minimum input from the animal.[2] Yet the many animal subjects were still at work restructuring the temporality of the device – not just its frame rate and shutter speed, but the evenness of frames. Braun reports that Marey refused to integrate sprockets which would have solved his temporal woes, because he wished to still be able to vary the width and height of the film according to its subjects (Braun 1994: 156).

---

2   *Muybridge did later integrate a 'motor-clock' into his system of image making (Scharf 1975: 126).*

INTERFACE D: ENFRAMING FLIGHT, OR 'GET THIS THING FROM OFF MY WING!'

The explorations of the mechanisms of flight began with insects. An insect was held with forceps and passed through a blackened cylinder (Marey 1879: 182–183). Its wings would brush against the cylinder and make marks, thus being another, perhaps more perfect, example of autography. Though instructive, the limitations of this method became apparent to Marey, as the resistance caused by the 'brushing' of the insect wings would actually slow their rhythm (Marey 1879: 184). Another method was thus created in response – gilding the wings of the wasp to create a luminous trace (Braun 1994: 31–32).

As Marey's practice was at this point pre-photographic, there was no way to automatically transcribe this trace as the practice commanded. The next turn was to the myograph – a device perfected within physiological practice for measuring the contractions of muscles. This apparatus was attached to the bird's pectoral, but – like the brushing of the insect wings against the cylinder – the physical properties of the instrumentation changed the patterns of flight, making their readings unreliable. The solution was a clever inversion, evocatively described by Dagognet:

> *To put it simply, the bird moved within the mega-apparatus without having to carry it. Because it was not possible to 'miniaturize' the measuring device, Marey inverted the terms and put the bird – without compromising its freedom of motion in the air – into the contraption.* (Dagognet 1992: 84)

The interaction between the agency of the myograph,

that of the bird and the framework of evaluation within physiology had necessitated a radical reimagining. The advent of chronophotographic instruments would again switch around the forms of relation. Proceeding from Janssen's chronophotographic revolver, used to transcribe the transit of Venus, Marey developed a chronophotographic gun that could be used to take twelve stills of a bird in flight within a single instant. No longer would the bird need to be framed by an apparatus of air tubes or electromagnetic signals – light itself provided a way of taking measurement without restraining the bird.

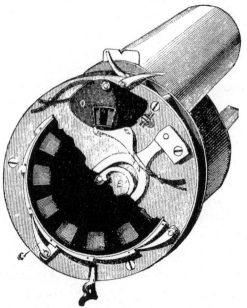

Figure 5: The internal workings of the chronophotographic gun.

We can trace a movement here. The development begins with equipment which is intrusive to the animal being studied. For insects, it interfered with their wings; for birds, the weight of the equipment was an impediment. At the same time, the specific agency of each creature's physiology is expressed sometimes directly (the insect's autography) or through a form of mediation that is specifically configured to it. A number of reversals were attempted – the luminous insect wings, the enframing bird contraption. In the end, however, a more generalised solution was found – chronophotography – which paradoxically allowed the subject far greater freedom of movement whilst reducing its level of agency over the apparatus itself.

We might also note that the switch from insects to birds shows that it is not always true that instruments were adapted to animals rather than vice versa. Here, the specific animal is chosen at least in part according to the extent that it can accommodate the various requirements of the instrument.[3]

INTERFACE E: THE SKATE THAT WON'T KEEP IN SHOT

In 1888, the chronophotographic apparatus was brought more closely to bear upon marine life. An aquarium was installed facing out into sunlight. Behind it, the chronophotographic camera was placed, so aquatic animals could be recorded against the daylight. Sometimes a white cloth was used to produce a more satisfactory silhouette. Lines were traced upon the aquarium glass to create a rectangular frame – the photographer would simply wait for the creature to cross into the rectangle. This proved an especially good method for jellyfish – their transparent bodies even placed their internal

3   There is also the question of whether the animal is expressing agency, if the animal is writing, in instances where it is photographed. We will leave this consideration to the end.

movements in full view. However, some creatures were far less compliant with this set-up – particularly the skate:

> *The difficulty which arises in this experiment is that of keeping the fish in a convenient position, so as to show its movements clearly. Left to itself in an aquarium, the skate remains motionless at the bottom; yet if disturbed it swims to the surface, and causes a disturbance of the water by flapping its fins, and it is but seldom that it swims quietly in a forward direction.* (Marey 1972: 218)

Figure 6: The skate restrained.

Skates instinctively cling to the bottom of the waters, where in their natural habitat they might find clams, shrimp and other creatures to eat. They are not prone to swimming openly and regularly in a manner that would make them easy to photograph. The solution that Marey describes, however, is more complicated than our previous examples if we wish to think of the animal as an active component of the system:

> *A flat strip of iron has its two ends bent at right angles; holes are bored in corresponding positions in the two uprights, and two iron wires are passed through them, and tightly stretched. On these two wires two glass tubes are threaded and united by cross-bars. The latter are provided with clips for holding the fish. One of the tubes is fitted with a toothed forceps for holding the front part of the fish; the other is provided with a plate on which the tail end*

rests, and to which it is fastened by means of a ligature. (Marey 1972: 219)

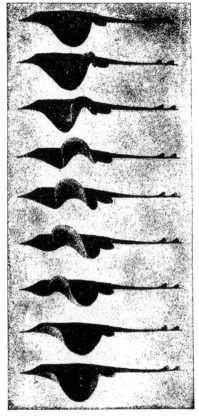

Figure 7: Skate undulating – side view. Proceeds from bottom to top.

Of course, the animal here is still actively shaping the system. Each part of this equipment is, as much as any other part of Marey's apparatuses, configured to the physiology of its subject – in the length of each bar, and the choice of each fastener (forceps for the front, which needs to be grasped; ligature for the tail, which needs only be tied). However, the modifications take the form of a restraint that bypasses the agency and desires of the skate in favour of that of the chronophotographic recording equipment, which requires particular conditions and behaviour from the skate to do its work. The skate does retain some agency, which it expresses by *not* moving, until it is physically irritated into doing so with a stick – and even then it is not possible to know how perfectly this undulating motion compares to the skate's natural propulsion.

It should be clear that the initial movement observed in the discussion of flying animals – a decrease in agency but an increase in freedom of movement – does not universally apply to all species. Had Marey continued down the track of myography and the graphic method in general, it may have been that a less restrictive apparatus for the skate would have been developed. As it stood, the chronophotographic apparatus required the skate to be almost entirely restrained.

INTERFACE F: ANIMALCULES ASK FOR A LITTLE LESS LIGHT

In 1891, the microscope was integrated into chronophotography, and deployed to record the motions of micro-organisms. Here, the study was made possible by the ready existence of an instrument tuned to observe microscopic life. But despite this ingenious integration, the production of protozoa chronophotograms proved even more difficult than recording insects, owing mainly to the rapid movements of protozoa:

Infusoria cross the field of the microscope in a moment, and execute an immense number of movements which the eye cannot follow. The vibrating cilia, for instance, which serves as locomotor appendages in many of these animalcules, vibrate with such rapidity that they are absolutely invisible and only come into view when the animals are dead. (Marey 1972: 293)

Figure 8: Apparatus for taking microscopic chronophotograms.

The speed of such motions necessitated adjusting the shutter time to be as short as possible. This meant more light was required. However, attempts to bring the necessary light onto the microscopic creatures via a lens would make the environment too hot and kill the organisms. Like the sows in Coppin's essay 'Crate and Mangle' (2008), who perish under mistreatment within intensive farming, the protozoa express agency over the instrumentation by dying. Rather than a light dimmer being made, an alternative path was uncovered that fulfilled the needs of both instrument and animal: the light source was modified to flash for less than 1/1000 of a second, synchronised with the photographic recording mechanism.

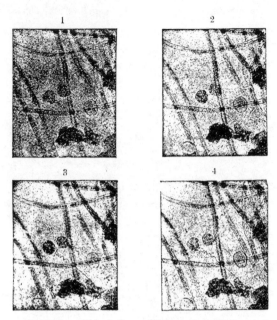

Figure 9: Recordings of vorticellae and the reaction of their spiral stalks.

The protozoa are a very direct case of observation potentially changing the object in a very straightforward manner. Too much light and they will fry. The images of the protozoa play into a sense that is present throughout a selection of image sequences: what orders them is the instruction and the imperative that they be ordered.[4] For instance, if Marey had told us that the images of the skate in figure 7 ran from top to bottom, not bottom to top, would we be any the wiser? This is different in the cases of the graphed horse in figure 4, the falling cat and the semi-continuous sequence of the bird in

4   *An alternative direction for chronophotography – the temporal 'stacking' of images to reveal a range of movements rather than a sequence – was explored later by Uexküll. See Pollman (2013).*

flight. The extent to which certain creatures express a particular dynamism, whereas others can be perpetually resequenced, is another combined expression of the intermingled agencies of animal, apparatus and the design of the experimenter.

What of the protozoa's agency over the film itself? That is to say: it is clear that the technical development of dry plates and celluloid depends on the possibilities of their deployment, of how they react to the subject they are attempting to capture. But there is a more difficult question: when a subject is photographed, is this is a form of autography? Are the protozoa writing themselves onto celluloid?

I don't propose to provide an answer to this question, which I take to be fundamentally unanswerable as it is presently posed. But reframing it may help us think about agency at work here. We cannot coherently refer to mediated processes such as the pneumatic rubber balls under horse hooves or the wings of insects against a wax cylinder as autography, and then deny it to chronophotographed animalcules. Whether such action is mediated by air-moved instruments, waxed paper or light-sensitive chemicals cannot make a difference here. The meaning of the term wavers and loses focus under such considerations. However, we can continue to meaningfully reflect on the differences in modes of address, the different patterns of agency enabled in each medium.

These considerations, in a spin that the chronophotographic revolver was designed never to perform, bring us back to the start – to the gardener's cat. For the cat may have had less decisive agency than some of the other animals over the instrumentation itself, though one should note the unusual shape of the images produced. And the cat did not really contradict Newton's law – this would have been too big an irony for the mechanist Marey – though the problem of its seeming ability to do so remained for some time. It might make us wonder what thoughts Newton might have had if a cat had fallen from the tree rather than an apple. But more than this, the sequence it created was something different from mere representation. In a sense, it magnified the agency of the cat so as to bring a problem to light, to show *it*, this dynamic cat, hadn't been properly taken into account. But that the integrity of the cat was respected – that no lasting harm was done – feels crucial here. Would we, could we, speak in such a way if a vivisection was being performed?

It has been argued by Väliaho, following Agamben, that cinema creates a 'zone of indistinction' between the naked life of the subject and the *bios* that comes from being a part of a political community (Väliaho 2010: 19–20). Agamben's division – between naked life and political being – has been criticised by Cary Wolfe, following others such as LaCapra, for it leaves animals always on one side of the division, as always already abjected. It does not provide the tools 'to think a highly differentiated and nuanced biopolitical field' (Wolfe 2013: 27). This division appears yet more precarious when we are presented with the animal recorded and yet transformed – the naked life of the animal cannot have been revealed if that was all there ever was. What these considerations might suggest is a more complex, multiplicitous approach to the forms of life enabled and revealed through their entanglements with science, that the life of the horse uncovered by pneumatic instrumentation is not that revealed by chronophotographic graphing, that neither are the motions of the skate, and so on. Perhaps in chronophotographic practice, its alternative cinematics, we can still find new ways to think about life, time and the world, as the modernists of the early twentieth century did. But perhaps these considerations could form the basis of a different kind of practice, one that, rather than attempting to create ordered and metrical tracings, could create operational systems tuned in sympathy to the temporal rhythms of those bodies from which it is composed.

References

Albera, F. (2010) 'The Case for an Epistemography of Montage', in F. Albera and M. Tortajada (eds) *Cinema beyond Film: Media Epistemology in the Modern Era*, Amsterdam: Amsterdam University Press.

Braun, M. (1994) *Picturing Time: The Work of Etienne-Jules Marey* (1830–1904), Chicago: University of Chicago Press.

Coppin, D. (2008) 'Crate and Mangle: Questions of Agency in Confinement Livestock Facilities', in A. Pickering and K. Guzik (eds) *The Mangle in Practice: Science, Society, and Becoming*, Durham: Duke University Press.

Dagognet, F. (1992) *Etienne-Jules Marey: A Passion for the Trace*, New York; Cambridge, MA: Zone Books; distributed by the MIT Press.

Hillier, M. (1988) *Automata & Mechanical Toys: An Illustrated History*, London: Bloomsbury.

Mamber, S. (2004) 'Marey, the Analytic, and the Digital', in J. Fullerton and J. Olsson (eds) *Allegories of Communication: Intermedial Concerns from Cinema to the Digital*, Rome: John Libbey.

Manovich, L. (2002) *The Language of New Media*, Cambridge, MA: MIT Press.

Marey, E.-J. (1972) *Movement*, New York: Arno Press.

Marey, E.-J. (1879) *Animal Mechanism*, New York: D. Appleton and Co.

Mayer, A. (2010) 'The Physiological Circus: Knowing, Representing, and Training Horses in Motion in Nineteenth-Century France', *Representations*, 111(1), pp. 88–120.

McDonald, D. (1960) 'How Does a Cat Fall on Its Feet?', *New Scientist*, 7(189), pp. 1647–1649.

Newhall, B. (1972) *The History of Photography from 1839 to the Present Day*, New York: Museum of Modern Art.

Pickering, A. (1995) *The Mangle of Practice: Time, Agency, and Science*, Chicago: University of Chicago Press.

Pollman, I. (2013) 'Invisible Worlds, Visible: Uexküll's *Umwelt*, Film, and Film Theory', *Critical Inquiry*, 39(4).

Scharf, A. (1975) *Pioneers of Photography: An Album of Pictures and Words*, London: BBC.

Väliaho, P. (2010) *Mapping the Moving Image: Gesture, Thought and Cinema circa 1900*, Amsterdam: Amsterdam University Press.

Wolfe, C. (2013) *Before the Law: Humans and Other Animals in a Biopolitical Frame*, Chicago; London: University of Chicago Press.

MARK WALDRON

&

A cat called Orangey was in a number of movies,

BUT HE DIDN'T know he was. He didn't even know
he was in *Breakfast at Tiffany's.*

Obviously he knew nothing about it. All he registered
were the peculiar new locations, the heat of the lights,

and a vague sense of fear as well as bursts of affection
coming from the people around him.

Of course cats know just about nothing
of the human world at all.

They live in a parallel universe *inside* the human world.
Mostly smaller than it and fitting into it,

though in places its boundaries stretch beyond
the boundaries of our experience in soft tubular fingers.

Their consciousness would be repellent to us if we could
inhabit it.

Its lack of words and its meat and the fur that we might
experience as being in our mouths.

The paucity of its dimensions, that flatness, would press us
to the ground, make our heads split.

The configuration of their genes is such that they would
bring us down,

would make us blind to everything that from up here
we are able to see,

and open up, at last, a sharp slick world full of certainty
and ease of feeling.

KEVIN M. FLANAGAN

❧

Machine-Age Comedy Gone Rural: Hustlin' Hank *(1923)*
and the Problem of Animals on Film

Comic cowboy Will Rogers made some of his early silent
shorts for Hal Roach Studios, an arrangement that he later
spoke about with derision: 'All I ever do on the Roach lot is run
around barns and lose my pants' (Rogers quoted in Yagoda 2000:
206). While Rogers might view these early movies as routine
exercises in slapstick, they do have residual value in that they
tell us about the narrative scenarios that were intelligible to
audiences as comedy. *Hustlin' Hank* (1923, Scott Pembroke) is a
curious example, ostensibly a star vehicle for Rogers – a chance
to at first charm and then poke fun at urban filmgoers with
his rural persona and fish-out-of-water sensibilities – that
reads today as a self-conscious attempt at staging an encounter

between the performance stylings of human actors (steeped in stage melodrama and the physical histrionics of the silent screen) and the unpredictable 'naturalness' of filmed animals. In *Hustlin' Hank*, Hank (Rogers) is hired to photograph a group of unruly farm animals, a task at which he fails, in the process showing the ways in which animals challenge the technological stillness and assumed staginess of both silent cinema and portrait photography. Even though *Hustlin' Hank* is not part of the instantly familiar canon of silent shorts, its illustration of the problems of putting animals on screen connects it to some of the major themes that continue to occupy scholars and fans of the period.

The 1920s are when cinema began to engage with modernity and mechanisation at a fever pitch. Conventional wisdom holds that this period – long commemorated for the widespread visualisation of the city, as well as for the thorough instantiation of Fordist principles of production in capitalist endeavour – is dominated by an industrial kind of modernity. For Michael North, the ubiquity of the machine brings with it a new kind of comedy, one not based on pure spontaneity, but rather occasioned by the automatic nature of industrial production (as well as visual reproduction) (North 2008: 5). Following Walter Benjamin and his famous questioning of the role of mechanical reproducibility in contemporary life, North ponders the emergence of this new sensibility, where the unruly clown (say, Chaplin) does not just subject himself to the camera as a means of recording a natural performance, but becomes a robot, using the body to approximate the workings of something mechanical (North 2008: 5; Benjamin 1968: 235). The kind of comedy that thus becomes most closely associated with the machine age is a mode of slapstick performance that turns the human performer into a hybrid of human and machine, at once a recognisable person *and* an automaton. As the famous Chaplin performances (the funhouse sequence in *The Circus* [1928], or the opening factory sequence in *Modern Times* [1936]) remind us, it is the Tramp's ability to inhabit two worlds simultaneously – man and machine – that endear him to us. For Alex Clayton (here working with Henri Bergson's claims about how we laugh as a corrective to man's propensity to appear too rigid and machine-like), Chaplin succeeds through performative ingenuity, precision and the elasticity of his body's movements, not through a total surrender to the repetitious nature of the machine (Clayton 2007: 15–16; for more on Bergson's theory of the comic, see Bergson 2008). Thus, a main current of silent comedy showcases a conscious hybridity and adaptability as requisite means of getting along in the world.

Even a casual survey of comedy from the 1920s uncovers the basic problem of seeing silent slapstick's engagement with industry and the city as totally dominant. Many of Buster Keaton's famous roles – his turn as Johnnie Grey in *The General* (1926) comes to mind – take place in rural environments (and in the historical past). In *The Frozen North* (1922), the humour of the tundra (meant to house a comprehensive send-up of William S. Hart's wilderness melodramas) relies just as much on Keaton's flight from a bear, or his tripping over a dog, as it does on his faulty assembly of a snowmobile. Even *Sunrise* (1927) (a film that explicitly dramatises the morals of the country against the temptations of the city, where, to be fair, time is split between the two different environments) contains a hilarious sequence of an apparently drunk pig running rampant through a crowded restaurant. That animals and machines could both interface with humans for comic effect, and sometimes towards the same ends, might seem banal to the point of cliché. But can animals and machines be conceptualised in the same way?

Eadweard Muybridge's photo study *The Attitudes of Animals in Motion* (1881), especially his investigation of the movement of horses (*Horses, Running, Sallie G.*), suggests a strong and lasting comparison between animal and machine (Solnit 2003: 182–183). For Étienne-Jules Marey, the figure of the 'animal-machine' offered a way to think of organisms in terms of man-made creations. Francois Dagognet writes that

> *Marey always defended the theory of the 'animal-machine,' as long as this machine was no longer conceived as a simple assemblage of pulleys, wheel and wires, but rather as a veritable 'animated motor,' a living machine, at the source of activation (locomotion, voice and so on).* (Dagognet 1992: 44)

The movement and elegance of a machine could be based on observed nature, just as the natural organism could be rendered intelligible through comparisons with man-made technological objects.

While practitioners like Muybridge and Marey might see animals as corresponding to machines, they arguably inhabit a quite different ontological position from purely mechanical devices. Mark Rowlands has put forth an approach to animals that recognises them as autonomous beings, ones who have preferences, feel pain, experience happiness and make choices (Rowlands 2002: 22). Writing in the late 1930s, E. Keith Robinson reminds readers that the training of animals (the type of training that would enable an animal to 'perform' in a movie) usually means subjecting them to some form or other of cruelty, and that film sets (often hot, crowded and surprisingly claustrophobic spaces) cause animals to suffer

(Robinson 1939: 8–10). As biological entities, animals cannot be patched together with replacement parts. Even though animals can be trained, they cannot be programmed to perfectly replicate tasks in an absolutely exact way (their compulsions to repeat differ from the machine's in kind, quality and motive). Animals can approximate some of the same movements and comedic gestures as machine-like humans – they can repeat tasks, physically assault or push others, participate in chase scenes and express discomfort or dissatisfaction – but they are not offering consciously replicated performances in the same way as Chaplin or Keaton.

Animals in silent comedy occupy a strange position: they are frequently in scenarios as machine-like props, but they are just as often offered as supporting players, as beings that are on camera to do a task, whether by accident or through training. As much as animals may seem like natural parts of films, *Hustlin' Hank* visualises how seemingly natural and idyllic things like rural landscapes and both farmyard and wild animals prove problematic subjects for motion pictures.

Hustlin' Hank was made during a strange moment in Will Rogers's career. Oklahoma's most famous performer, Rogers made his name doing vaudeville, channelling his cowboy roots into comedy that showcased his technical competence and his verbal wit. Rogers started making films during the silent era, prompting a trade-off: he would reach audiences as never before, but with no synchronised sound, his comedy would have to spring from physicality alone. Rogers used silent cinema, especially his time with Hal Roach Studios, as a stepping stone. He would go on to make bigger movies that better showcased his skills, and he would arguably reach the biggest possible audience through his syndicated newspaper columns. Richard Lewis Ward surmises that

The failure of Will Rogers to make an impact in silent pictures, despite the fame and popularity he had already obtained on the stage, may be attributed to Rogers's heavily verbal, not visual, style of humor. The Roach films show him shifting uncomfortably between forced slapstick (getting soaked by a lawn sprinkler and eating a lace coaster in Our Congressman*) and more characteristic Rogers' wit delivered via wordy and too-frequent title cards.* (Ward 2005: 50)

When Ben Yagoda describes Will Rogers's early Hal Roach Studios films as being 'loaded with pratfalls and leaps into lakes', he seems to have had *Hustlin' Hank* in mind (Yagoda 2000: 206). Rogers-as-Hank spends much of *Hustlin' Hank* avoiding work, but when he is spurred into action, it is either because he's been given an order or because he is being pursued by an animal. The main source of conflict between humans in *Hustlin' Hank* is the forcing of 'city' values onto the 'rural' ranch. Verbena Pitt, sister of ranch owner Jim Pitt, arrives by car with retinue in tow. Pitt wants to take photographs of wild animals in their natural settings, and even fancies some staged shots that combine animals and humans. 'Hardhead' Hobbs, one of Hank's associates, summarises the conflict in values in a title card: 'What's this dame's idea o' shootin' wild game with a camera? It's hard 'nough to hit 'em with a gun.' The difference between Hank/Hobbs and Ms Pitt's people does not just have to do with how they regard animals (the farm folk know how stubborn and dangerous animals can be; the city-dwellers expect animals to behave for their photo session). There is a telling sequence where Pitt provides high tea both for her entourage and for the farmhands. Hank does not know how to properly eat the dainty food, and only proceeds to use his hands to eat his cake after he sees someone else do it.

Even though *Hustlin' Hank* is explicitly about photography, it subtextually speaks to antagonisms between animal and human. The camera, as Paul Virilio famously suggests, can be equated to a gun (this complicates Hobbs's differentiation of the two objects), and its ability to fix and render visible can enable a kind of symbolic violence. Marey's chronophotographic gun encapsulates this duality: it is a technically harmless object whose physical style and association with wartime technology gives it new valences. The humans are enacting a sort of safari that uses the camera as a gun to secure mementos. But, in a curious nod to the ontological equality between people and animals, the film visualises a way in which animals 'hunt' and visually mark humans. When animals such as the angry donkey in the farmyard go after a person, the camera temporarily takes their point of view and an iris singles out their prey. While the iris was a visual cue often used in early cinema to prompt an audience's focus – that is one way that it functions here, to be sure – it also visually replicates the act of looking through the scope of a rifle. Humans hunt with the camera-gun; animal-machines hunt with their on-board instincts and resources.

The film carefully parses the differences in kind between a human being's relation to machines and an animal's. In *Hustlin' Hank*, animals are conceived either as unselfconscious pieces of scenery – note the dogs and chickens milling about the grounds in the early moments of the film – or as berserk robots whose routines have broken down. The bear that hounds the wilderness photo shoot is revealed to be a trained cub that escaped its master, while the donkey that hounds everyone at the ranch during the first half of the film is an uncooperative beast of burden. When lazy Hank attaches a pail of water to the donkey's mouth – this fits his character, who avoids labour of his own for as long as possible – the donkey drops the water and kicks over a stack of crates. Hank's desire to anthropomorphise the donkey, to pass off work on the animal as if it were a colleague, is shut down quickly. Moreover, this scene illustrates that animals are not quite machines in the reliable, labour-saving sense that dominated some modern discourse (as Larry Stewart notes, in relation to attitudes about the uptake of new technologies for agriculture and industry during the late eighteenth and early nineteenth centuries, machines can disrupt and alter the flow of labour as much as they can help it; see Stewart 1998: 260). Instead, animals are self-possessed beings capable of occasional cooperation, but more often guided by intensely personal concerns.

Pitt seems to think that her photography is just a trifle, an indulgence that is of no harm or consequence to the animals she wants to see. Much of the conflict in the film arises when human agents attempt to get animals to behave in certain ways, whether for the camera or for doing farm work. Before the photo expedition proper, one of Pitt's city-dwelling associates attempts to take photographs of grazing cattle. This photographer's seemingly benign act prompts a donkey to attack. The donkey is subsequently locked up behind a fence, but later breaks free and chases Hank throughout the ranch. This sequence illustrates the primary way that *Hustlin' Hank* approaches the relationship between animals and humans on screen: the sequence appears 'natural' and unrehearsed, suggesting that the donkey's actions are merely prompted by the context or environment at a specific moment (in this way, the basic message of the film is 'We never know how animals will respond, so regard them as dangerous and wild'). But knowledge of the production conditions of fictional filmmaking suggests that we also respond knowing that each moment is scripted, staged, rehearsed and perfected. The human actors learn blocking and practise actions. Trainers and treats (and potentially some cruel physical treatment) prompt the animals, such that they perfect repetitive actions and give a polished performance. Thus, the sequence of the donkey chasing Hank attempts to casually present this seemingly spontaneous encounter, but the route followed is so calculated – to the extent that both Rogers and the donkey enter a side-building and jump through an open window – that the film's explicit messages about the dangers of photographing animals are in some ways solved by the film's realisation and completion. In other words, if it is so difficult to film animals, then how did Pembroke and his crew manage to do it in *Hustlin' Hank*?

If the film suggests that animals are wild and unpredictable, it also attempts to illustrate how photographic technologies are ill-suited to their representation. This is mainly related by how difficult it is for Hank to set up a valid shot. While the film establishes that Hank is a lazy amateur with no professional knowledge of the camera, he still gets enlisted to serve as the principal photographer for Pitt's shoot, which is to be a mix of animals in their supposedly natural habitats and tableaux of humans having nominal interactions with animals. Hank is prompted to begin shooting upon realising that the bear cub has wandered into the camp. Armed with a boxy camera and tripod, he scrambles to take some pictures. His bumbling stab at getting a few snaps is one of the film's funniest sequences. This camera apparatus is too awkward for the immediacy and quick action needed to capture images of how animals really are. Hank cannot figure out how to set up the tripod, which flails around his body like the tentacles of an octopus. The bellows of this plate camera stretch out, in the process becoming an accordion in his hands.[1] By the time Hank has a chance at framing a shot, the bear has moved away, prompting Hank to follow. Even though it is revealed that this bear cub had been trained, and therefore was used to human interaction, it is still shown to have no regard for the technical problems that come with taking a photograph. The episode is doubly humorous in that Hank has not loaded a plate into the camera (a title card offers that 'The bear don't know that'), a shortcoming rendered even more inconsequential by the fact that the long exposure time for the plate would have necessitated a relatively still bear.

The plot offers some comeuppance for Pitt and her misunderstanding of what it takes to take photos in the wild. Her enthusiastic attempts at inhabiting the same space as a bear cub (however trained) gets her chased out of frame after an accident burns down their camp and the animal becomes startled. This sort-of validates Hank's laziness – why bother even trying to force this behaviour on a potentially dangerous beast? – and brings a note of closure to the city/country plotline, where the ways of the ranch and the wild work best when not subjected to the schemes of city folk. This film likely played well to contemporary audiences, especially ones from rural environs, thanks to its siding with Rogers and his good-natured inhabitation of country values. The film was just one in a series of Hal Roach-produced films for which he was the principal attraction (and for which he was paid a record-breaking sum of $2000 a week) (R. J. Maturi and M. B. Maturi 1999: 86). *Hustlin' Hank* saw moderate critical success. *Motion Picture World* described it as 'all very good entertainment' (quoted in R. J. Maturi and M. B. Maturi 1999: 226). But Rogers would go on to bigger movies and bigger fame, reaching an

---

[1]   *For more on the transformation of objects into living things in the context of silent comedy, see Aragon (2000: 53).*

apex in popularity just before his tragic death in an airplane crash in 1935.

Viewed today, *Hustlin' Hank* is an incredibly contradictory film. It wants an audience to laugh at the problems of trying to make images of animals, yet it is a film that was able to make moving images of animals in the first place thanks to an ability to overcome the inherent problems presented. It offers that both animals and humans, even though they interact with, and occasionally take on, the interests of machines, in fact have different relationships to the camera and to what it takes to construct a performance. Even though the film edits together sequences to suggest motivation and autonomy for animals, it also features some fine shots of people and animals interacting in the same frame, thus touching on the kind of realism that André Bazin lauds in his seminal essay 'The Virtues and Limitations of Montage': despite training and rehearsal, some of the interactions between the bear and the actors in *Hustlin' Hank* give off the real threat of danger (Bazin 2004: 52).[2] Overall, *Hustlin' Hank* takes the dominant features of silent comedy – its relation to cities and its fascination with machines – and fuses it with the Western and rural world of Will Rogers. Many of the problems offered by *Hustlin' Hank* with regard to animals in film have since been rectified. Flexible and microscopic digital equipment enables relatively unobtrusive observation. Any animal too dangerous to physically interact with a human actor can be summoned during post-production thanks to computer-generated imagery. Still, viewed ninety years on, *Hustlin' Hank* combines problems and issues of the day with a kind of comic physicality that will never go out of style.

---

2   *Bazin especially praises the scene from* The Circus *between Chaplin and a tiger, who are trapped in the same cage.*

References

Aragon, Louis (2000) 'On Décor', in Paul Hammond (ed.) *The Shadow and Its Shadow*, third edition, San Francisco, CA: City Lights Books.

Bazin, André (2004) 'The Virtues and Limitations of Montage', in *What Is Cinema?*, volume I, trans. Hugh Gray, Berkeley, CA: University of California Press.

Benjamin, Walter (1968) 'The Work of Art in the Age of Mechanical Reproduction', in *Illuminations*, ed. Hannah Arendt, trans. Harry Zohn, New York: Schocken.

Bergson, Henri (2008) *Laughter: An Essay on the Meaning of the Comic*, trans. Cloudsley Brereton and Fred Rothwell, Rockville, MD: Arc Manor (also available through Project Gutenberg: www.gutenberg. org/ebooks/4352).

Dagognet, Francois (1992) *Étienne-Jules Marey: A Passion for the Trace*, trans. Robert Galeta with Jeanine Herman, New York: Zone Books.

Maturi, Richard J. and Mary Buckingham Maturi (1999) *Will Rogers, Performer: An Illustrated Biography*, with a Filmography, Jefferson, NC: McFarland.

North, Michael (2008) *Machine-Age Comedy*, Oxford, UK: Oxford University Press.

Robinson, E. Keith (1939) 'Wild Animals and the Films', *Sight and Sound*, 8(29), pp. 8–10.

Rowlands, Mark (2002) *Animals Like Us*, London: Verso.

Solnit, Rebecca (2003) *Motion Studies: Eadweard Muybridge and the Technological Wild West*, London: Bloomsbury.

Stewart, Larry (1998) 'A Meaning for Machines: Modernity, Utility, and the Eighteenth-Century British Public', *Journal of Modern History*, 70(2), pp. 259–294.

Ward, Richard Lewis (2005) *A History of the Hal Roach Studios*, Carbondale, IL: Southern Illinois University Press.

Yagoda, Ben (2000) *Will Rogers: A Biography*, Norman, OK: University of Oklahoma Press.

ABIGAIL PARRY

❧

The Wolf Man

Of course I believe that The Wolf Man *is the best of my horror films – because he is* mine.

– LON CHANEY JR.

Y OU CAN'T **know how it feels –**
to have the blood

bark backwards through the heart,
and every nerve snap shut.

That's how it was, each time
I saw that name, my father's name, mine

265

but not mine.
                    The man himself

played twenty roles a week, could lose
both legs and break his back by close of day.

The Miracle Man, *The Hunchback*, *The Unknown*,
the man with a thousand faces, every one

his own. The work of a craftsman.
I watched him grind the lenses,

strap himself in homemade trusses,
bind his limbs, bend over backwards

till his back was broke for good, spine buckled,
his eyes spent. Everyone had a piece:

the studio took his arms, his legs,
his face a thousand times. The talkies

killed the pantomime, but even his voice
was acrobat – till that went too.

Then only his name was left
                              – and I took that.

The day they repossessed the car, it was –
furniture gone already, business sunk.

Only his name was left. I couldn't hock it,

so I wore it. It swallowed me in one gulp.

Those years were hungry years, scavenging
bits and scraps, giving away a good name

for third-billings and extras,
stunt work, cowboys, thrillers.

And Christ, the man's shadow! Sure,
it opened doors, but then each night

it grew long and tall, and came capering
up behind me, like the hard-

faced harbourmaster, waving *go back go back*.
Go back to what? The country starved.

I grew thin behind that name, impalpable.
I grew cold behind that name, insatiable.

A thickset ghost with a heavy burden,
uncertain, lumbering. A ghoul. That is,

till I found the Wolf.

                   Makeup took the credit,

but the Wolf was mine,
I found him in me. Only I knew the Wolf,

how I'd nursed him in the stony, coldest
part of myself, chewing on nothings,

mouthfuls of ash and a brain of diamonds,
a bellyful of ice and a brain in ribbons.

"A man lost in the mazes of his own mind"
But when I walked, I felt the sprung

piston of haunch and shank, a tread too
firm to be faked. And when I opened my mouth,

I spoke from far off,
a lean and craggy country,

and behind it piped the high
grave falsetto of the Wolf. And oh, oh,

"When the Autumn moon is bright..."
Those hours were mine. *Mine.*

A word to follow home.
A word to bite down on.

Sebastian Manley

☙

'Does zoology include people?' Human and Animal Identity in Hitchcock's Marnie *(1964) and* The Birds *(1963)*

Tʜᴇʀᴇ ɪs a lot of anguish and not much reassurance in Hitchcock's two great Tippi Hedren films, the earlier of which fits into what George Butte calls without hyperbole the director's 'trilogy of despair' (*Vertigo, Psycho* and *The Birds*) and the later of which would no doubt make it into a tetralogy of despair or something similar, despite the superficially more positive-romantic ending (2004: 220). Both films focus on characters whose relationships are defined by anxiety, compulsion, angst and dark secrets. At the same time, both films offer a wider and often disconcerting reflection on knowledge, self-definition and, more specifically, the relationship between human nature and animal nature, a question that began to increase dramatically in importance in academic and other spheres in the decades after the end of Hitchcock's career.

In *The Birds*, a forerunner of the animal-monster horror cycle (later entries included *Jaws*, *The Swarm* and *Arachnophobia*) and a serious slice of art cinema in the mould of Antonioni, a small town in California called Bodega Bay is subject to a series of violent bird attacks, thought by some to be somehow caused by the film's main character, Melanie Daniels (Tippi Hedren), an outsider who has come to the town in the hopes of continuing a strange flirtatious relationship with a local man called Mitch Brenner (Rod Taylor). The subject of *Marnie* is another strange romance, in this case between Marnie Edgar (Hedren again), a compulsive liar and thief who is repulsed by sex and fears the colour red, and Mark Rutland (Sean Connery), a rich widower who blackmails Marnie into marrying him and tries to 'cure' her by subjecting her to some particularly uncomfortable sessions of amateur psychoanalysis. Part of what is both pleasurable and unnerving about the two films is, as many critics have noted, the way in which the lead characters frequently put on different identities, to hide, to flirt or just to make things easier for themselves. Melanie and Mitch in *The Birds* first meet in a pet shop, where Mitch initially mistakes her for a salesperson; unexpectedly, Melanie does not correct him, and proceeds to play the role of a salesperson. Melanie thinks she is giving a good performance, but in fact Mitch saw through her act almost immediately and, having recognised her as the prominent socialite Melanie Daniels, is just playing along. Mitch keeps up his *own* charade until he shows his hand by making a witty-cruel comparison between Melanie and one of the pet-shop birds ('Back in your gilded cage, Melanie Daniels', he says, returning a bird that has briefly got free to an actual gilded cage). In the first minutes of *Marnie*, we see a dark-haired woman on the run from the law enter a hotel, discard her old clothes for new ones, and literally pick a new identity from a selection of Social Security cards: 'Mary Taylor', 'Martha Heilbron' and 'Margaret Edgar'. As 'Margaret Edgar', or 'Marnie', the woman goes to the bathroom to wash the inky dye from her hair – finally bringing her in line with our image of the film's star, cool blonde Tippi Hedren – before stepping out into the street, ready to start another life of crime and deception. Marnie's masquerade, it quickly becomes apparent, is more than just a way to evade the law. She performs her 'straight' identity – law-abiding, professional, emotionally balanced – to gain the approval of others and in a way to try to escape herself, to deny some trauma or wound of which she is only dimly aware. In this way Marnie and Melanie seem to be almost sisters: both sustain a kind of confident glamour that turns out to be something closer to a nacreous shell, concealing in both cases a mysterious vulnerability and sadness (both Melanie's and Marnie's problems seem to relate, in a not unambiguous way, to a lack of maternal love). They are two of Hitchcock's most compelling figures, inscrutable sometimes even to themselves.

In the same way that the characters' identities as individuals are in question, so are the characters' identities as human beings – or, at least, human beings as they are usually conceived of as a special category of beings separate from other kinds of animal beings. Via a series of typically Hitchcockian doublings and inversions, each film calls into doubt various common ideas about the essential difference between the human and the animal. *Marnie*, the more inward and obviously psychological of the two films, draws our attention to the animal nature of human nature, the human *as* animal, a topic explicitly broached early on in the film when Marnie asks in response to Mark's talk of his aborted career as a zoologist whether 'zoology include[s] people'. *The Birds* offers a larger-scale, more spectacular and, at first glance, more conventional vision of the relationship between humans and animals in which animals are a kind of alien force, but a closer look reveals a different picture, where birds and humans seem to exchange or share characteristics. Both films employ dark humour and disturbing, almost surreal narrative forms in provoking us to think again about our place in the animal world.

THE BIRDS

A little over halfway through *The Birds*, in a scene following the famous sequence in which the birds amass at the town school's playground and attack the schoolchildren, Melanie starts to talk to an amateur ornithologist called Mrs Bundy (wonderfully played by English actor Ethel Griffies). Evidently a familiar face at the Tides restaurant, where Melanie has come to seek shelter and a phone, Mrs Bundy greets Melanie's reports of the bird attacks with an amusingly brisk scepticism, asserting that birds are not aggressive creatures before starting to make a point about the aggressiveness of *humankind*. At this point she is cut off by the waitress, who is calling for an order of fried chicken – a bird, that is, killed by a human. This unexpected but expressive illustration of Mrs Bundy's point – a classic bit of Hitchcockian wit – serves to momentarily realign the film's moral coordinates, directing sympathy away from the human protagonists and towards the 'monsters', the birds whose acts of aggression seem suddenly just an echo of the human acts of aggression directed against birds (confinement, killing, eating) every day as a 'natural' part of human culture.

Strange parallels and inversions through which birds come to seem human or humans come to seem bird-like are everywhere in the film. As Scott Calef notes in his essay on the concept of humanity in Hitchcock's film, birds are on several occasions associated with speech – one of the characteristics traditionally seen to distinguish humans from animals – while humans are often associated with extreme inarticulacy and muteness. The first conversation of the film, for example, is between the woman at the pet-shop desk and Melanie, who has come in to pick up a myna bird who she expects to be able to talk (she's right, although she'll have to give him lessons); the same bird is mentioned again later, when Melanie tells Mitch how she plans to teach the bird to say obscenities so as to shock her aunt. Human characters, meanwhile, are at several points during the film struck mysteriously dumb. Calef cites two horrific scenes that are somehow made more shocking by the fact that the characters do not cry out as they might be expected to: the scene where Mitch's mother, Lydia, comes across the bloodied corpse of Dan Fawcett and runs out with her mouth open but making no sound; and the scene where Melanie is attacked by birds in the Brenner attic, an utterly overwhelming experience for the character and the viewer that leaves Melanie almost entirely mute, even when revived by Mitch some moments later (2007: 82).

Calef also notes that while the birds seem to display intelligence and planning in their attacks – contradicting Mrs Bundy's blithe assurance that birds' 'brain pans aren't large enough' for such things – the human characters often display a kind of herd behaviour that links them to the animal world (as it is stereotypically conceived of by humans). People ignore the facts of the attacks simply because they don't seem likely to them. They have very little idea what is going on or what to do about it (the phrase 'I don't know' is the film's most persistent leitmotif, as Calef notes). And they tend to succumb easily to panic and instinctive actions, as when Mitch, incredibly, decides to throw a rock at a flock of birds that he knows perfectly well could kill him and Melanie in retaliation; he just isn't thinking and cannot help himself (Calef 2007: 80–81, 83–84). As well as acting like birds, Mitch and many of the other characters, in this and other scenes, come to *look* like birds in certain shots, particularly the profile shot that Hitchcock scholar Richard Allen identifies as a recurring shot throughout the film, in which characters are shown looking into the distance, 'chins jutting forward', in such a way as to suggest 'the Janus face of the human being: half human, half bird' (2007: 194).

Hitchcock's narrative world becomes in these instances an almost surreal world where human reality and bird reality collapse or extend into one another. This is a vision of human–animal relations that seems to philosophically undermine the surface story sketched by the film of heroic humans battling evil animals – a class of narrative that took off in the decades after Hitchcock's film and that seems to reflect what would now be called 'speciesist' attitudes towards non-human animals. Human–animal studies scholar Randy Malamud, for example, describes animal-monster horror films, including *The Birds*, as representing one side of a cultural dichotomy that splits animals into 'good' pets and helpers (Lassie, Flipper, Old Yeller) and 'bad' or monstrous others that encourage our hatred (the shark in *Jaws*, Orca the killer whale). In Malamud's analysis, *The Birds*, in portraying the birds as frightening and as a threat to humans, indulges in a conventional objectification of animals equivalent to the conventional objectification of women in film: the animals like women are reduced to something alien and one-dimensional, something that exists less as a subject than as a dramatic function (2012: 75). But the self and the other in *The Birds*, as is so often the case in

Hitchcock's films, are in truth not so simplistically opposed. Much of what is commonly 'known' – in human culture and sometimes specifically in the world of the film – about birds and humans and the moral order in which they are suspended is questioned or outright rejected. If Malamud's dichotomising impulse threatens to immure us within a contrived world of human subjects and animal objects, Hitchcock's darkly imaginative fantasy gives us a more real world, in which belief in what philosopher Jeremy Bentham in 1780 called the 'insuperable line' between the human and non-human animal is revealed as a naïve fiction (2007: 311).

MARNIE

Scepticism about the essential difference between animals and humans in *The Birds* becomes scepticism about the very categorisation of humans as human rather than simply a variety of animal in *Marnie*, which figures its central romance as a kind of uncomfortable standoff, between the glamorous but cold Marnie and Mark, her would-be lover, who aims to reconnect Marnie with her instinctual drives and cure her of her neuroticism and frigidity. Throughout the film, dialogue spoken by both Mark and Marnie makes reference to the animal nature of humans, particularly at the levels of sex and desire. Mark describes his father as someone who judges a person 'by scent' and who admires 'animal lust'. In the 'hunt' metaphor that structures Mark and Marnie's romance – 'You don't love me. I'm just something you've caught. You think I'm some kind of animal you've trapped', Marnie says in response to Mark's first 'I love you' – Mark is cast as an animal predator-seducer driven by primal instinct. Marnie, delivering what seems to be both a valid criticism of Mark's chauvinism and a kind of script developed to cover her trauma, describes men as 'beasts' and wittily dismisses Mark's attempt to psychoanalyse her as really an act of animal lust (her reformulation of 'Me Tarzan, you Jane', 'You Freud, me Jane?' – inserting Mark the analyst into the position of the archetypal 'apeman' – is received with a smile from Mark).

A similar understanding of human nature as a sort of animal nature is conveyed in a more concrete, less potentially figurative way by a number of memorable narrative details. Mark, we are perhaps surprised to learn, given the exaggeratedly suave-macho persona he projects in the film's early scenes, is an amateur zoologist – a detail established in the first full dialogue scene between Mark and Marnie, when she visits his office at his request to do some clerical work. The flirtatious exchange in this scene indicates that Mark's interest in zoology is in some way coextensive with his interest in human behaviour or psychology: when Marnie queries the meaning of the term 'zoology', Mark defines it as the study of 'instinctual behaviour'. Mark's pointedly broad definition here (i.e. not just animal behaviour) elicits from Marnie the question referred to earlier about whether zoology includes people. Mark's reply is: 'Well, in a way. It includes all the animal ancestors from whom man derived his instincts'. Mark, it is clear, understands people *as* animals of a kind (possibly, though not necessarily, a 'superior' kind – but in any case not separate from animals in any essential way). Indeed, it is this understanding that means he is able to recognise Marnie's secret problems – which, briefly, amount to the *repression* of 'animal' instincts, a distaste for, and even aversion to, affection, the mating game and sex.

In its emphasis on the idea of the 'animal within', Hitchcock's film locates itself within a tradition of thought about the human as animal, or human 'animality', that Michael Lundblad identifies as rising to prominence with the publication of Darwin's *On the Origin of Species* (1859) and *The Descent of Man* (1871), and early works by Freud (*The Interpretation of Dreams*, 1900; *The Psychopathology of Everyday Life*, 1901; and *Three Essays on the Theory of Sexuality*, 1905) that 'translated Darwinist constructions of "real" animals into "animal instincts" within the human psyche' for influential American and European psychologists such as Richard von Krafft-Ebing, G. Stanley Hall and William James. Freud's psychoanalysis was founded in some ways on the recognition of the animal aspect of the human. As Lundblad notes, Freud saw the human mind as being driven by animal instincts for survival and reproduction. He warned against neglecting the 'animal part of our nature' in the critical fight against repression. And, following Darwin, he offered a brisk and explicit rejection of the 'insuperable line' often drawn between the human and non-human species: 'Man is not a being different from animals or superior to them; he himself is of animal descent, being more closely related to some species and more distantly to others' (Lundblad 2013: 4). For Freud in these works, then, as for Mark in *Marnie*, understanding animal instincts is the path to understanding human instincts.

If the film seems to draw on this kind of Darwinist-Freudian discourse, though, it hardly seems to endorse it, at least in its most simplistic form. The tragedy of Marnie's trauma clearly is that she has closed herself off to the 'animal' aspects of herself (indeed she sees marriage, which we can take to mean intimacy and sex, as 'degrading'). She comes across as an assemblage of glamour and mannerisms, a figure more mechanical than human, whose body, as Butte puts it, 'is a costume that she manipulates jerkily with levers and pulleys from some safe place inside' (2004: 222).[1] But Mark, guided in his actions by an idea of animality that reduces all to aggressive heterosexuality, cannot finally cure Marnie. If Marnie cannot accept the animal nature that is a part of her, Mark conceives of this animal nature too narrowly. He fails to see that Marnie's dysfunction relates to an inability to accept not just sexual intimacy, but also a larger and more open kind of human intimacy – an intimacy that is withheld from her by her mother and that she seems to feel only when riding her horse, Forio. The love Marnie experiences in these moments with Forio (emphasised by the swelling orchestral score) is clearly the kind of instinctual, primal but nonsexual love that Marnie's mother cannot or will not give her, but Mark, sadly, cannot remedy or even see this lack, because it does not figure within his rather stark, sex-oriented model of human-animal behaviour. At the end of the film, Mark takes Marnie to see her mother in an attempt to uncover the origins of her trauma, and at this point the repressed world of sex and violence that has pushed through into the narrative world in the form of a red blotting filling Marnie's vision and the screen itself is finally registered in full, as Marnie 'becomes' her child self and a sequence reveals to her and us the truth of the events that caused her fear of men and sex. But, as Allen notes, what is made clear in this sequence but remains unknowable to Mark is that Marnie's trauma is caused not just by the violent act Marnie performed as a child, but also by her mother's emotional abandonment of her, which has led her mother, in her guilt, to deny Marnie affection. The sense at the film's close

---

[1]   *Mark does refer casually to Marnie as an animal, but if she resembles an animal then it is Sophie, the jaguarondi Mark keeps a picture of in his office, with whom Marnie shares (to a comical degree, it seems to me) a kind of refined artificial glamour.*

is that Marnie is still ill, her marriage to Mark more a sentence than a solace (Allen 2007: 102–103).

In some ways, of course, *Marnie* relies on rather questionable or 'essentialist' conceptions of both animal and human nature that much modern thinking would have little time for. But one of the film's achievements is to probe our possibilities through rendering characters who, like some characters in *The Birds*, make mistakes about human and animal nature. As philosopher Robert Yanal suggests, *Marnie* is a 'counterexample to Descartes's idea that we are always certain of the contents of our mind' (2007: 258). Marnie does not know her mind. But maybe Hitchcock is also saying that she does not know her own nature, that we do not know, or should not be so sure of, our own nature, our identity as human beings. The disturbing but resonant truth of Hitchcock's two remarkable late films is that, as humans, we are not who we thought we were.

References

Allen, Richard (2007) *Hitchcock's Romantic Irony*, New York: Columbia University Press.

Bentham, Jeremy (2007) *An Introduction to the Principles of Morals and Legislation*, New York: Dover Publications.

Butte, George (2004) *I Know That You Know That I Know: Narrating Subjects from Moll Flanders to Marnie*, Columbus: Ohio State University Press.

Calef, Scott (2007) 'Featherless Bipeds: The Concept of Humanity in *The Birds*', in David Baggett and William A. Drumin (eds) *Hitchcock and Philosophy: Dial M for Metaphysics*, Chicago; La Salle, Illinois: Open Court.

Lundblad, Michael (2013) *The Birth of a Jungle: Animality in Progressive-Era U.S. Literature and Culture*, New York: Oxford University Press.

Malamud, Randy (2012) *An Introduction to Animals and Visual Culture*, Houndmills, Basingstoke, Hampshire; New York: Palgrave Macmillan.

Yanal, Robert J. (2007) '*Shadow of a Doubt* and *Marnie*: Entries into a Mind', in David Baggett and William A. Drumin (eds) *Hitchcock and Philosophy: Dial M for Metaphysics*, Chicago; La Salle, Illinois: Open Court.

JUDE C. MONTAGUE

❧

Empire of the Ants

*T*HE **FUTURE** is here. *You just have to see it.*
The breeze swoops vol-au-vents over Dreamland's fine sand.
Off-coast, Joe, nervous but resolute, heaves overboard
sealed barrels stencilled DO NOT OPEN.

Men stare past long side-partings;
their fringes flutter and jerk in the off-season current.
What do you think, fella?
Will these windy shores be a good investment?

Ssssssh. What they don't know
is that those barrels leaked
and tiny creatures never noticed before,
have ballooned into giants.

Maybe you don't like cheap scotch but it's free.
That's what Velma and I like the most.
What do you think lady?
The women push strands out of their eyes.

Fumbling away from the party,
 just out of a bad marriage,
Loulene and her lover stumble into a bloody corpse. *What?*
She spins her dollface to bury her lips in his cruel chest.

What could have caused wounds like that?
There's no kind of beast like that on this island.
A crocodile?
Oh my god.

This situation has already escalated.
Dan rows the newly bonded team downriver
heading for **Future Golf Course**,
to polystyrene scraped by a violin bow.

I can't stand it any longer, I have to get out of here.
The mangroves shake the water.
When the boat bangs on the shore
she jumps out onto the bank of the **Future Club House**.

Her glossy dark hair sweating
onto her beige culottes,
tousled in terror, she swings like a sexy cannon,
away from Dan's 'Come back!' towards the **Future Marina**.

only to find her dipping breasts
encased in many miniature circles
as we pull back
to reveal her compound scream.

Jᴀᴍᴇs Cᴏɢʜɪʟʟ

❧

Tallow

(From 'Djurmordäre': 4 poems after Bergman's En Passion*)*

Fᴏʀ ᴀ heaven of glue
and the dubious peace
of the knacker's yard

the djurmordäre
had come one last time,
to torch Olsson's barn.

You arrive without
remembering how
you'd got there,

you'd beaten yourself
desperate with tears,
put an axe in her shadow,

284

and this was somehow
the consequence:
the cattle blistering

in their stalls to guttering
grease haemorrhage
their hide, cracked

and peeling all through
the seismic pity
of their long death croon

the camera dares not
follow the firemen
inside, but contemplates,

instead, the horse
that broke out as they
broke in, doused

in petrol (Olsson tells us)
that lies dead, a whinnying
barrow, transformed

to cinder, helpless
repository for our bottomless
domesticating sympathy

that kills as it draws close,
damns each creature
as we breed it— innocent

but hardly blameless,
they fall with us—
Adamic victims, the sum

of our humiliations,
cruelties and freedoms
overflowing into the heart

of that mute caste:
the damn horse
just wouldn't die.

JULIE ANN SMITH

☙

*Death of a White-Tailed Deer
in David Lynch's* The Straight Story *(1999)*

DIRECTOR David Lynch portrays with perfect pitch the clichés
that human beings live by. Indeed, one never knows whether
he is celebrating middle-class mindsets or aiming to unsettle
them. One example occurs in two short sequential scenes
from *The Straight Story* wherein Lynch depicts the death of a
white-tailed deer in a car–deer collision. Both scenes depend
on stereotypes of hunting culture, and they reflect its larger
philosophical view that animals are incapable of any awareness
of their own experiences, including severe trauma. In other
words, the scenes incorporate cultural erasure of animals'
capacity to witness, that is, to understand that something
devastating is happening to them or to their fellows. To this
end, the scenes use three stereotypes from hunting discourse:
the animal lover, the hunter, and deer themselves. In the
end, however, we do not know whether Lynch is uncritically
adopting these stereotypes or using excess and contradiction
to destabilise them.

In *The Straight Story*, a seventy-three-year-old man, Alvin Straight (Richard Farnsworth), unable to qualify for a driver's licence, drives a tractor from Iowa to Wisconsin in order to see his ailing brother, from whom he has been estranged for ten years. Along the way, he engages with people from small towns and with strangers on the road. One encounter is with a woman who has just hit and killed a deer with her car. Alvin dismounts from the tractor to see if the woman is hurt. The 'Deer Woman' screams at Alvin – and the world at large – that she has tried but repeatedly failed to avoid collisions with deer. She then abruptly drives off. In the next scene, Alvin is roasting a large piece of meat, presumably from this deer, over his campfire. Surrounding him and apparently watching are deer statues similar to inexpensive lawn ornaments.

DAVID LYNCH AND WISCONSIN HUNTING CULTURE

These two scenes borrow motifs from hunting culture as played out in Wisconsin, motifs certainly understood by Lynch's screenwriters and to some extent Lynch himself. The screenplay for the film was written by Mary Sweeney and David Roach, both Wisconsin natives. Mary Sweeney was Lynch's domestic partner at the time she wrote the screenplay and Lynch filmed it, and she is the one who presented him with the project. During the 1990s and early years of the 2000s, the two of them and their son lived in a house on Lake Mendota in Madison as an alternate home to the Lynch house in Hollywood. *The Straight Story* was filmed in Iowa and western Wisconsin, specifically the Prairie du Chien area west of Madison. The Roach–Sweeney screenplay is based on an episode in the life of a man named Alvin Straight that took place in Iowa and Wisconsin. While what I am calling 'hunting culture' is nearly identical everywhere in America, I will focus on Wisconsin because this is where I have lived for decades and been exposed yearly to its discourse.

THE CRASH AND THE DEAD DEER

At the beginning of the scene of the deer crash, the camera focuses on the face of Alvin as a car speeds past him in a no-passing zone. He hears a crash and is visibly upset. He dismounts from his tractor and makes his way to the accident, where he sees the crumpled hood of a car spewing steam and a dead deer lying on the road. This scene depends on familiarity with the problem of deer overpopulation. Although overpopulation is never explicitly mentioned, it can be the only explanation for the crash. The woman complains: 'I have hit thirteen deer in seven weeks driving down this road, mister, and I have to drive this road every day' (Roach and Sweeney 1999: 84). In an interview, Lynch claimed that this 'deer serial killer' was based on an actual person, although one who never met Alvin: 'Some [episodes] were based on other true stories that got folded in like the Deer Lady [...] she does exist – a woman who, for some unknown reason, hit thirteen deer [Laughs]' (Rodley 1997: 251). The scene in the film has exaggerated her experiences by making the collisions all occur in seven weeks. Even though the Deer Lady is obviously reckless, the excessive number of crashes exploits a prevailing assumption that is part of hunting culture, that is, that car–deer collisions are caused by an overpopulation of deer that can only be managed by hunting. In other words, most people around here would say that a car–deer collision means 'We need hunting.'

That the opposite is the case – that hunting actually produces an overpopulation of deer – only began to be heard at about the time *The Straight Story* was being filmed. In 1999, the Wisconsin Wildlife Coalition, a subgroup of the Alliance for Animals of which I am a member, released a pamphlet that exposed the myths about deer overpopulation perpetrated by the hunting community, including the Department of Natural Resources. It showed that the intent of the Department of Natural Resources was and is to produce an enormous herd to satisfy the some 700,000 gun hunters that slaughter approximately 400,000 deer and wound another 200,000 (who die a slow death in the woods) during the annual nine-day deer-hunting season. The report showed that deer population in the state had dramatically increased from 1963 to 1999 because the DNR employed management techniques to intentionally create a yearly population explosion in order to give hunters a satisfactory hunting experience. Nevertheless, '[t]he principal argument presented to the public by the DNR for hunting deer is that the herd has over-populated and threatens the fields, farms and automobiles of the state' (Wisconsin Wildlife Coalition 1999: 5). The Deer Woman describes one of her failed strategies to avoid hitting deer as playing 'Public Enemy real loud'. Her comment only makes sense if 'Public Enemy' refers to the deer, a principal message of hunting promoters.

The dead deer on the road in the film closely correlates to the way dead deer are seen by the general population during and after the nine-day gun-deer hunt. Deer are never shown by the media as living creatures who suffer and die; they are always already dead. Deer are merely statistics reported as kill numbers or photographed as tagged carcasses. The death of the deer in the film likewise entails no experience of dying. The collision takes place off-screen; the deer shows no signs of expiring or even of ever having been alive and hit. As the screenwriters describe it, it is 'a nice eight point buck' (Roach and Sweeney 1999: 84), a characterisation signalling trophy hunting. In fact, the car is actually the site of greater trauma; while there is no deer blood on the road, there is an ugly smear of engine oil. Reports about car–deer collisions in Wisconsin are always about the impact on the automobile, and the deer is mentioned only as the cause of a scare or a financial inconvenience.

THE DEER WOMAN

The Deer Woman screams her tirade, flailing her arms wildly as she screeches, never letting Alvin have a word; she then jumps into her car and tears off. She will remind viewers of the dilemma of non-hunting citizens who do not want to kill deer but who do not want to wreck their cars in car–deer collisions either. The woman pats the deer carcass lying on the road and says, 'He's dead.' She starts to cry and then says, 'And I love deer' (Roach and Sweeney 1999: 85). Part of the joke on her is that she is guilty of 'serial bambicide' (Jackson 1999) even though she is an animal lover. If she wanted to avoid car–deer accidents, she would have to support hunting to reduce the herd, the narrative goes. Alternatively, without hunting, she would be killing the deer herself with her car due to overpopulation. Frustrated by repeated trauma to herself, she eventually would convert to a pro-hunting attitude, is the implied message of hunting discourse.

As a character, the Deer Woman depends on the influence of such myth-making. She is someone who is excessively emotional in her love of animals, a stereotype of the

291

animal protectionist. She is female, urban and sentimental yet drastically inept at assisting the animals she claims to love. She is reckless, as opposed to the outdoorsman, who maintains a careful relationship with the environment. She is ignorant of nature. She looks out onto the flat, empty agricultural landscape as alien territory from where loveable beings with incomprehensible behaviour emerge. She says with astonishment in a line added by Lynch, 'Where do they all come from?' While Lynch loves a dark, ominous mystery behind surface appearances, he here uses the theme to make the woman comically ignorant of biological facts. The woman's love of the deer seems tenuous at best because her excessive emotionalism puts her, rather than the deer, at the centre of the trauma. We are thus reminded that activists over-identify with animals and make themselves the victims.

Intentionally or not, Lynch perfectly captures in the Deer Woman the problems with surrogate witnessing for animals: namely the very real fact of silencing animals by overwhelming them with the performance of the human. Additionally, nullification of human witnessing for animals occurs through stereotyping the human witness.

ALVIN AS OUTDOORSMAN

When he hears the crash, which occurs off-camera, Alvin's face is visibly alarmed. He dismounts from his tractor to see if the woman is hurt, and when he sees that the victim is 'only a deer', he is visibly relieved. Alvin nudges it with his foot to see if it is still alive – a distancing, objectifying gesture. He listens to the woman's tirade politely but seems to suppress a condescending smile at the woman's emotionalism. After the woman drives off, a second scene shows Alvin roasting a deer steak over a campfire with artificial deer behind him. The next morning as he drives away, we see deer antlers mounted on his trailer displayed in the manner of a hunting trophy.

In many ways, Alvin represents a stereotype of a hunter, albeit an old and disabled and now former one. Earlier in the film Alvin says that he was assigned the job of sniper in World War II because of the shooting skills he had learned through a lifetime of hunting. The Ace Hardware where he hangs out with his buddies in his home town has animal heads mounted on the wall. The John Deere tractor that he rides carries the logo of a rampant buck. We have no doubt that we are in a place that naturalises hunting. Alvin has the practical sensibilities that see deer as meat and trophy. This is often expressed by hunters as their alignment with a Native American land ethic. As one critic has approvingly written:

> *The hurrying woman who works in an office killed the deer, but slow-moving Alvin, who lives closer to the earth, knows how to honor the creature. Like a Native American who respects the animal's life he takes so that he may live, Alvin cooks and enjoys the deer's flesh and mounts its proud antlers on his trailer.* (Olson 2008: 474)

A different critic sees Alvin's 'closeness to the land' more cynically:

> *Alvin and the woman exemplify two types: the hysterical stranger, the outsider, living against nature, and the instinctual naturalist, who laments the deer's death but skins and eats it anyway. To drive the point home, as it were, the woman tears off in her perennially wrecked car while Alvin mounts the horns of the deer*

on his trailer – a bit of crude posturing given that the kill wasn't
his – and, well fortified by this God-delivered meal, soldiers on.
(Johnson 2004: 142)

Tim Kreider makes an additional point that mounted antlers and hunting trophies in Lynch's work generally symbolise human violence and its often disastrous effects on the innocent (2000: 29–30).

The scene plays with hunter self-mythologising to implausible and even comic effect. The Native American ethic towards animals requires full and idealised engagement with the animal body in the act of transforming it for human use, including care to waste nothing. Only able to walk with two canes, Alvin could not possibly have dragged the carcass off the road, gutted it and processed it for eating. In fact, we never see the body again, only one piece of meat. Furthermore, having a hunter eat roadkill exposes the hunting pretence of down-to-earth practicality. Hunters would find it unthinkable, the kill being the critical part of the hunt. Additionally, hunting culture validates all sorts of absurd posturing by hunters who are 'over the hill' as they engage in creative ways to validate hunting when no longer able to participate. The year before *The Straight Story* was released, a man in Dodgeville, Wisconsin, made the front page of the local section of the newspaper by mounting a deer head on his tractor in a fashion similar to the way Lynch has Alvin mount the deer antlers, except that the Dodgeville man mounted the entire taxidermic head. If Lynch was influenced by this image, he rendered it with a restraint not in the source.

Figure 1. Deer head mounted to tractor in downtown Dodgeville, Wisconsin. Joseph W. Jackson III, Wisconsin State Journal, 14 November 1998, 1B.

THE WITNESSING DEER STATUES

In both scenes, the possibility of an animal witnessing its own trauma is foreclosed. The emotionalism of the woman replaces the experience of the animal. Alvin's rendering of the deer into food and trophy silences the deer as a living being capable of a point of view on events happening to it. The last part of the second scene explicitly raises the issue of animal witnessing but does so in a most vexed way.

As Alvin roasts a piece of deer meat over the fire, a group of animal statues look on. The setting is an empty lot out in the country. We see a derelict shack leaning on its side and several statues of animals scattered about in the tall grass. Most are deer, but there is also a sheep; the species of many is hard to identify, but all look as if they have been discarded there. A group of four deer closest to Alvin stare with blank expressions. Alvin looks at them over his shoulder and shifts position self-consciously to put his back more directly to them, as if feeling guilty for eating one of their friends in their view.

Figure 2. A group of animal statues 'watch' as Alvin eats some deer meat.

The deer witnesses are not in the script but were added by Lynch himself. Greg Olson asked Lynch about them and received this enigmatic answer:

> *Lynch says that these concrete figures are an example of the 'strange places' one encounters in the rural Midwest. And he laughs in appreciation of his viewers' imaginations when I tell him that some people think that the figures are part of a memorial cemetery that the Deer Woman erected.* (Olson 2008: 476).

What strange places Lynch has in mind is unclear. However, deer statues are everywhere in Wisconsin as lawn ornaments and are often displayed by hunters.

A hunting neighbour of mine had two 'Bambi' statues in front of his house, which he lovingly painted with unfortunate results. Also, about the time of the release of *The Straight Story*, the DNR launched its 'Earn a buck' programme, which required that a hunter first kill a female or a fawn (called by the DNR an

Figure 3. Deer family statues, Janesville, Wisconsin. Author's photograph, 6 August 2013.

'antlerless deer') in order to earn the privilege of killing a male. Thus, the 'antlerless deer' statues of this scene are relevant to deer hunting practices.

Clearly the deer witnessing scene is a joke, as statues do not watch people and make them self-conscious about their behaviour. But is the joke on the Deer Woman, on Alvin, or on the deer? The Deer Woman gave deer human-like importance through caring about what happened to them. She seems to anthropomorphise them, just as they are excessively anthropomorphised here, perhaps as a way to make fun of her. Alvin is also a target of the joke in that he appears to have been infected by the Deer Lady's 'Bambi syndrome'. In spite of his detachment from animal death, he seems to be vulnerable to thinking about deer as beings with awareness. However, he quickly comes to his senses. He smiles at his own discomfort; and he masters his lapse into sentimentality by mounting the antlers on his trailer as object-trophy.

What makes the viewer so uncomfortable about this scene is that it seems also to make fun of the deer, the victims. Such jokes are everywhere in the environment. For example, one sees deer heads used as hat racks or deer carcasses propped up in beds of pickup trucks in crude tableaux. I have seen recently killed deer propped up around a card table with cards fastened to their hoofs. Here the joke is that the deer statues seem to witness what humans have done to them. The scene deploys the familiar cultural strategy of first denying animal sentience by making the animal witnesses inert, and then masking that denial by granting them preposterous abilities. Deer do not gather together to watch a predator eat a fellow deer. Deer do not recognise in deer steaks someone whom they used to know. Humans could not do this either. But by suggesting this fantastic capacity, Alvin erases the kind of witnessing that they are capable of – an understanding that something devastating is happening to them or to others in their social group.

One effect of the joke is to create a 'what if' scenario that renders viewers exceedingly uncomfortable: what if animals could know the role of human agency in their trauma? What if they could accuse? Another animal statue associated with Lynch a year later seems also to suggest these questions. In 1998 the city of Zurich organised an event it called 'Land in Sicht' or 'Countryside in View'. Officials gave selected artists and schoolchildren fiberglass cows, which they were to decorate with cultural themes pertinent to city life. When finished, the cows were distributed around prominent areas of town as a public art exhibit and then auctioned off. In spite of the irony of thinking that one can bring the country to the city by means of painted fibreglass animals, the idea took off worldwide. In 1999, the city of Chicago, two hours from Madison, organised its own 'cow parade'; and in 2000, about 500 such decorated fibreglass cows were exhibited in New York. Lynch submitted an entry to the New York exhibit, but it was summarily refused. It depicted a cow that was decapitated, had its back hollowed out, was smeared in fake blood and had knives and forks sticking out of its rump. Written across its body were the words 'eat my fear'. Thus Lynch used animal statues on two occasions to depict and even trigger the considerable cultural energy routinely deployed by humans to deny animal witnessing.

THE MEANING OF ANIMAL WITNESSING

The deer that is the victim of the car–deer collision essentially fails to be present to its own experiences, and thus Lynch seems to recapitulate the typical cultural silencing of animal witnessing. To most of us, witnessing means providing verbal testimony after the fact concerning matters that we have been in a position to observe. But another definition of 'to witness' is 'to give evidence of by one's behaviour; to make evident; to evince' (*OED*). This definition implies both a capacity to know that one is undergoing trauma – although such knowledge is necessarily circumscribed during the event itself (see below) – and a making manifest of that trauma through behaviour. In this sense, then, animals may serve as witnesses to their own extreme-limit experiences.

At the heart of the claim that animals cannot know that they are experiencing trauma is a cultural tradition that maintains that animals cannot experience death. In his *Electric Animal* (2000), Akira Mizuta Lippit traces the Western philosophical tradition that holds that because animals do not have the capacity to conceptualise non-existence, they cannot really die in the same way humans do. This is because they lack the power of an imagination that exceeds the givens of the present and moves the individual towards the unperceived, in this case death. Thus, lacking the ability to imagine and fear death, they cannot really die. Lippit writes, 'Since animals are denied the faculties of language, they remain incapable of reflection, which is bound by finitude, and carries with it an awareness of death. Undying, animals simply expire, transpire, shift their animus to other animal bodies.' Lippit cites Bataille on the complete absence of death among animals: 'Not only do animals not have this consciousness [of death], they can't even recognize the difference between the fellow creature that is dead and the one that is alive' (2000: 188).

Such thinking is routinely applied to animals' capacity to know their own trauma. Within the philosophical tradition, 'knowing' means reflection from a distance that is only possible once information is 'off-loaded' through language or some other form of representation (Smith and Mitchell 2012: 343). But I take 'knowing' here to mean a capacity to experience the wound of dissolution that is at the core of catastrophe, a state between obliviousness and full cognisance that one communicates in non-languaged ways. It is important to realise that in the act of undergoing trauma, humans do not have full knowledge of it either. Borrowing insights from the brilliant work of those who have theorised Holocaust testimony, I would note that Michael Bernard-Donals and Richard Glejzer, following Freud, write that the victim of trauma is never fully conscious during the event itself; the event at the time it occurs is unavailable as knowledge, is not *conceptualised* as such (2001: 57–58). Thus, humans understand that even other human beings undergoing traumatic experiences cannot grasp the event *as knowledge* at the time it happens. Nevertheless they require from animals demonstration of a capacity to understand a crisis at the moment of occurrence and to signify this in ways comprehensible to humans. Without this, they are thought to be having no experiences at all. In the case of both human and animal, trauma must be understood as experience without the possibility of detached knowledge expressible by language.

As Holocaust theorists have made clear, the experience of catastrophe requires a response: not just assistance in response to physical assault but a response to forestall the anguish of psychic collapse – loss of a sense of orientation towards oneself, others and the world, an experience of shock at being alone and without recourse when one is most helpless, of being an unaddressed and unaddressable other. Without a responsive 'other', the psychic confusion of trauma cannot be mitigated. In other words, the empathetic response has foundational importance, creating an affective loop between two entities, one responding to self-destroying experience, the other capable of receiving and validating that response. Failing to apply the point to non-human animals, but writing movingly in terms that ought to include them, Tal Correm links reciprocity in trauma not to languaged communication but to a reading of the body:

In The Straight Story *and* The Elephant Man, *Lynch shows that the possibility of ethical relations arises with the understanding of the centrality of our body in our experience; he also depicts the horrible consequences when the body as a lived body is ignored. Empathy is a necessary condition for reciprocal relations between people because it discloses both persons as subjects. [...] Only when a body is perceived as a lived body, as a communicative and expressive body, can ethical relations be established.*

The body's initial communication, openness, uniqueness, and sensitivity require responsibility, reciprocity, and mutual recognition. This understanding illumines The Elephant Man: *so long as his body is objectified, and alienated, or, in other words, is being seen merely as objective body, Merrick suffers abuse and torture. [...] In contrast to the objectified body, the lived body communicates and requires empathetic response. Ethical relations are established through the exchange of address and response. The vulnerability of the body demands responsibility and reciprocity.* (Correm 2011: 140–141)

What reason is there to suppose that a non-human animal might not suffer from programmatically unanswered or even unrecognised address in the face of their trauma? If the self emerges through participation in relationships of address and response, then animals, highly social beings that they are, might also suffer from the absence of affective response during experience of calamity. Although the nature of a self may not be the same as that of humans, still the sociability of many species presumes that something important is lost without response. Human beings often express their trauma by means more expressive than language can bear – gestures and utterances, embodied modes that they share with non-human animals. We might say, then, that the animal witnessing scene in *The Straight Story* acquires its power by showing one typical human being refusing address and response to non-human animals.

CONCLUSION

Critics of *The Straight Story* agree that the film is about fundamental values played out in the American heartland. But they profoundly disagree about Lynch's take on them. Some see him as celebrating its rugged individualism, family and community. Others are searing in their scorn of his sell-out to the underside of such values. In any case, hunting is included in the film because hunting culture tirelessly represents itself as a repository of the same core American values that are the subject of the film. Whatever his view of the hunting myth or his lack of one, Lynch has brilliantly delineated mindsets that are integral to hunting culture and to American assumptions about animals' incapacities to grasp their own experiences.

References

Bernard-Donals, Michael (2001) 'Beyond the Question of Authenticity: Witness and Testimony in the Fragments Controversy', *Publications of the Modern Language Association*, 116(5), pp. 1302–1315.

Bernard-Donals, Michael and Richard Glejzer (2001) *Beyond Witness and Testimony: The Holocaust and the Limits of Representation*, New York: State University of New York.

Correm, Tal (2011) 'Constellations of the Flesh: The Embodied Self in *The Straight Story* and *The Elephant Man*', in William J. Devlin and Shai Biderman (eds) *The Philosophy of David Lynch*, Lexington, KY: University of Kentucky Press.

Jackson, Kevin (1999) '*The Straight Story*' (review), *Sight and Sound*, 9(12), pp. 57–58.

Johnson, Jeff (2004) *Pervert in the Pulpit: Morality in the Works of David Lynch*, Jefferson, NC: McFarland & Company, Inc.

Kreider, Tim (2000) 'The Straight Story' (review), *Film Quarterly*, 54(1), pp. 26–33.

Lippit, Akira Mizuta (2000) *Electric Animal: Toward a Rhetoric of Wildlife*, Minneapolis; London: University of Minnesota Press.

McGowan, Todd (2007) *The Impossible David Lynch*, New York: Columbia University Press.

Olson, Greg (2008) *David Lynch: Beautiful Dark*, Lanham, MD: Scarecrow Press.

Roach, John and Mary Sweeney (1999), *The Straight Story: A Screenplay*, New York: Hyperion.

Rodley, Chris (ed.) (1997) *Lynch on Lynch*, London: Faber and Faber.

Smith, Julie A. and Robert Mitchell (2012) 'Animal Ethics and Animals Minds: Reflections', in Julie A. Smith and Robert Mitchell (eds) *Experiencing Animal Minds*, New York: Columbia University Press.

Wisconsin Wildlife Coalition (1999) *Wisconsin Wildlife Report*, Madison, WI: Alliance for Animals.

NICK MURRAY

A Very Special Case

I

I'M GONNA make you a star
A dozen faces
gargoyled round the room
wrench into buoy-headed agreement

    Keiko remains unfazed

A star I tell's ya
Those fins would be on every billboard
from coast to coast

    Keiko remembers

Just bat those white ghost eyes
A double will do all the hard work

Learn the positive spin, loop
and up through the rigging

II

Hands against the glass
of an off-season merry-go-round
kids trace the letters under the zeppelin shadow.
Keiko – and living honestly so,
unlike the half dozen Shamus
to bear the title
like a profession.

Life is all slow circles
in between films.
Cheap tricks and
trying to remember
you're at the apex of your career.

III

Lean back on your coral rocking chair
and remember the old days.
When robots couldn't get wet
and the swimming was good.

But even your hydraulic corollary
is out of practice now.
Imaginary orcas make all the fish

these days, and no one petitions
the habitable space on a hard drive.

One last trip, they say,
for old times' sake.
They say it's nice up in Norway.
To live out those last few shows.
Cheers from overcurious gulls
and cameras that must be just out of sight.

RICHARD EVANS

&

The Pitch

Harry Flint, comedy actor, hyper-hipster, heretical saint
kills himself on a stardrunk night, February 1972.
One hundred years a failure. Rehab royal. Reprobate.
Swans off to the bardos to meet his final review:
irrecoverable flop. Harry Flint deceased, in a downward drift.
Flash of form in human dress, with the head of a dog.
And it's ten years on, the-movie-in-the-movie pitch:
Harry Flint, The Life of a Wag. Fame, drink, love, drink,
disease, drink and done in a hundred-minute flash of jokes
gone almost bad, in the decade's intermission,
but still with that Harry charm, that depth-note of dread
we all recognised behind every success:
awards, the comeback, the comeback again, to the very last
    shot –
grey, taut, already a ghost – and those awkward last gigs:
exhuming the gags, but hollow or cruel.
Flash to the suburbs, Hollywood smiles,
Harry Flint deceased, reborn as Fred,
an affable Deutscher hound with fine dispensation
to artistic direction, perfect comic timing,

that wry tilt of a head. Sit Freddie.
Walk Freddie. Sing Freddie. Dance.
First gig, a bit part: *The Life of a Wag*,
Joey, Harry Flint's loyal friend to the end
as the lighter press gushed. Licking the stars' swinging feet.
Whimpering for a week, before the ex popped by
with an average review to cheer Harry up.
So that's how Harry, now Freddie, plays Joey. Gets dragged
through his own plot, with some doofus as the lead:
flirting with his wife, wincing sympathetic at his kids,
in a salt-and-pepper wig, not at all like his old hair.
Wrecking all his lines, the electric pulse of speech
ringing phoney, hammy, Good Morning Vietnumb.
Fucker thinks he's a better Harry!
Kills each dismal scene, and then kills them both –
sets them up to swing from fame and love and everything
into wherever the movie goes when the credits end.

OLLY GRUNER

ॐ

Easy Rovers, Raging Fur Balls: How Animals Did a Wee-Wee on Hollywood and Humped Louis Mayer's Favourite Armchair

If I could walk with the animals, talk with the animals, grunt and squeak and squawk with the animals. And they could talk to me!
 – Doctor Dolittle

All that 'talk with the animals' crap we were getting back then, you'd think someone might once have actually listened.
 – Mr Tibbles, star of *The Godfather*

DECEMBER 1967: Hollywood braces itself for a month of animal madness. The fangs are out as two big-budget epics prepare to do battle for the Christmas box office. One is about a man with a gift for bestial communication; the other follows a little boy's adventures in the jungle. With its disastrously expensive production costs, dull songs and convoluted narrative, *Doctor Doolittle* went on to become one of the film industry's biggest flops of all time. *The Jungle Book*, on the other hand, roared into cinemas. It reached the box-office top ten and provided Disney with its first animated hit for almost a decade.

313

If their commercial fortunes differed drastically, *Doolittle* and *The Jungle Book* did at least have one thing in common. They were representative of a dying breed: the last gasps of an old Hollywood about to be rocked to its foundations. Just at the moment these innocuous animal flicks were doing the rounds, the film industry was in the throes of revolution. The sixties had finally hit Tinsel Town and a new generation of filmmakers were dosing up their movies with lashings of sex, drugs and rock-'n'-roll. Blockbusters like *The Graduate* and *Bonnie and Clyde* (both 1967) contained a hip counterculture sensibility that shocked middle America while enthralling its kids. They were but the prologue to a decade's worth of cultural upheaval. Indeed, as the countless exposés of late 1960s/early 1970s Hollywood have informed us, hedonistic excess – both in front of and behind the camera – quickly became just another way of saying 'Let's do lunch.'[1] The exploits of filmmakers Dennis Hopper, Jack Nicholson, Warren Beatty, Francis Ford Coppola, Jane and Peter Fonda et al. titillate movie buffs the world over. Salacious histories and magazine articles on the 'sex and drugs generation' have colonised middle-class coffee tables like so many piles of cocaine.

Yet within this mountain of literature one group of Hollywood luminaries remains underrepresented. This is all the more surprising given that they were the creative forces behind such classics as *The Godfather*, *Jaws*, *The Long Goodbye*, *The Panic in Needle Park* and *Mean Streets*, not to mention underrated masterpieces like *Benji* and *Charlotte's Web*. They were the feral generation – the animals that saved Hollywood. For a few short years, these four-legged thespians sought to challenge the

---

1   *The most famous exponent of this story being Peter Biskind's classic Hollywood tell-all,* Easy Riders, Raging Bulls: How the Sex 'n' Drugs 'n' Rock 'n' Roll Generation Saved Hollywood *(1998).*

dumb clichés that pervaded films like *Doolittle* and *The Jungle Book* and created some of the most enduring pictures ever to grace the silver screen.

What follows, then, is first and foremost a celebration of the animals that remade Hollywood. Focusing on the films themselves and the lives of prominent individuals, I hope this article goes some way towards redressing the human-centric imbalance that has heretofore defined writing on the subject. The candid – and at times explicit – background history has been included for the sake of context. I would like, here, to thank all animals that agreed to be interviewed for this piece and to clarify that I have no desire to besmirch the honour of any dog, horse, pig or cat active during those heady days. In fact, if this article has any purpose, it is simply to reaffirm an old saying that seems to have been lost somewhere along the line. When it comes to Hollywood: four legs good, two legs bad.

BONE TO BE WILD

By 1967, the cinematic animal was in an advanced state of decline. *Doctor Doolittle* and *The Jungle Book* were but prominent additions to the cliché-riddled puff that had been emanating from Los Angeles for decades. In the movies, animals had four choices. Role number one: the monster (as in *King Kong*). Role two: the cheerful lackey who helps some little brat solve a crime (the *Flipper* syndrome). Role three: the mischievous troublemaker who exasperates and entertains their human masters (*à la Bringing Up Baby*). Or role four: the tragic companion driven to an unfortunate death thanks to their unwavering loyalty (tearjerkers of the *Old Yeller* ilk). In other words, the choice was thus: be a villain or be a sap.

Surprisingly, it was the heroic characters that drew the most ire from my interviewees. If rampant gorillas and werewolves displayed a penchant for human flesh that few real animals could understand, they were at least allowed the luxury of independence. When it came to 'good' animals, however, an obsequious bark for Mr and Mrs Jones was about as far as most scripts went. Underpinning every heroic role was an all-encompassing *love* for their human masters.

'Love is an understatement', says Pickles Gabor, who would later go on to play *Rocky*, Al Pacino's suicidal spaniel in *The Panic in Needle Park* (1971). 'We were supposed to worship the ground they walked on.' For a pup growing up in the 1960s, popular culture offered little more than a distorted window onto a world of faithful doggies and fawning masters. Gabor recalls watching his first episode of *The Adventures of Rin Tin Tin* when he was six months old. 'I remember the blast of the bugle and this majestic German Shepherd standing there to attention.

'From the moment I saw him he was my hero. Defending his home from Indian raids – I idolised him for the rest of my childhood.' Gabor is still sentimental about RTT. 'He was our John Wayne. You might grow to hate the lies he told you, but you can never forget what he represented: strength, loyalty, courage – he was America as my childish mind imagined it to be.' But the impact of Rin Tin Tin on pop-culture dog representations was far-reaching, and not necessarily positive. The countless imitations and rip-offs – from *Ace the Wonder Dog* to *Lassie* – presented cookie-cutter images of heroic, servile dogs. The space for innovative portrayals was severely limited.

'I'll tell you what the problem was', says Gabor. 'Loyalty. The "man's best friend" thing was cool to begin with, but when it consumes a character at the expense of every other quality it becomes an issue.

'I think it led us down a pretty dark road. You started getting this fad for mercy killings. The first time I watched *Old Yeller* I remember thinking "Why can't the kid get rabies? Why always the dog?" A bullet in the head for years of servitude, no thanks. I still cringe thinking of [Elvis] Presley singing that awful song "Old Shep". Boy and dog grow up together, dog is faithful to boy, dog gets old and wants to retire? Hell no. He's passed his prime so Presley blows his brains out. Man, I watched [the Elvis movie] *Girl Happy*; if anyone needed to be put out of his misery, it was Elvis.'

In many ways Gabor's performance in *The Panic in Needle Park* was a response to these previous stereotypes. Midway through the film Bobby (Al Pacino) and Helen (Kitty Winn) purchase a spaniel, Rocky. For a few brief moments Rocky seems to signify the couple's blossoming relationship and desire to quit their old lives as heroin addicts. But events quickly take a turn for the tragic. While riding home on the Staten Island Ferry, Bobby and Helen decide to shoot up. They leave Rocky to prowl the deck alone. When Helen emerges from the bathroom, she only has time to hear a last plaintive bark and watch as Rocky charges off the hull and into the sea.

This scene has often been misinterpreted as symbolic of Bobby and Helen's drug addiction and the destructive impact it has on their emotional relationships. Yet Gabor explains that his motivation was far more complex. 'As usual, people read it from a human perspective. You know: "Screw the dog, he's just a stand in for marriage counselling." When I prepared for the film, I was thinking about all those loyal pooches of the past, the ones who serve humans and are killed or, at best, tied up in their kennels night after night.

'So I made a decision. Better to die and be master of my own fate than live and be slave to a couple of junkies. I'd been

317

reading a lot of Dostoevsky at the time and was fascinated by the ambiguities that surrounded acts of suicide in his novels. *Panic in Needle Park* allowed me to work through my own anxieties: is a life without freedom a life worth living? How does a dog keep his faith when all around, his brothers are in chains, etcetera?

'The best thing about my performance was that it had this strong emotional kick, for animals *and* humans. Al and Kitty buy a dog, hoping I'll symbolise a new stability, domesticity even, in their relationship. What do couples do when they settle down? They buy a dog. But my response is to take that away, leaving them to flounder in their own sea of uncertainty. By empowering myself I disempower them. Life isn't as simple as setting up a home and buying a puppy any more. The absent dog came to symbolise turbulent times ahead.'

Many canine stars of the period concur. Daisy Villiers, whose brief turn as the excitable terrier chasing Jeff Bridges and Cybil Shepard in *The Last Picture Show* (1971) garnered much acclaim amongst her peers, sees the situation thus: 'In a sense, our performances could make or break a film. Pickles proved it in *The Panic in Needle Park*; the poodles from *Midnight Cowboy* were brilliantly camp as that old lady's chaperones. I tried for something similar in *Picture Show*. It was clear that Peter [Bogdanovich, the director] wanted his movie to explore the social and psychological impact of modernity on small-town America. Restless youth, the sexual revolution, the death of the Old West – the times they were a changing. So I hammed it up. Barked like I was a prophet of doom, totally freaked out.

'Looking back at my performance now, I cringe a little. But it felt fresh at the time, and freshness was what we all wanted. In the early 1970s, a lot of dogs were searching for an image, an identity. The old role models, the Rin Tin Tins, the Lassies, didn't chime with our lives at that point. We needed new icons. I suppose that was why Benji was so important. He gave us a voice. Without Benji we'd probably all have given up.'

'I FEEL LOVE': BENJI STORMS HOLLYWOOD

Benjamin Higgins Samuels III, or 'Benji' as he would be better known after his eponymous film debut stormed America in the fall of 1974, was an unlikely superstar. Born in Porchester, Texas, in 1970, he spent the first three years of his life travelling between various military bases. His father, a German shepherd, was a career war dog, having served two tours of Vietnam by the time his son arrived. His mother, a Yorkshire terrier called Pebbles, worked as a children's entertainer.

Life was a whirlwind for the young family. From Texas they moved on to Fort Sherwin in California. 'I first met Benji in California around 1972', recalls Snoopy O'Brien, a childhood friend. 'He'd just moved into the installation. Both our fathers were about to leave for the 'Nam. We started hanging out together.' O'Brien is just one of many friends and acquaintances who remember Benji as a shy dog who kept himself to himself and barked only during Independence Day fireworks. The friends would sneak into the base's common room to hunt for dropped peanuts and catch late-night movies.

O'Brien remembers *Dr Doolittle* being broadcast one night. 'There was a whole bunch of us young dogs there. We were, like, "Is this for real?" Here was a man claiming to be able to talk to the animals. But he couldn't understand a word. The animals would say something about politics or the weather and he'd just go [and here O'Brien adopted a faux English accent] "Ah, Mrs Tabatha has come for her toothpaste." It was a farce. There's a priceless moment in the film where Doolittle's doing one of his self-important "talk to the animals" skits and the golden retriever, Frank, says out of nowhere: "Up yours, buddy." Of course the good doctor doesn't have a clue. We all cracked up at that. It became this long-running joke between us. We had to have a sense of humour about these things, otherwise we'd all have gone mad.'

For Benji, however, it was painful to see his fellow animals so misrepresented on the big screen. 'The film hit Benji a lot harder than it did the rest of us', recalls O'Brien. 'One time, it must have been a few weeks later, I was sitting with him in his room smoking a Jay, I remember it so clearly, he turned to me and said, "My father's in Vietnam serving his country, my mother makes children laugh, but to them they are nothing but dumb mutts. Fucking *mutts*, man. That's all we are." I think it was around that time Benji decided he was going to make a movie.'

In January of 1974, Benji finally got his break. MGM was looking for a new star to helm a dog-themed picture. There would be open auditions that week. It was here that a performance since enshrined in Hollywood folklore took place. The 'armchair incident', as it is now known, is the story told to every aspiring dog actor. A tale of triumph over adversity, a reminder that persistence pays off, this five-minute episode made Benji the legend that he is today. It also got him his movie contract.

Pete Weisberg, a Jack Russell working for MGM as a continuity assistant, was one of the few dogs to witness Benji's audition. 'We'd already had a day of competent but bland performances: the usual stuff, dogs catching balls, standing on their hind legs and so forth. And then Benji walked in. He was a striking cross-breed, and even before he did anything it was hard to take your eyes off him.' Benji did not *do* a great deal in that audition. In fact, it was this refreshing insouciance that was so endearing. 'You had to be there, man, it was incredible. Here we were sat in the great mogul Louis B. Mayer's old office, used to animals coming in and literally begging for jobs. But Benji, he just walked in, looked at us and then looked over at the chair.' It was a solid piece of furniture, a French Louis-style armchair that had once belonged to Mayer. 'It all happened in a blur. He walked over to the chair, wrapped himself around one of the legs and started humping it. He did this for about five minutes and no one said a word. We were too dumbstruck. When he'd finished, all he said was "Thank you gentlemen" and walked out.

'We didn't bother auditioning anyone else after that.'

Released in October 1974, *Benji* appeared as America was facing a mountain of crises. The economy was in its worst state since the Great Depression; defeat in Vietnam had shattered the country's self-esteem. Two months earlier, Richard Nixon had resigned his presidency, disgraced by the Watergate scandal. The film's promotional tagline seemed to directly address a nation in need of cheering up: 'It's a very special motion picture that just plain makes you feel good.'

Benji was a 'feel good' film, but one which spoke to issues bedevilling mid-1970s America. The first shot, a zoom on a smashed window with Benji's head poking outside, drips with metaphorical potency. The decrepit house represents the United States at that time. Benji's appearance is like a ray of hope, a declaration that from even the most arid of landscapes goodness can grow.

The entire opening sequence is devoted to its shaggy-haired troubadour hero roaming the streets of a small town. Benji skips down a dirt road and through a residential district. Each tree he passes receives a splash of Benji's piss, as if he were marking the entire town as his own territory. Then comes the sequence's most famous moment: Benji has just wandered through the town centre and eventually arrives at an opulent mansion, in front of which is a lawn. 'Keep off the grass', a sign implores. But our hero ignores the sign and walks straight across the lawn. This brief moment of rebelliousness became a cult phenomenon amongst young dogs, who interpreted it as a reference to marijuana smoking. 'Hey, we all knew Benji liked to smoke a little grass', says Jill Puddles, who was working as a guide dog in 1974. 'It was like a "fuck you" to human rules and regulations.'

If the opening sequence suggests Benji to be a carefree hedonist floating on the winds of fate, the film's remainder presents something a little more complicated. This is a dog with a painful past. An interesting creative decision was made to have Benji experience several traumatic flashbacks. The first occurs when he sees one of the film's villains holding a shotgun. Benji suddenly remembers his days working as a police dog and being shot at by a criminal. Again, later in the movie, as he is trying to save two children from their kidnappers, we see glimpses of his life by way of a flashback. His past traumas hang like an iron cross upon his psyche.

Professor Duke Poocher, head of canine studies at Kennel University, reads Benji's flashbacks as intersecting with a broader cycle of 'trauma' films appearing in the 1970s. 'Hollywood in the 1970s was responding to events like Vietnam and Watergate, producing paranoid political thrillers, cynical revisionist westerns, films about returning veterans. The old myths of American exceptionalism, faith in God, country and family were being eroded. The flashback was often mobilised as a figment of a tortured psyche – history coming back to haunt an individual just as it was haunting our nation. In popular culture they become prominently associated with Vietnam veterans – films like *The Deer Hunter, Coming Home, Welcome Home Soldier Boys, Taxi Driver,* were about emotionally scarred vets reliving their combat experiences and finding it impossible to assimilate back into American society. I think *Benji*'s themes in many ways complemented this cycle. Here was an outsider who, to begin with at least, is rejected by "decent" society. He experiences traumatic flashbacks and is forced into fighting a war in his back yard. I'd say that films like *Rambo* owe a lot to Benji. The opening sequence from *First Blood* (1982) sees a shaggy veteran, Sylvester Stallone, wandering through small-town America. He too is an outcast, pushed into violence when he only wanted peace and quiet.'

Benji rescued Hollywood from decades of mediocrity. Yet, his was but one voice amongst a cacophony of others. Indeed, at the very time he was putting together his cinematic masterpiece, the howls of revolution were keeping Los Angeles awake at night. And the single, repeated refrain: 'Everybody wants to be a cat.'

'I BELIEVE IN AMERICA': MARLON BRANDO'S CAT

Mr Tibbles was an extraordinary cat trapped in a very ordinary name. Ever since his youth he'd been an extrovert, always performing for family and friends, as if to compensate for the common title his parents had bequeathed him. 'Imagine taking your evening constitutional when suddenly from a house somewhere a voice yells "Tibbles", then another voice yells "Tibbles", and another and another. As early as I can remember I've been fighting my own insignificance.' It was only after the release of Francis Ford Coppola's mafia epic *The Godfather* (1972) that he came to accept who he was. 'I didn't feel ordinary after *The Godfather*.'

Tibbles's performance was certainly not ordinary. *The Godfather*'s opening sequence is significant in highlighting the different outlooks of key characters Bonasera (Salvatore Cassito) and Don Corleone (Marlon Brando). The former has attempted to play it straight, live as a good American, follow the rules. For his efforts he is treated like a second-class citizen and his daughter lies in a hospital bed. Corleone, on the other hand, plays by his own rules and puts no faith in the American system. For his efforts he sits in an opulent mansion surrounded by wealth and luxury – all the trappings of the American Dream. The irony of *The Godfather* is that crime and murder, not honesty and hard work, lead to assimilation. It is left to Mr Tibbles to emphasise this point.

Brando's cat appears three-and-a-half minutes into the film. Stretched out on the Godfather's lap, he looks entirely at ease with his human companion. 'The great thing about cats is we're able to signify warmth and stability or discomfort and fear through the smallest of gestures. When we purr and stretch we're the ultimate symbol of a happy, comfortable home. When we arch our backs and hiss we become these fearsome feral monsters, suggestive of social and psychological disarray (think Val Lewton's *Cat People*).' In *The Godfather*, Tibbles maintained a relaxed demeanour. In doing so, he added metaphorical weight to the idea that it was the Corleone family, not the Bonasera family, that was assimilated into American life.

'It would never have worked with a dog', explains Tibbles. 'Dogs have too much association with blind loyalty. A cat, on the other hand, is more discerning in terms of the company he keeps. We are powerful creatures who gravitate toward other powerful creatures. Thus, my relationship with Marlon was really a meeting of two men of similar stature. He needed me to secure his place in American society; I needed him to tickle my belly. I suppose it was a gentleman's agreement of sorts.'

Most striking for film viewers is how Tibbles is able to dominate a three-hour film through a performance that lasts barely minutes. This, however, was not unusual for the time, as he points out: 'Think about the monkeys in *The Graduate*, or the lion cub in *Mean Streets*. In minor roles, these animals were able to capture the tone of their respective films (i.e. the absurdity of modern life in *The Graduate*, and the youthful rage that underpins *Mean Streets*). For me, the best example of this was in [Robert] Altman's *The Long Goodbye*. The cat in that movie plays her part with unparalleled brilliance.'

An adaptation of Raymond Chandler's detective novel, *The Long Goodbye* (1973) offered a challenging portrayal of Chandler's iconic private dick, Philip Marlowe. Famously played by Humphrey Bogart in *The Big Sleep* (1946), Marlowe was the hard-boiled detective *par excellence*. As played by Bogart, he was tough, cynical, weather-beaten and sharp talking. This is the film image that had lasted through the years. All the more surprising, then, that *The Long Goodbye* would digress from this archetype and present a quasi-hippie Marlowe (played by Elliot Gould), whose defining traits seem to be gentleness and a love for cats.

Given the critical acclaim that greeted her performance, it is surprising to hear that Ginger Purrs, who played Marlowe's feline companion in *The Long Goodbye*, was, at one point, on the brink of being fired. Director Robert Altman had begun on the film's opening sequence, where Marlowe tries to feed his cat. Initially, it was supposed to be a thirty-second scene – he dishes the food into a bowl, she eats the food. But Purrs refused to play ball. 'I'd come along to give Ginger a little moral support', remembers Tabby Jones, a friend and fellow actor, 'and she was in tears, saying "I won't eat that crap." She was an upper-class dame and was used to being fed fresh tuna and chicken breasts. Robert tried at first to coax her, but after about six hours of take after take he snapped. Fired her there on the spot and asked an assistant to find him another "moggie".' It was only an intervention by the Cat Union chief Felix Hoffa that prevented her career from being over before it started. 'Felix was fantastic, this great old Siberian who always smoked a big cigar and, when needed, had movie directors for lunch.'

Union trouble was the last thing Altman needed on this low-budget project. 'Felix just looked him hard in the eye and said, in that guttural voice of his: "The cat stays in the picture!" That was it, Altman capitulated, rewrote the whole opening scene so as to accommodate a cat that wouldn't eat her food. Now we had Marlowe driving off in the middle of the night to shop for something acceptable to Ginger's refined palette. It gave birth to a whole new, and very funny, scene, which I think worked a lot better.'

Ginger Purrs's contribution to *The Long Goodbye* was immense. She was the symbol of Marlowe's gentler side. She was fond of telling friends that, while she respected Bogart's acting, she didn't agree with his interpretation of the private detective. She felt Chandler's Marlowe was far softer, boyish even. The opening lines to Chandler's novel, *The Big Sleep*, were a favourite: 'I was wearing my powder-blue suit, with dark blue shirt, tie and display handkerchief, black brogues, black wool socks with dark blue clocks on them.'[2] The idea of Bogart discussing his socks with dark blue clocks on them was ridiculous; he would have sounded like a schoolboy, or an

2   *Raymond Chandler,* The Big Sleep *(1939), p. 1.*

interior designer. Purrs felt that her and Gould's interpretation of Marlowe, on the other hand, managed to explore this side of Marlowe: a slightly neurotic, obsessive detective more interested in finding his missing cat than solving a crime.

The Long Goodbye's lacklustre performance at the box office hit Ginger Purrs for six. Thinking she'd created something genuinely original, she was disappointed to find it didn't take with the American public. In need of a break from the stresses of filmmaking, Purrs threw herself into her other passion – radical politics. 'We'd all seen *The Aristocats*', says Mr Tibbles with a nostalgic look in his eye. 'That celebration of the humble alley cat [played in the film by Thomas O'Malley], and call for cats to take control of their own lives. You know "Everybody wants to be a cat … A cat's the only cat who knows where it's at." It was galvanising. It definitely pushed a lot of younger felines into politics.' Ginger Purrs was one of them. Her story is both inspiring and tragic.

Not long after *The Long Goodbye* reached cinemas, Purrs hit the road. She planned to give a lecture tour of America, espousing her political ideology. Thousands of cats turned out to hear her speeches on self-determination and sticking it to the Man. 'The FBI were on her back the whole tour', explains Thomas O'Malley, whose alley cat portrayal in *The Aristocats* had been an inspiration. 'The government was terrified they were going to have a revolution on their hands. Cats would quit their armchairs and rugs by the fireplace and take to the streets.'

In November 1974, Purrs met a campus radical at Beakley Campus, California – a bird by the name of Tweety Pie. While natural foes, cat and bird seemed to hit it off, both wanting freedom for their respective species. 'That bird was a fraud', argues Tibbles. 'An FBI stooge.' About a month into their acquaintance, Tweety Pie started interrogating Purrs on her political commitment. He asked her how she could call herself a revolutionary when her cat comrades – lions, tigers, panthers – were imprisoned in cages across America. What was she doing for them?

Tweety Pie's attack hit its target. Purrs was adamant she needed to do something for her fellow cats in cages. Thus it was announced that 17 December 1974 would herald the first in a series of 'black panther fundraisers'. At 9am on the day of the event, Purrs stood before America's media and announced that today (17 December) was 'Freedom Day' for big cats. Los Angeles zoo was packed to the gills as she climbed up the panther cage and raised her paw in salute. 'I begged her not to do it. I told her to let the panthers fight their own war', says O'Malley. 'But she just kept repeating, "They're cats, we're cats, we should stand together."' There was a hush as she jumped from the railings and into the cage.

Within two minutes Ginger Purrs was no more.

'It really was the beginning of the end', said Tibbles. 'For us cats and animals in general. When you realise the extent to which the FBI and government were willing to go to halt our revolution.' Independent, open-minded animals were scared to enter the film industry lest they suffered a similar fate. Cinematic representations also seemed to become more conservative, reverting to the old stereotypes that the feral generation had tried to reverse. No portrayal was more indicative of this trend than that of a shark by the name of Bruce.

The one thing on which all of my interviewees agree is that Bruce Fairfax was a really nice guy. 'He was the sweetest shark ever', gushes Charlotte Jones, who played the matriarchal spider in her eponymously titled *Charlotte's Web* (1973). 'Sometimes he'd turn up unannounced at my apartment with croissants and we'd sit and have breakfast together watching the sun come up.' Others concur. 'Maybe in your life you meet one or two people without a bad bone in their body', says Gustavo Fidatov, the football-playing donkey from *Gus* (1976). 'Bruce was definitely one. He really helped me with my English when I first arrived in America, introduced me to movie people. He was a good friend.'

The wall of defensiveness that Hollywood's animals put up around Bruce has made it difficult to obtain much information about his personal life. We know that he arrived in Los Angeles around 1972 and was approached to star in a 'shark-themed film' the following year. The story goes that Bruce was under the impression he'd signed up for a celebration of marine life (the title 'Jaws' being a reference to the importance of dental hygiene for sea creatures). By the time shooting commenced it was too late to back out.

'I remember all of us turned up at the premiere', says Pickles Gabor. 'We were so pleased our good friend Bruce had finally got his break.' But when they arrived at the cinema Bruce was nowhere to be seen. 'We assumed he must be hob-nobbing with the executives; word on the street was *Jaws* was going to be massive.' As the lights went down the auditorium fell silent.

Everyone in the cinema knew something was wrong. This was not the celebration of marine life they'd been expecting, but a horrific tale of murder on the high seas. Screams echoed through the hall as Bruce committed his first atrocity, the savaging of a female skinny dipper. While the animals were used to a little suspension of disbelief at the movies, seeing their friend Bruce – Hollywood's consummate 'nice guy' – tearing about in a murderous fury was too much. 'It was like the 1950s all over again', says Tibbles. 'The cat beast from Mars. In the space of two hours Hollywood seemed to reverse everything that we had fought for. The old stereotypes had returned.'

It turned out poor Bruce had not been hob-nobbing with executives. He was simply too ashamed to attend his debut. 'He thought he'd let us down.' According to his dolphin roommate, Bruce Fairfax skipped Los Angeles on the night of *Jaws*'s premiere. He has not been seen since. 'It really wasn't Bruce's fault', argues Gabor. 'There were forces beyond his control. The tide was turning in Hollywood. Younger filmmakers, less interested in art than in getting bang for their buck, were calling the shots. The Spielbergs, the Lucases, etc. It was all about the bottom line. After *Jaws*, I think we all knew the game was up.'

When studio executives discovered the economic rewards available from big-budget, conservative blockbusters, the space for innovation rapidly contracted. Bruce Fairfax's ordeal was but a harbinger of things to come. By the fall of 1976, most of my interviewees had either left Hollywood or were sniffing around for minor bit parts. Ginger Purrs was dead. Benji went off the rails. He was last seen in 1979, sprawled out in a dingy hotel on the outskirts of LA, his only company a bottle of Jameson's and a few of the leeches from *Apocalypse Now*. Mr Tibbles quit filmmaking, bought himself a vineyard in Southern California and now runs a successful wine business. Daisy Villiers continues to work in the industry, but sticks to low-budget independent features. Pickles Gabor now serves as consultant at the Ridgeley Institute for Animal Actors, training the next generation of canine stars. He likes to tell them about the old days, 'the last great time in Hollywood', as he puts it. 'Don't get me wrong, the Hooches, the K-9s, the Beethovens – they starred in fun movies. But the spark had gone, they were repeating the same old formula.' Gabor is doubtful we'll ever see a return to the golden days of the 1970s. 'Too much money is at stake. The studios won't risk it.' But he remains sanguine. 'The movies live on, they continue to move us, perhaps someday they'll inspire the next Benji, the next Mr Tibbles.

'Whatever.' He shrugs. 'No one can take away my memories. We were the feral generation, man, the animals that saved Hollywood.'

Writers' Biographies

ANTHONY ADLER turned to poetry as an alternative to bear-baiting. He is a member of Burn After Reading and Ver Poets. Follow him on Twitter as @AnthonyAdler.

SIMON BARRACLOUGH is the author of the Forward Prize-finalist debut *Los Alamos Mon Amour* (Salt, 2008), *Bonjour Tetris* (Penned in the Margins, 2010) and *Neptune Blue* (Salt, 2011). He is also the editor of the collaborative Hitchcock homage *Psycho Poetica* (Sidekick Books, 2012) and co-author of *The Debris Field* (Sidekick Books, 2013). His most recent full-length book, *Sunspots*, is also a live event, and he was poet in residence at the Mullard Space Science Laboratory throughout 2014.

JOHN CLEGG was born in 1986. His first collection, *Antler*, was published by Salt. In 2014, the Emma Press made a pamphlet of his long poem *Captain Love and the Five Joaquins*. He won an Eric Gregory award in 2013.

ANGELA CLELAND was born in Inverness in 1977 and grew up in Dingwall by the Cromarty Firth. She completed a Master's in Creative and Life Writing at Goldsmiths College, London in 2003. Her published works include the pamphlet *Waiting to Burn* (Templar Poetry, 2006), the poetry collections *And in Here the Menagerie* (Templar Poetry, 2007) and *Room of Thieves* (Salt Publishing, 2013), and the science fiction novel *Sequela*, published under the name Cleland Smith. Cleland currently lives in Surrey with her husband, her two sons and her cat Loki. *www.angelacleland.co.uk*

JAMES COGHILL has had poems published in a smattering of places, including Lighthouse *Literary Journal*, *IS&T*, *Fuselit*, *Belleville Park Pages*, the *Emma Press Anthology of Homesickness and Exile* and the *Emma Press Anthology of Dance*. He has a strong interest in animal studies and Swedish culture and has recently finished a sequence about giant anteaters.

RICHARD EVANS has written two collections of poetry, *The Zoo Keeper* (Egg Box, 2003) and *Orbiting* (Moth Light Press, 2009). He currently lives in Southampton but is soon moving to Chester, to live with his girlfriend. It was her, in fact, who came up with the premise for this poem, but was too humble to accept co-authorship. He works as a freelance tutor.

KEVIN M. FLANAGAN is a PhD candidate in the Critical and Cultural Studies Programme at the University of Pittsburgh, where he is completing a dissertation on war representation and discourse in British cinema and television between 1939 and 1980. He is editor of *Ken Russell: Re-Viewing England's Last Mannerist* (Scarecrow Press, 2009) and has contributed essays to *Framework*, *Media Fields Journal* and *Proteus: A Journal of Ideas*.

CAROL FREEMAN is an Adjunct Researcher at the University of Tasmania and former editor of the quarterly *Australian Animal Studies Group News Bulletin*. Her work on visual representations of animals, bioethics and the role of popular culture in wildlife conservation has appeared in a range of journals and the essay collections *Leonardo's Choice: Genetic Technologies and Animals* and *Animal Death*. She is co-editor, with Elle Leane and Yvette Watt, of *Considering Animals: Contemporary Studies in Human-Animal Relations*. A new edition of her book is now out, titled *Paper Tiger: How Pictures Shaped the Thylacine* (Forty South, 2014).

AMANDA GILROY teaches media and animal studies in the American Studies department at the University of Groningen. She writes on film and TV for *PopMatters*. Currently she is working on a cross-media study of *Black Beauty*. Her life companions are two horses, two humans, a dog and four cats.

OLLY GRUNER teaches Visual Culture at the University of Portsmouth. When he isn't trying to talk to animals, he researches and writes about contemporary American cinema, the historical film and cultural memory. He is currently writing a book on Hollywood representations of the 1960s.

CLIFF HAMMETT is an artist and writer who develops investigations into phenomena as diverse as jokes in software, the political ecology of bat detection and the forms of time that inhere in domestic activities.

ANGELA HOFSTETTER received her PhD from Indiana University in Comparative Literature in 2009. She began teaching courses in Composition, Victorian Literature and Comparative Literature at Butler University over a decade ago. Her real passion is combining a first-year seminar that focuses on animals in nineteenth-century fiction with service learning, creating a dynamic space to explore the tensions between the literal and figurative animal with real-world applications. Her current research explores the intersection of aesthetics, ideology and animal studies. An avid hiker and passionate student of classical dressage, she shares her rural home with Great Danes and Baroque horses.

LOREDANA LOY is a PhD student in the Department of Sociology at Cornell University in the United States. She also holds an interdisciplinary master's degree in Media and Sociology from New York University. One of her research interests is the intersection of popular culture and social change with a focus on the relationship between animals and society. Loredana is also the newsletter editor for the American Sociological Association, Animals & Society section.

SOPHIE MAYER has three books forthcoming in 2015, spanning film – *Political Animals: The New Feminist Cinema* (I.B. Tauris) – and poetry: *(O)* (Arc) and *kaolin, or How Did a Girl Like You Get to Be a Girl Like You?* (Lark Books and Writing Studio, US). For more, visit *www.sophiemayer.net*.

WALTER C. METZ is a Professor in the Department of Cinema and Photography at Southern Illinois University. He holds two bachelor's degrees, one in Materials Science and Engineering and the other in the Humanities. He has a master's degree in Communication Studies from the University of Iowa, and a PhD in Radio-Television-Film from the University of Texas at Austin. He is the author of three books: *Engaging Film Criticism: Film History and Contemporary American Cinema* (2004), *Bewitched* (2007) and *Gilligan's Island* (2012). Currently, he is drafting a book manuscript entitled *Molecular Cinema*, a new theoretical exploration of materialism in cinema as a way of rethinking the relationship between science and film.

JUDE C. MONTAGUE is a writer, artist and composer/ musician based in London. As a professional media archivist (ITN/Reuters/freelance) she often creates art in response to international news agency material, including her third collection of poems, *The Wires, 2012* (Dark Windows Press). She curates a radio show, *The News Agents*, for Resonance FM.

NICK MURRAY is a live literature producer, writer, musician and founder of Annexe Press, based in London. Enjoying life as a generalist has allowed him to turn his hand to a multitude of things without feeling like he should knuckle down and focus on just one. His work has appeared in publications such as *inc. Magazine, The Bohemyth, Belleville Park Pages, Litmus* and the anthology *Jawbreakers*.

ABIGAIL PARRY is an award-winning poet and sometime circus performer. She can most commonly be found writing about B-movie monsters, seductive animals and mischief.

DR NICOLAS PILLAI is a researcher in the School of Media at Birmingham City University and an Associate Fellow of the University of Warwick. His doctoral thesis explored portrayals of happy marriage in Hollywood films, with two chapters devoted to the Thin Man films. He is currently researching and writing a book on jazz and screen modernism. In 2014, Nicolas gave the keynote address at Cardiff University's 'Jazz and Cinema' conference and curated the 'Jazzprojector' season at the Vortex Jazz Club.

SAMUEL PRINCE lives and works in London. His poems have appeared in various print and online journals, as well as the anthologies *Birdbook 2: Freshwater Habitats* and *Coin Opera 2: Fulminare's Revenge*, both from Sidekick Books.

JULIE ANN SMITH is retired from the Department of Languages and Literatures at the University of Wisconsin, Whitewater. Her articles focus on representations of animals' minds in cultural discourse, particularly in literary works. She is active in animal rights and animal welfare, and she founded the Wisconsin chapter of the House Rabbit Society. She co-edited *Experiencing Animal Minds* (Columbia University Press, 2012) and is currently working on a book on rabbit consciousness.

JON STONE was born in Derby and lives in London. His poems have appeared in anthologies of imitation, formal innovation, science fiction, erotic and comic book poetry. *School of Forgery* (Salt, 2012) brings all these elements together, while he also collates, collaborates and anthologises through Sidekick Books. He won a Society of Authors Eric Gregory Award in 2012 and the Poetry London competition in 2014.

TÂNIA REGINA VIZACHRI researches animal representations and the impact of these representations on childhood education. She has a master's degree in Cultural Studies from USP (São Paulo University) and is a high school sociology teacher. Her favourite animal films are *Chicken Run* and *Planet of the Apes*.

MARK WALDRON's first collection, *The Brand New Dark*, was published by Salt in 2008. His second, *The Itchy Sea*, came out in September 2011. His work appears in *Identity Parade: New British and Irish Poets* (Bloodaxe, 2010) and *Best British Poetry 2012, 2013* and *2014* (all Salt). He's been named one of the 2014 Next Generation Poets by the Poetry Book Society.

PROFESSOR PAUL WELLS is Director of the Animation Academy, Loughborough University, UK. He has published widely on animated film, including *The Animated Bestiary* (Rutgers University Press, 2008). He is also an established writer and director for film, TV, radio and theatre, conducting

workshops and consultancies worldwide based on
Scriptwriting (AVA Publishing, 2007). Recent docun
include *Mackinnon & Saunders: A Model Studio*, featu
Burton, and *Whispers & Wererabbits: Claire Jennings*, w
Park, creator of *Wallace & Gromit*.

MIKE WEST writes and performs comedy and po
used to host London's legendary variety night 'The
School of Enlightenment'. On Twitter he's @camdenli

REBECCA WIGMORE is an artist and writer living i
East London. Her favourite animal is the wombat ;
website is rebeccawigmorefeelsyou.tumblr.com. Thank
your interest.

CHRISSY WILLIAMS lives in London, and is directo
Poetry Book Fair. She is the author of five poetry par
and runs a monthly informal poetry and comics worksl